Personas of Holy Pretence

Personas of Holy Pretence

Zahir Kaleem

Viva Books

New Delhi | Mumbai | Chennai | Kolkata | Bengaluru | Hyderabad | Kochi | Guwahati

Publisher's note

First Published 2013

Viva Books Private Limited

- 4737/23, Ansari Road, Daryaganj, New Delhi 110 002
  Tel. 42242200, 23258325, 23283121, Email: vivadelhi@vivagroupindia.net
- 76, Service Industries, Shirvane, Sector 1, Nerul, Navi Mumbai 400 706
  Tel. 27721273, 27721274, Email: vivamumbai@vivagroupindia.net
- Jamals Fazal Chambers, 26 Greams Road, Chennai 600 006
  Tel. 28294241, 28290304, Email: vivachennai@vivagroupindia.net
- B-103, Jindal Towers, 21/1A/3 Darga Road, Kolkata 700 017
  Tel. 22816713, Email: vivakolkata@vivagroupindia.net
- 7, GF, Sovereign Park Aptts., 56-58, K. R. Road, Basavanagudi, Bengaluru 560 004
  Tel. 26607409, Email: vivabangalore@vivagroupindia.net
- 101-102, Moghal Marc Apartments, 3-4-637 to 641, Narayanguda, Hyderabad 500 029, Tel. 27564481, Email: vivahyderabad@vivagroupindia.net
- First Floor, Beevi Towers, SRM Road, Kaloor, Kochi 682 018
  Tel. 0484-2403055, 2403056, Email: vivakochi@vivagroupindia.net
- 232, GNB Road, Beside UCO Bank, Silpukhuri, Guwahati 781 003
  Tel. 0361-2666386, Email: vivaguwahati@vivagroupindia.net

www.vivagroupindia.com

ISBN: 978-81-309-2273-7

Published by Vinod Vasishtha for Viva Books Private Limited, 4737/23 Ansari Road, Daryaganj, New Delhi 110 002.

Printed and bound by Syndicate Binders, New Delhi.

S0000/X0000

Contents

Foreword & acknowledgement

A lot of authors tend to thank a multitude of famous people for inspiration and assistance, some from the mighty Julius Caesar to Barack Obama. While many of them may have inspired a lot of people indirectly through their roles and contributions in history, as the author of this book I feel more obliged to thank those with whom I have had the pleasure and privilege of interacting through various phases of life. The first acknowledgement must go to the circumstances that triggered the obsessive desire to write this book in the first place. It is difficult to imagine how the current events and circumstances cannot impact on all living beings, directly or indirectly. If the global and national milieu was different today in a positive way, who knows I might have chosen to pursue another passion.

When I started this project well over a year ago, I lost sight of the fact that the current year would represent the 100th anniversary of the greatest poet and intellectual the country, if not the sub-continent has ever produced. It therefore took me a fraction of a second to decide that in some major way a dedication had to be made to Faiz Ahmad Faiz, whose poetry and philosophy are loaded with inspiration and excellence in every line of his huge collection of works. That influence will be obvious throughout the text in the chapters to follow. In fact the very opening chapter leans on his shoulder for the most apt description of the tragedy that presently casts its shadow on the nation, on individual citizens – home and abroad – and indeed on interpersonal and international relationships.

Therefore dedicating this effort to him in largest measure is both an obligation and an honour, the obligation a national duty; the honour a personal devotion.

I am delighted that his elder daughter, the brilliantly creative Professor Salima Hashmi very kindly agreed to contribute the following piece, a daughter's tribute to a great father:

"Commenting on the world we inhabit today is a challenging task, trying to make sense of it, is even more daunting. Living in Pakistan, we have witnessed the collapse of political structures, civil wars, ethnic strife and pervasive extremism in our very short history as a nation state. Against a backdrop of turbulence, there have been many who have taken the people's woes unto their hearts. They have struggled for social justice, for representation, for sanity, for dignity. So many battles have been lost and yet hope persists in ways that lift the heart and rejuvenate the soul. Traditionally, it is the poet, the musician, the artist, the philosopher who gives voice to the sorrows and joys of human experience. Here, we have been lucky. We have had both words and music to live by; our champions when we have no others. Among them was Faiz Ahmed Faiz, who gave his 'land of yellowing leaves', words of courage wrapped in intense lyricism.

Zahir Kaleem dedicates this book to Faiz Ahmed Faiz, which is only appropriate. His vast experience in countries like ours, coupled with his concerns for ordinary people is what propels his writing. He joins those who believe in the distant dawn".

On a personal note, I must start with the biggest thank you to my wife Sophia in particular for her unflinching support and tolerance in the face of excessive and erratic work hours as well as my frequent travels, especially over the two recent decades. Also like to record my gratitude to my elder son Sahir who provided invaluable support in matters of information technology, his field of expertise and my younger son Rameez for his positively critical feedbacks at various stages, my daughter-in-law Anqa for her very keen interest and constructive involvement. Above all, I make this special dedication to my little angel granddaughter Raameen, who may not yet have started to speak but by her mere delightfully innocent presence has been an inspiration and joy in equal measure.

Every individual has role models and mentors in life. The first immense influence and encouragement for me came from the highly knowledgeable and respected Dr. Mohammad Ajmal as my professor during college days. More is said about him later. The second great influence was through my late father-in-law, Sardar Mohammad Nasim, a man of unimpeachable integrity, warmth in relationships, unlimited hospitality and amazing fair-mindedness in all matters. The third and final major influence came later in professional life in the form of my former boss and current friend and mentor in most matters professional and inter-personal relationships. He is Sheikh Sajjad Hassan, a former chairman of the Federal Board of Revenue and subsequently federal secretary to the government of Pakistan. He combines the rare attributes of professional excellence and the art of firm administration but with benevolent undertones, not to forget his brilliant sense of humour.

A note of gratitude to my brother Aneeq Khawar and his family for their exceptional support and involvement. There are several other friends and family members to thank for their role and friendly contributions in adding value and facilitating this effort. My friend since 1984 T. S. Krishnamurthy in India who as an experienced author himself offered wise counsel to help me start this effort; my very good friend and former Commonwealth colleague Dr. Ved Goel for his impartial sharing of experiences on a number of topics; my niece Sana Saif in Lahore for her most helpful liaising role in publication related matters; my Malaysian friend and neighbour Kwan Loo for generously sharing his experience of on-line publishing. Most of all, to each and every one of those who have played a part but cannot each be listed here for practical limitations.

Zahir Kaleem

1

For Whom the Book Tolls

آج کے نام؛ اور آج کے غم کے نام

Aaj ke naam; aur aaj ke gham ke naam

[Dedicated to today; and to today's sorrows]
Faiz Ahmad Faiz

This is by and large the story of less than five per cent of the population of Pakistan; those who are and have been since Mohammad Ali Jinnah's death the movers and shakers of the country's destiny and its current misfortunes. While wealth and luxuries are probably better protected than nuclear assets in the confines of their high private boundaries, the blame and abuse for their misdeeds are burdened on the nation as a whole. It is unfair and completely underserved for the overwhelming majority of the country's population.

In more recent times, this is sadly also the story of a substantial chunk of the formerly "exploited" population too, an experiment in the name of a holy transformation meant to be conducted under strictly controlled conditions but one which has gone horribly wrong. The outcome of it all, a sub-nation in the form of a large group with no attributes of a nation but all those of a crowd passing through progressive stages of deterioration. Initially from directionless assemblies of benign onlookers of events to becoming more proactive miscreants, progressing to unruly gatherings, then aggravating to impromptu angry violent rallies and currently stooping into the thoughtless behaviour patterns of lynching mobs. The recent tragic events in Sialkot where two young brothers were hunted down by a mob worse than a pack of hungry wolves, in broad daylight, right under the watchful eyes of so called law enforcers are graphic illustrations of the degeneration of a once very peaceful, extremely hospitable and tolerant society into an unrecognisably transformed bunch with attributes that are the extreme opposite. There is hardly room for further deterioration because the final crossing line is anarchy and historically it is an end game.

Caught between the two, is the overwhelming majority of the rest of the population; who simply wish to continue to lead normal lives as before despite all the odds but they have no control over either the ruling class or the hate mobs. They are actually hostage to and at the mercy of the agendas and activities of both.

Whereas the object of analysis is mainly Muslim thought processes, more specifically that of Pakistani nationals, home and abroad, human thinking and behavioural patterns are universal in many ways. Therefore, a number of analysed situations will lead readers from other religions, races or cultures to associate some analysis with their own situations and indigenous problems. The probability of that being the case increases further with the use of "*Analytical Psychology*" as the principal work tool, which was founded by *Carl Gustav Jung* on very broad concepts like universal archetypes and the collective unconscious.

Drivers of hate and violence

Before you embark on a journey of revenge, dig two graves
Confucius

The past few decades have been afflicted by an increasingly high number of confrontations, minor conflicts and all out wars in the name of or using religion as the basis at national and international levels, both inter-religious and intra-religious. Self-appointed wardens of religions have set in motion abrasive agendas that can only lead to grief and sorrow in the long run for all parties involved. Unfortunately even more so for those not party to any of this, as the fatalities and the mutilated survivors of the senseless and brutal "*to whom it may concern*" suicide bombings have demonstrated in the most tragic and painful manner in many parts of the world. From the *Talibans* on the one hand offering the generous choice of "*either you follow our commandments or you are infidels*" to *George Bush* on the other hand threatening similarly "*either you are with us or against us*" there are far more venomous gases in the atmosphere than life saving oxygen. To back up their positions, all sides of such religious divides claim some kind of direct communication with and guidance from God and justify their actions accordingly in the light of the respectively proclaimed divine guidance.

It wasn't too long ago that *Zia-ul-Haq*, the most brutal and wicked of military dictators, whose name has recently been expunged from the national constitution of Pakistan used to go into what he dubbed regular "*Istakharas*" [*a prayer for guidance*] in the darkness of the night and return in the morning to inflict another savage act of torture on his opponents or the entire nation in the name of divine guidance. A lot of Muslims with strong religious inclinations engage in the practice of "*Istakhara*" from the goodness of their hearts and genuinely held beliefs but for noble intents only. But in Zia's case, it was pure and unadulterated dishonesty aimed at exploiting the religious beliefs of unsuspecting citizens with the sole purpose of wrapping himself around power like a lethal snake. ***Shakespeare*** describes such a character in his typically articulate style in "*The Merchant of Venice*" saying that the "**The devil can cite Scripture for his purpose.**" The quote refers to the temptation offered to *Christ* by the *Devil* in a passage from the Old Testament. Zia's name may have been deleted from the country's constitution but the deep and repeated wounds he inflicted on the nation in prolongation of his Satanically personal agenda continue to bleed profusely, the hatreds he induced and parochial groups he created under his "*divide and misrule*" principle carry on blood-spattering street vendettas without the slightest hint of repentance, guilt and remorse. Zia and his axis of devils took it upon themselves to sort out their surroundings, to discipline those who did not think or behave like them, to drive an invading army not out of his own country but a neighbouring country that we never thought highly of as a neighbour and to do that, use innocent, unwanted and excess kids from poverty stricken families, indoctrinate them into becoming fighting robots and later human bombs in Afghanistan so that his wobbly rule at the time could be prolonged in the name of religion. He embarked on his journey of deception and greed in the garb of a holy mission. In the process he volunteered a lead role in digging graves in alien land but forgot the wise words of Confucius that for each grave dug abroad, two would eventually be dug back home. It is now left to a bewildered and traumatised nation to bury their dead almost every day, killed in the streets, in mosques, police stations, colleges, market places, beauty parlours in market centres and even on the motorways.

In doing all that, did he not cultivate the seeds for what the nation is getting today, even though he was an unconstitutional power grabber? It is obvious that our political masters committed some serious wrongs in the past. Does it not make sense to revisit our past with an open mind, take an honest look into our own conduct and having accepted our faults, make honest corrections? More importantly, not to carry on as before because all that the country will continue to get from its present line of conduct is more of what it has always got in return.

While most religions may be afflicted at present in varying degrees with extreme positions of intolerance within their ranks, unfortunately a particular misguided breed in the current generation of Muslims are in the lead role. In such times, leaders should be expected to navigate their followers out of potentially explosive possibilities with integrity and vision but when most of them are themselves at the forefront of hate campaigns driving the country to a point of no return, nothing good can be expected from the current sorry lot of political leadership. The present state of affairs demands a deep analysis at the earliest of how and why the nation allowed itself to be so easily sucked into a near impossible state of affairs.

Psychological perspectives

Anger and hostility are natural human reactions to long spells of frustration and under-achievement. It is not for Muslims in general to analyse the role of others or for others to give direction or counsel to Muslims, but it is certainly what Muslims themselves need to do on their own. A self-analysis that focuses only on what we need to do on our side to promote and advance our own future but more importantly, sort out our present.

There are several approaches to analysis of problems, analysis of mental processes being one of them. A fundamental principle of problem solving in psychoanalysis is the belief and professional conviction that problems encountered by the mind can only be corrected when the forgotten or repressed source of a problem resident in the deep unconscious sectors of the psyche is brought back to consciousness. Awareness is half the cure. This is therefore also an attempt to bring back to surface the hidden psychological sources of problems in the hope that awareness will at the least trigger problem solving desires, even if solutions appear to be a long way off.

Most issues are not always as straightforward as they might appear to be at face value. Attempting to analyse the hidden agendas, vested interests, and dynamics of the forces for maintenance of status quo where this can only be done by blocking the path of progress of those at whose cost vested interests remain in their respective positions of privilege, exploitation, power, control or other wicked pursuits is therefore never a straightforward task.

Sigmund Freud is generally accepted as the father of modern psychoanalysis. However, none of his well-known disciples or close associates followed Freudian concepts as espoused by Freud himself. Two main arguments against the validity and reliability of his theories were, firstly that his thinking was greatly influenced by the confines of the largely matriarchal Jewish society in Vienna that he was born into, which manifests itself in the significantly dominating role that the mother plays throughout his analysis of the human mind. Secondly, and in my view the more potent argument was put forward by his most brilliant and talented associate, *Carl Gustav Jung*.

In his words the problem with Freud was that he never came across a sane person in his life. Freud's theories were limited to the problems that generally infect the abnormal mind. They did not go beyond that to look into how the healthy, creative and normal mind thinks and operates.

Having taken that uncomplimentary position about the parochial parameters of Freud's understanding of the human mind, Jung spread the scope of his quest for establishing the truth to almost all parts of the globe. I was privileged to have been a student of the legendary *Dr. Mohammad Ajmal* for four years as a *Ravian* [*called so because of the local River Ravi*] at the prestigious Government College in the historical city of Lahore and offer no apologies for also being a devoted follower of the theories of Carl Gustav Jung in the subject of psychology. Dr. Ajmal served as head of department of Psychology for a long time, later served Principal of the same college, Vice Chancellor of the Punjab University and as Secretary Education in the Government of Z.A. Bhutto. He was also invited as a visiting professor at the prestigious Chicago University during that period. I have to mention him as a mentor and one of the greatest influences for me and countless other students during developmental stages of higher education. He was immensely articulate, intellectually honest and benevolently firm as an administrator, dedicated educationist and intellectual, all those fine attributes packed in one mortal frame. That breed of educationists and intellectuals is what the country sadly misses at present.

Jung's vast travels led him to several conclusions. Principle among them was his inference that the human mind had several universal patterns of behaviour some of which transcended generations, which he referred to as "***archetypical patterns of behaviour***". These were resident in a massive aggregate database of humanity which he referred to as the "***collective unconscious***". He met people from all religions and races as well as those without any religious beliefs in various far away parts of the world such as East Africa and as far as India. He also observed that people believed in various religions and some believed in none and concluded that whether a human being stood on one side of the religious fence or the other, the fact remained that the idea or concept of God influenced every human mind without exception and Jung considered it his business to simply study those influences and how they impacted on the behaviour and psyche of individuals or groups of individuals in an impartial manner. He therefore went on to study even the relatively obscure disciplines of Sufism, Alchemy, etc. in order to develop a better and more balanced understanding of the human mind. His approach was global and included the healthy or creative mind as much as the deviant ones, a study of mankind, not just local societies. His school of thought came to be known as "***analytical psychology***", which is reflected in the title; the concepts of *persona* and *shadow* archetypes being fundamental to Jung's theories. This is primarily a comparison of the current confrontational and intolerant breed in society responsible for almost all present troubles and sorrows with members of the society as it existed before religious fanaticism was injected as a political doctrine in the mid-1970s. The analysis applies equally to Pakistani expatriates in particular and Muslims expatriates from elsewhere in general living in various parts of the globe but manifesting home grown isolationist attitudes in adopted alien environments.

Structural & functional societies

This is another key theme in understanding the dynamics of socio-cultural milieus. As important as individual human behaviour is, it is influenced by and affects the group or society within which individuals exist and operate. For present purposes, we will take one most relevant classification of groups or societies in social psychology as our second simultaneous tool of analysis; "*Structural vs Functional societies*". In a nutshell, structural societies place more emphasis on how things or people look or should look in outwards appearance from the perspective of the society or beliefs held; whereas functional societies are more focused on outcomes or results rather than external presentation; placing more emphasis on the spirit in which an action is performed instead of the physical form in which it is delivered. The society in Pakistan can be classified as an extreme form of structuralism and we will see how this attribute has served or failed to serve the nation's best interests in its relatively short history.

Change adaption

Self-praise is no praise; it is a craving of the mind for reassurance especially when the chips are down, a longing for social approval to enhance self-esteem. Some people need to stand in front of a mirror every hour, to station themselves before it in self-admiration until they can self-certify an exceptional personality or at least a socially presentable look. It takes three lines to complete this complimentary analysis! But looking for one's own faults, having the courage to laugh at oneself, accepting that one could be or may have been wrong, having the grace to concede that someone else could presently be better than oneself and that everyone could learn from others, that one can make suggestions to others which he thinks will be of benefit to them, but NEVER insist that his way of life is a "*take it or leave it*" proposition. All this requires a generous degree of tolerance, humility and willingness to change. When it comes to matters of evolution and change, very few people would want to challenge ***Charles Darwin*** on the subject. His view on change and progress is "**It is not the strongest of the species that survive, nor the most intelligent, but the one most responsive to change**." We are blessed to have lived on this planet at a time when life moves forward literally every second at blinding speed. Many of us have crossed the historical time line of the second millennium, which will only return in history almost a thousand years from now. We have no option but to keep pace with the speed of change and the changing world. Nations have lived far too long in the comfort zone of a make belief life that is hooked to the "*glorious yesterday*". Yesterday was yesterday; it cannot be today, even less it cannot be tomorrow. Those who achieved glory in their yesterday, lived in that yesterday, not in the day before.

The world is in unprecedented turmoil at present, led by the threat of religious extremism and consequently terrorism. Many see Muslims as the main villains and most Muslims in turn are full of anger and counter complaints. There has been no shortage of the complaints versions from Muslims in present times. This is a strictly a non-religious attempt using *psychoanalytical* tools to bring to consciousness the mental processes at work that have created current mind sets. Also an attempt to explain to Muslims that many problems are predominantly self-created and in large measure Muslims alone can find solutions to them not through free flowing hatred that distorts the thought processes at present but through a rational and analytical approach to problems and solutions that offer a glimmer of hope for a more promising future for ourselves **along with, rather than against the rest of the world**.

Contempt, anger, hatred and other negative emotions can devastate potentially healthy and prosperous possibilities. It is great to learn from the success of others; even more beneficial to learn from the failures of known people because the proof and consequences of failure in each case are there for everyone to see, not just to speculate. I recall watching a movie on ***Richard Nixon's*** disastrous period in power. After having self-destruct and leaving behind a horrible legacy, in one of his soliloquies, the character says, "**Those who hate you never win. Not until you start hating them back. That is when you begin to destroy yourself**"! Profound words uttered with the benefit of hindsight if we can momentarily ignore the negative image of the author, it is most relevant to what the world is witnessing today in the form of hate generated happenings. Too many people today from all over the world, from all religions, races, colours, nationalities allow their judgements to be dictated far too easily by hatred of others than be driven by their own best interests.

Secondary objectives

While an objective analysis of the path of change in mind sets during the past six or seven decades is the primary objective of this book, I hope to encapsulate in the process, a few secondary objectives too.

Amongst them is the need to introduce to our current younger generation in particular, some of our forgotten literary and cultural icons; not through dull descriptive accounts but by using their known and popular masterpieces to reconstruct current themes, crises and real life or time scenarios. A lot of migrant population from the sub-continent all over the world can speak and understand the Urdu and Punjabi languages but are unable to read the script for lack of exposure abroad. With that in mind all text in both languages is supported by the *Roman* script versions to facilitate comprehension.

Another objective is to attempt to do justice to some of our unsung national heroes like the legendary social worker *Abdul Sattar Edhi*, intellectuals and a rare breed of judges who defied Zia and passed judicial orders independent of commandments issued to them, unknown freedom fighters who set themselves ablaze in the streets of major cities to draw international attention towards the inhumane practices and policies of Zia-ul-Haq.

Perhaps the most important of secondary objectives is to try to rekindle the lost intellectual creativity and spontaneity of the common citizen. The standard thinking process in society has become so predictably modular that not only can responses to various stimuli be anticipated in advance; one can even guess the repetitive language that is likely to be used. Until a couple of decades ago, some words and expressions simply did not exist in public jargon. Some of the present ones employed these days were introduced in more recent times through state media in official press briefings and absorbed by everyone in society almost in the same behavioural pattern as was associated with strictly regimented communist societies of the cold war period. Communism by its totalitarian approach was averse to any creative and spontaneous thinking that could have had the aptitude to exceed the boundaries of Communist party philosophy.

Let us look at only one example here very briefly by way of illustration. All through school and college life of our generation, when any person or event was referred to in conversation, a variety of words and expressions were used, such as "*Iss silsiley mein*", *Iss barey mein*", "*Iss ke mutalak*" and so on. Each expression meant more or less the same [*in this context or connection*] whether to book mark a news item in conversation, statement or event, etc. or simply to recall a relevant precedent. During *Pervaiz Musharaf's* period, most press briefings started to use a new expression "*Iss hawaley se*" which also means the same thing. However, it has since become almost a national catchphrase. Every conversation starts with this singular use to the exclusion of all other alternates and synonyms. There is nothing wrong by itself in the use of this expression, if used intermittently with other variables. But when thinking becomes so stagnated and creativity so completely intimidated into submission, people resort to standard expressions and words that the mind is comfortable with as a safer option. The attitude is symptomatic of psycho-economics; a concept that refers to a mind's predisposition to expend the least amount of mental effort at all times that is necessary to achieve any or every purpose. From official briefings to national news bulletins, chat shows on electronic media, comments by judges and legislators, social conversation, off the cuff conversations by the man on the street – everyone using the same expression reflects very unhealthy and under exercised minds. It may seem no big deal and probably is not for its scale of impact but what it represents metaphorically is an alarming downhill slide in national IQs and a general lack of creative energy. It is the exact opposite of what is referred to in psychoanalytical terms as "**automatic unwinding of the libido**", a natural and unhindered release of thought processes. The current mental state makes it so much easier for agents of control and manipulation to influence individual and collective minds of automatons that are inherently inclined to accept everything thrown at them without thinking or analysis, instead of having to deal with individuals with creative ability and freedom of thinking processes.

Throughout my tenure with the Commonwealth, my preferred approach with member countries was that it was not our role to dictate solutions to sovereign states. Instead of that we endeavoured to introduce best practices in all professional matters and left it to the members to select those options that they deemed most suitable for themselves as end users. Management approaches adopted for various purposes need to be customised according to the aims and objectives. It will be my endeavour to conclude my point of view and analysis of various situations throughout this book with short questions for the reader to consider for himself, a stimulus to apply one's mind in pursuit of solutions and possibilities rather than giving a subjective "*take it or leave it*" perspective. The current intellectual inertia needs to be tutored and jump-started back into proactive modules in place of the current fatalistic patterns of responses.

There are similar additional secondary objectives that will come up as we go along. In some situations, it will be necessary and important to name persons but in some others, creating and using a fictional fall guy instead of real names where possible will be the preferred option; the point or issue being more important than individual actors.

2

Madness, but with a unholy method

Religion and religious role players

Religion and genuinely held religious beliefs are one set of subject matter in themselves; religious parties, leaders and social actors with religious masks constitute a completely different subject matter altogether. Criticism of the self-appointed "*ground staff*" for religious matters should not be equated or confused with criticism of religion itself. ***It is of utmost importance never to lose sight of this distinction or be misled into mixing the two; not at any stage in this book and even more importantly in all aspects of practical life.***

Theory & practice

Theory is almost always simpler than practice. An immaculate time tested theory can be let down by faulty implementation, vested interest or other logistical fallacies. In some cases, theory itself can be flawed but if it works in most other cases but has not worked in one particular case, in all probability the cause of failure will be in the implementation process. Wrongful or dishonest enactment or administration of a theory, doctrine, belief or a national constitution does not mean that any of these is inherently flawed. Getting this analysis right is often the vital difference between success and failure, advancement and decline or decay. Identifying the difference between theory and actual practice is also often the best analytical approach to determining which of the two is at fault. Judging events and actions by this analytical approach will provide answers to many crises we have faced in our short history and will continue to face if perennial habits and practices do not perish quickly.

With apologies for those who do not read or understand the Urdu language, I want to start with a brief poem that is a sad commentary on our present state, before we take a deeper look at specifics. Amongst the several secondary objectives referred to earlier, one is to reintroduce to the senior generation and introduce to our younger generation, some of the nation's unsung heroes, intellectuals, artists who did not get a fair deal nor their deserved share of recognition during their life time or even posthumously, having lived in a predominantly uninformed and traditionalist society. The following piece is a humble tribute to the great *Faiz Ahmad Faiz*, an immensely gifted poet, the finest of his generation, an intellectual giant, champion of noble causes like freedom of expression and equal rights, and winner of Lenin Prize in 1962. This attempt is styled on one of his many masterpieces.

ہم جو تاریک راہوں میں مارے گۓ
جاگیریں بچانے کو وارے گۓ
اسکری لاٹھیوں سے پچھاڑے گۓ
دینی سبق سب کو سکھانے گۓ
امن و سکوں خُد ہمارے گۓ
سنسار بھر میں دھتکارے گۓ

اپنے ہاتھوں میں اپنی تقدیر تھی
راہ جو چنی اپنی ہی تدبیر تھی
کیسا شکوہ اور کس منہ سے کریں
گر حاقمیت کے آمرانہ سلسلے
تباہی کی راہوں سے سب جا ملے
ہم جو تاریک راہوں میں مارے گۓ

Hum jo tareeq rahoan mein marey gaye
Jagirein bachanein ko warey gaye
Askari lathaliyon se pecharey gaye
Deeni sabak sab ko sikhaney gaye
Amn-o-sakoon khud hamarey gaye
Sansaar bhar mein dhutkare gaye

Apney hathoon mein apni taqdeer thi
Rah jo chunni apni hi tadbeer thi
Kaisa shikwa, aur kis moun se karain
Gar hakamiyat ke aamirana silsiley
Tabahi ki rahoon se sab ja miley
Hum jo tareeq rahoan mein marey gaye

"Jinnah" the betrayed and abandoned father figure

Conservative and liberal camps exist in most countries and societies. The difference is in the intensity of opposing viewpoints and the degree of tolerance or accommodation of opposite perspectives. From a psychological standpoint, the higher the degree of tolerance of ambiguity or disagreement, the healthier the mind is likely to be. That holds true for all groups, societies and nations too. There is no dispute that the case for an independent Pakistan consisting of Muslim majority provinces was lead almost under the singular and undisputed stewardship of Quaid-e-Azam, Mohammad Ali Jinnah, the now seemingly ignored, if not forgotten "*Father of the Nation*"! That lack of dispute is not always entirely from the goodness of all hearts but is nevertheless a rare consensus, partly from fear of retribution from the vast majority who still hold Jinnah in high reverence.

From the man on the street to the most educated Muslim then, Jinnah was the only source of information, guidance and decision making at the time. Jinnah himself never said publicly or privately that Pakistan was created in the name of religion. Those who said so used a sort of reverse logic to the one used by Zia in his referendum; if the voters supported Islam, it was his victory. In this case, if a homeland was envisaged for Muslims in the hope of a better future, it had to be for religious reasons only.

Muslim majority provinces being the natural basis of self-governance meant that Muslims from any province not being a Muslim majority province had a choice to make. They had an optional right to migrate to Pakistan from any Muslim minority province in the sub-continent but that was purely a personal choice based on either imminent threats to their existence or perception of brighter future for their generations to follow in a new country, but Pakistan was only primarily meant for Muslim majority provinces. Likewise Hindus and Sikhs who migrated to India had personal choices to make based on similar considerations. Millions of Muslims stayed back in India and today constitute a bigger group of population than the Muslim population of Pakistan.

The creation of Bangladesh in 1971 further reinforced the principle of self-governance by the majority because that is what the people of Bangladesh eventually felt they were being deprived of, not the right to offer their prayers! In fact it was the "litmus test" argument or illustration in favour of majority rule being the only basis for an independent Pakistan.

Mohammad Ali Jinnah's personal life style and dress code throughout his early life and the independence struggle period provided circumstantial evidence of his socio-cultural leanings. But with vested interest so determined to blur that image, more direct evidence was needed. Two most focused and unswerving quotes from Jinnah leave no room for doubt. None was required by his admirers anyway but vested interest needed not only to propagate their twisted version but also to try to destroy any evidence that threatened to make their concocted case weaker. These direct quotes from Jinnah that leave no room for an iota of doubt have rarely been in public view. Was this just a coincidence or oversight; an innocent oversight of the very basis on which Jinnah carried out a long struggle for an independent state? Most unlikely.

The campaign for Jinnah's posthumous character reform reached its climax during the devilish period of General Zia. Jinnah's framed photos in "western dress" hung in government offices since independence were removed and substituted by artificial paintings showing Jinnah clad in a "*sherwani*", a dress not a common wear in any of the five provinces that constituted Pakistan in 1947. The change of dress in itself is not the issue; the motives of deception behind the move are the real issue, as if the Father of the Nation needed additional demonstrative certification of his patriotic credentials. The two quotes from Jinnah in reference are:

1. **"You are free; you are free to go to your temples, you are free to go to your mosques or to any other place of worship in this State of Pakistan. You may belong to any religion or caste or creed – that has nothing to do with the business of the State.... You will find that in course of time Hindus would cease to be Hindus and Muslims would cease to be Muslims, not in the religious sense, because that is the personal faith of each individual, but in the political sense as citizens of the State.** [*Aug 11, 1947, Jinnah's address to the First Constituent Assembly*].

2. **"Pakistan is not going to be a theocratic state to be ruled by priests with a divine mission. We have many non-Muslims- Hindus, Christians and Parsis – but they are all Pakistanis. They will enjoy the same rights and privileges as any other citizens and will play their rightful part in the affairs of Pakistan."** [*Feb. 1948, Jinnah's broadcast address to the people of the United States of America*].

So direct evidence, supporting circumstantial evidence and forensic evidence consisting of Jinnah's personal belongings, still in display till today in the museum next to his dignified resting place in Karachi all showcase with loudness and clarity a consistent argument.

Having abandoned a crystal clear national vision provided by Jinnah, with such guilt free ease and having opted or fallen instead for exactly what he had specifically forbidden, do we have any case for being surprised or frustrated at where we stand today? Should we even wonder why religious fanaticism has come to haunt us when it was carefully programmed in a manner that institutes of technical and vocational education which provided possibilities and opportunities for at least self-employment to young technicians were instead incrementally fizzled out to be replaced by a network of uncontrolled and unregulated "*deeni madrassas*" [*religious schools*] owned and managed by quarrelsome and militant religious sub-groups? Could this approach to nation building, creating the present lot of young so-called students who come out of religious schools and have no other career prospects than the narrow channels into which they are launched from early childhood have led to any outcome other than what is on display today?

The national leaders betrayed its founding father as soon as he passed away, consequently the nation lost its way and the rot set in from the beginning; the journey has been downhill ever since. It had to be. A mass of people moving in different directions, for destinations unknown does not make a nation. It has to have all the attributes of a crowd. A crowd is easier to mislead than an organised group or nation. A distinct feature of a crowd is that individual identities are consumed by the chaotic mob mentality. Is it difficult to figure out who could have gained from this induced madness? It could not have been Jinnah's followers and admirers; it had to be only those who stood to lose from the adoption of Jinnah's guidelines and political vision of nationhood.

One wonders if our rulers would have betrayed Jinnah even if he had lived on for a longer period of time. Had Jinnah lived on to see himself being betrayed in his life time, it would have been the ultimate insult for him, to witness betrayal by those for whose well-being he even concealed his terminal illness, because disclosure could have triggered a manipulated fatal delay in the nation's destiny, in the clear knowledge that with him removed from the scene, the movement would lose momentum and direction to die a natural death. The fact that he did not live long enough to witness his own betrayal will have spared him the agony in his last moments but it does not lessen the disgraceful conduct of those who still do lip service to his name but exclude and insult every basic value he epitomised, from their private and public lives. It was madness but certainly not without a well-conceived and disguised method. Does the country now have any other option whatsoever other than to regroup under Jinnah's original guiding principles ONLY and to make a fresh start? Better late, than never, that is if it is not already too late!

Before partition, the majority of feudal landlords called "*waderas*" in the province of Sind were Hindus. Muslims aspiring to be in similar positions of privilege and local power found it hard to compete and dislodge them. When Jinnah set the goal for a separate homeland the Muslim waderas and those gunning for economic opportunities declared their allegiance and support for him and the Muslim League, not out of love for the cause but because the opportunity it offered to drive away Hindu waderas was too good to miss out. Given Jinnah's political philosophy, there was no common ground at all but finding common ground with Jinnah was not the burning desire; using the opportunity to take over large agricultural estates was the driving motivation from the outset. As soon as Jinnah passed away, the only threat to their long term interest was gone. Getting rid of his guidelines in a hurry was the insurance policy for perpetuation of the landed aristocracy. To do that, the ruling class enlisted the support of willing volunteers in vital state organs and the social influence wielding clergy. The plot of the soap opera was well and truly laid out and it continues till today. The majority were kept out of decision making in nation building, and education kept out of the majority to render them incapable of comprehending the master plan, staying so overwhelmed about daily livelihoods that they would hardly have time for involvement in matters of governance that impacted directly on their lives. As and when it was required, effective interventions were made by the judiciary, executive, military and the clergy on behalf of stakeholders to ensure status quo. No wonder even till today, statements of political forecasts are commonly issued through the residential hideouts of some well-known *waderas* and *Pirs*.

The thinking process will not have been too different in other provinces to the extent of aligning with Jinnah and his Muslim League solely from selfish motives of self-preservation. It was only logical and natural for all such conspiring passengers on board the Muslim League train to jump off and run their solo races once the driver was no longer in control. The country and its population are today facing the consequences of their selfish personal agendas wearing deceptive personas of nationalism in one form or another.

Analysing thought processes – causes & effects

"The area is capable of producing large earthquakes because of the compression created when what is now India slammed against the Asian continent millions of years ago".
Caruso

Was Caruso talking rubbish in establishing a virtually timeless relationship in trying to explain the cause of an earthquake? A causal relationship between a recent earthquake and a seismic movement millions of years ago! That is the strength and timeless linkage between cause and effect in nature's rules of governance and cosmic management. My primary objective is not to make a political analysis, but to set the scene for analysing the causal relationships between our horribly flawed choices and the current mess we find ourselves in. Respecting the dynamics of cause and effect relationship is one of the building blocks for that broader analysis.

Events happen and developments take place in present times because causes are set in motion years, if not decades in advance. Causes need to be addressed ahead of consequences to find permanent solutions. Deep lying diseases, physical, social, cultural or economic can never be cured by patching up superficial symptoms. It is a universally accepted scientific concept that hardly needs more elaboration.

Everyone instinctively wants to know why something happened the way it happened, or why something did not happen the way we wanted it to? The cause leading to a response or reaction can be a person, thing, event, state, or some action or lack of action. Each stimulus will trigger a response or condition of some sort. It may differ for each individual or situation but there will always be a link between cause and effect. Take for example the vision of Pakistan as stated by the Father of the Nation. Discarding that vision has resulted in developments that are neither desirable nor beneficial. If that vision had been kept in focus and followed in letter and spirit, the consequences would have been different. The differences can be inferred in logical steps. If the logic followed in not adopting a principle is accepted, the corresponding logical sequence that could have developed if Jinnah's guiding vision of the new state had been followed should be equally reliable.

I am writing this book as an effect because events today give enough cause to be concerned about the future. If our national situation had been different today as a cause, I might have opted for something else as a pursuit instead as an effect. Global warming is the effect, caused by the abuse of earth's natural balance of elements; ill health is generally the effect of lack of exercise or excess of rich food that overloads the system, which constitutes the cause. If high blood pressure is not controlled effectively as a cause, it will invariably lead to one of the known and documented medical effects. It will not lead directly to low blood pressure because there is no logical or causal relationship to that likelihood. Social unrest and frustration can be the result of acute inequalities in wealth, opportunities or injustices. Finding the right cause and effect relationship is the key to a good and reliable analysis.

At the outset, I did not give myself a complete brief on contents for this book. As events have unfolded since this pursuit was envisaged a couple of years ago, many topics and sub-topics have found their own places in various chapter topics and sub-plots. A causal relationship is always at work, whether clearly visible or not, whether fully understood or not. The fault may be in individual perception, lack of understanding and comprehension of objective realities or simply a deliberately dishonest interpretation but never in the honesty and reliability of logic itself or in nature's law of causal relationships.

Our fictional fall guy

The two most dominant factors that affect or control the explicit and concealed thought processes and behavioural patterns in our society are religion and feudal or medieval socio-cultural control mechanisms. Our fictional fall guy must therefore encapsulate some very common or popular symbolic presence of both influences. Let the religious part be represented by the name *Ramzan* [*Muslim month of fasting*], the feudal part by *Chaudhry*. Since Chaudhrys are normally associated with the biggest province of Punjab, let us also add *Khan* to the name to make it a national character. That completes the full name, "***Chaudhry Ramzan Khan***". If our friends in the provinces of Sind and Baluchistan feel neglected or abandoned in any way, please don't because that is not the intention. If it makes more satisfying reading for anyone, please read "*wadera*" or *"sardar"* for *"chaudhary" or "khan"*, respectively wherever the fictional character appears in the text.

We can add one more variant to meet another character emphasis. Where the character is meant to be more in a feudal mind-set role, we will refer to him as "***Chaudhry Ramzan***". Where the text refers to a religious character, we will reverse it to ***"Ramzan Chaudhry"***. Since those referred to positively would prefer to be quoted as real life characters, references to the fall guy will be mainly uncomplimentary by necessity. It is therefore importance to get this out of the way; that the character is purely fictional and any resemblance to a real life existence will be purely a coincidence.

3

Accountability or destiny; a defining choice

Adam & Eves

Unless a person subscribes fully to the theory of evolution over the religious version of the origin of mankind, there is broad agreement amongst all religions that *Adam,* referred to by Muslims as *Hazrat 'Ād̲ām* was the first male human being God created. There are differences in minor details as to the circumstances under which Adam was expatriated from Heaven to earth. Despite those minor differences in detail, there is agreement that in essence it came about as a result of breach of unambiguous guidelines from God to Adam as to what was allowed or not allowed to be eaten from the *Garden of Eden.* The Christian version states that God "planted the Garden of Eden and set Adam there, to work on it and watch over it", permitting him to eat from all the trees in the garden except the Tree of Knowledge of Good and Evil.

Hazrat 'Ād̲ām takes a prominent role in Islamic traditions concerning the fall of Satan. It is said that when God announced his intention of creating Adam, some of the angels expressed disappointment wondering why God would create a being that could eventually indulge in evil. God subsequently created Eve [*Ama Ḥawwā*] for Adam's company. It seems very important and interesting that Eve was to be his social company, not to act as a creation for control or domination.

In the Muslim tradition the accepted notion is that angels were creations that would not be accountable since they were not blessed with "free will". When God commanded the angels to bow to Adam as his highest creation, Satan was also present but refused to bow and was consequently banished from Heaven. In retaliation Satan tempted Ama Ḥawwā to eat from the forbidden tree and she in turn gave the fruit to Hazrat 'Ā̱dām, who fell for the bait. For that act of disobedience or defiance, God sent Hazrat 'Ā̱dām and Ama Ḥawwā to earth, arriving first at mountain peaks outside Mecca; Adam on *Safa*, and Eve on *Marwa* in Saudi Arabia.

The minimum common denominators in all versions are, firstly that Adam and Eve were the first two human beings initially resident in Heaven and subsequently exiled to earth. Secondly, that God gave clear guidelines for strict obedience and with a warning of consequences for non-compliance. Thirdly, that both were drawn into temptation by Satan and that punishment for non-compliance was swift and appropriate. With no major disagreements on these three core issues, other details whether similar or variable in different religions do not matter for present purposes.

Accountability or destiny

With this scene setting, we can turn to our main thesis for this chapter. Two apparently conflicting religious beliefs are commonly referred to in daily life. The first relates to the concept of reward and punishment [***"Jaza"*** aur ***"Saza"***], Heaven, Hell and accountability in life hereinafter for deeds or misdeeds on planet earth. The second concept is that of preordained or predetermined destiny, a set path with time and space for each individual or events to inevitably take place; an arrangement of continual divine control at all times for everything that takes place during the life span of individuals or even nations on earth.

It is obvious from the very outset that both set of beliefs contradict each other. So let us try to analyse which of these two concepts applies more to real life situations and how? There is no better way to start than at the origin of mankind. The concept of accountability requires subjugation by man to all given codes of moral conduct. Adam was put in a trial situation and was told what was right and to be strictly followed; also told which actions were unacceptable and would invoke strict punitive consequences. We are also told that angels are not subject to accountability, having not been blessed with free will to choose between compliance and non-compliance. Man was however, blessed with a free will, the ability to decide between alternate, even multiple courses of actions or choices. Irrespective of the reasons for which he did, Adam violated the code of conduct and the rest as we say is history.

So the very first test man faced has two clearly identifiable characteristics. Firstly, Adam acting independent of control and with the ability to think with freedom which led him to eventually take a decision in favour of the forbidden guideline, and secondly, having made an independent choice, he then faced immediate accountability and divine retribution. It had to be so; a cause in the form of an act of defiance leading to the logical effect of punishment as forewarned. It would simply not add up if Adam and Eve were pre-destined to violate the given orders and still be held accountable for having committed an act that they were programmed to commit anyway, and to that effect the programme notes were carved out in the palm of their hands, as those commonly known as palmists would lead innocent human beings into believing. If this were not the case, would the fundamental belief about Heaven and Hell still be relevant? Why would God give His greatest creation the ability to think and a free will to choose his actions if every man and women had already been checked into Heaven or Hell even before landing on earth? How can someone be sent to earth with a destiny to stay a labourer or a slave or a beggar on the street all his life with no option whatsoever for a change for the better no matter how hard or for how long he or his subsequent generations tried? Those obstacles, physical and psychological are the creation of human mind and invariably work in support of the agents of control and exploitation.

It is worth repeating in order to leave no doubt in the mind of any reader that both are essentially religiously held views and very fundamental ones too. The aspect which needs attention is that both seemingly cut across each other and therefore there is a case for selecting or at least preferring one over the other as a guiding principle of life. Individuals and consequently societies and nations can favour either line of belief more than the other because religious choices are purely a personal matter between God and an individual. To me the version of accountability subject to independent decision making makes common and logical sense but many amongst my friends and family tilt towards the opposite view. Importantly, however, is the vital psychological hypothesis that depending on which of the two alternate views is favoured or followed by a particular person or a society will largely influence their general decision making and approach to life.

Those individuals and societies that believe more firmly in destiny will normally be more structural in chemistry where explicit form, rituals, ancestral practices and associated values will dominate decision making, interpersonal preferences and relationships. Those individuals or societies that are more focused on the aspect of a system of accountability in next life based on deeds or misdeeds on earth will tend to tilt as a group towards functionalism, concentrating on aims, objectives and moral rationale of decision making or behaviour, believing that every action taken or decision made will have a causal reaction, both in this life and up in the heavens.

Consequently standards of justice and accountability in the latter category of societies are generally higher and better established than in structural ones. It is therefore not surprising that in extreme forms of structuralism like in our case, justice and accountability in private and public life are subservient to other influences, if not non-existent.

God's ultimate gift to man

How can then free will gifted to man by his Creator be taken away from him by man himself in the garb of any cause or belief? How does the conviction that nothing moves or happens without God's will fit into life's scheme of things? What is the meaning of God's complete control of the universe? Looking at real life and events, it means exactly what it says. The immaculate manner in which the universe is run is proof of perfection. The sun, earth, other planets, moon, stars, etc. move flawlessly within a system. So flawlessly and immaculately that for centuries the sun has never been late in rising in any part of the earth even by a fraction of a second and with such impeccable exactness that experts can ascertain with insured accuracy years in advance the exact time, day, duration and proportion of a solar or lunar eclipse in a particular part of the globe. The divine control is not limited just to planet earth but encompasses the whole universe. It also implies that God has unlimited power to intervene in any matter but whether He does so to regulate the day to day and minute to minute lives of ordinary mortals in a way that dilutes the free will He constructed in man is a different matter altogether. If He does control and programme our thoughts and actions as many make us believe, then the logical question is where does that leave us with the divine accountability process in life hereafter? Divine control is for running the system of the universe, including the earth and the perfection we observe is proof of divine management. The manner in which the affairs of planet earth have been run for centuries is proof of man management. The point is well expressed in a rather light hearted recent quote about the affairs of planet earth, light hearted but with a serious message too. "**After one look at this planet any visitor from outer space would say, I want to see the manager**" ***William Burroughs.*** That impression is surely not reflective of divine management but is definitely a commentary on the consequences of an unending series of man-made disasters.

Anyone who tries to explain this tool of "*feudal management*" control which has no relevance at all to religion, except in its misuse, is sent into a name calling spin such as a "*kafir*" [*non-believer*] or a secular agent, a communist, etc. to sustain current artificial advantages. ***Faiz Ahmad Faiz*** spent most of his life behind bars but stuck to his convictions. That is not an easy option. Most people when put on the spot prefer to recoil and display a "*did not see*" or "*wrongly quoted*" signboard for fear of a short visit to a police station that could cause unnecessary inconvenience. Such rare national heroes, people with conviction and armed with knowledge that can contribute to the collective welfare of society rather than lead to the setting up of a sugar or steel mill as part of the family empire are worth their weight in gold. We have never paused to think about it and are therefore faced with the consequences of our own ignorance, inattentiveness and neglect. One can ignore a routine flu but only at the risk of letting it grow into a life threatening pneumonia. That is exactly what we have done to ourselves. Faiz poetically put this point across as follows:

الم نسیبوں جگر فگاروں کی صبحح افلاک پر نہیں ہے
جہاں پے ہم تم کھڑے ہیں دوںوں روشن عفق یہیں ہے

Alum nasiboon, jigar figaroon ki subha aflak par naheen hai
Jahain pe hum tum kharey hein donoon, shar ka roshan ufaq yahein hai

[Deliverance of the down trodden is not etched in the skies,
It is here, on this earth where you and I stand]

It is important to try to analyse the practical impact and consequences of pursuing life based on either accountability or destiny beliefs or indeed on mixed interpretations? Does the immaculate operation of the universe compared to shortcomings of life on earth throughout history and what continues to happen today, confirm two different levels of control? This is the benchmark for analysis of real life situations for individuals, societies, entire nations and in some instances, humanity as a whole.

As for accountability itself, it has to be to Him alone, not to any self-appointed human administrator on His behalf! No man has the right to arrogate to himself any divine role playing that aims to restrict or control the actions of their fellow beings. The *Talibans* of our present times are the fieriest advocates and self-appointed enforces of God's will. Could the manner of their operations and devastations be the laid out scheme of a sanctioned life in any sense? Them on the one side positioning themselves and scheming all along for self-destruction in the name of religion and a divine message. Their Muslim opponents on the other hand, trying to do their best to get to them or destroy them before they self-destruct and destroy hundreds of others in the process? What could possibly be predetermined destiny in this tale of horrors?

Like most matters in life, reliance on destiny has its positive and negative implications. It is a source of great healing of the mind when faced with or coming out of a hugely traumatic experience. A sudden accidental death in a family is always a mental energy exhausting experience. There is no element of choice or options in such experiences. There could have been a choice before such a tragedy hits such as driving more carefully, choosing between staying home or going out alone late at night, even deciding between travel by air or road and so on, but no choices to be made to reverse events once the present becomes the past. These kind of tragic experiences are tailor made to provide a most effective source of solace to the mind in the shortest time frame that no other alternate or professional counselling can provide; reconciling to all events as their fate. From a social and psychological standpoint, it is important to have that recourse to allow social life to run in a customary way because when a normal mind collapses under trauma, it cannot be predicted with certainty which way it might go. For a physical comparison, it is like a person falling unconscious from a standing position. He could land safely on a soft floor and recover with time or hit his head in the process of falling causing a severe injury that may take a long time to heal. In most unfortunate cases, the fall can even be fatal.

Societies which have high levels of lawlessness, which are devoid of legal privileges and high on discrimination in treatment of its citizens offer cognitive consonance for the mind through rationalisation with fate or destiny. This also implies that in societies where the ratio of injustices, denial of rights and opportunities, high levels of insecurity, most minds will rely heavily on accepting outcomes as the dictates of fate. Taking that option away would lead to far more cases of mental breakdowns than will be the case otherwise and leave a huge curative gap in helping the human mind in its quest for restoration of calm and respite.

This is true with all faiths, just as Jung found out in his treatment of his clients. Those he discovered were stronger in their belief in

Christianity were easier to heal than those who were less anchored with their religion. It is the average mind's "*get out of stress*" clause. Unfortunately, it is sometimes also the "*get out of jail*" clause for culprits if society starts to take accidents and criminal acts as events that were destined to happen anyway.

The solution lies in changing conditions that leave inflicted minds with no alternate psychological process of emerging from high levels of stress, frustration, anger and even hatred towards those seen as the cause, whether real or imaginary, from their suffering and injustices. That can only happen when society as a whole becomes more progressive, inequalities in wealth and opportunities are comparatively less but most importantly the level of respect for and rule of law, and recourse to seeking justice are within reach and affordability of average citizens. It is more often a mind's state of helplessness in seeking justice in the face of denial of rights or physical intimidation that nudges it unconsciously towards acceptance of events in the healing sanctuary of fate or destiny.

The country's current mess is that of the making of its own successive leadership and wrong choices, with the exception of one or two periods. The fact that many people very often seem bewildered at how have we receded into our present condition, surprises many observers in turn. The following piece of poetry attempts to portray how several acts and deeds over decades have led the country to the present mess and now into this psychological state of denial of responsibility. In pursuance of one secondary objective, the scene is set for introduction of a very popular poem later made even more popular as a song, written by ***Hafeez Jalandhuri***, author of the National Anthem of Pakistan. The original poem is named "**Abhi to mein jawan houn**" [*I am still young*]. That poem was reflective of immensely better times long gone and radiates a mood of benign naughtiness all the way, which is consistent with how people then freely expressed their views, were in control of their way of life and thinking before insanity was gradually injected into society. My attempt is reflective of our painful present that has none of the relaxing and positive moods of the contents relevant at the time. It only borrows the style and rhyme of the original popular piece by way of a compliment and fond recollection of better times:

Ab bhi mein nadaan kyon? Ab bhi mein hairan kyon?	اب بھی میں نادان کیوں؟ اب بھی میں ہیران کیوں؟
Hawa gard-o-ghubar hai Chahroon pe bas bukhaar hai Bahar bin bahar hai Taranum sarhad par hai	ہوا گرد و غبار ہے چہروں بس بخار ہے بہار بن بہار ہے ترنم سرحد پار ہے
Kahan gaya tu sakiya Idhar ko loat, ghar ko aa Arey ab dekhata hai kya Har sha hune ko hai tabha Jis had tak ja sakey nazar Khair ki mile na ik khabar	کہاں گیا تُو ساقیا ادھر کو لوٹ گھر کو آ ارے اب دیکھتا ہے کیا؟ ہر شے ہونے کو ہے تباہ جس حد تک جا سکے نظر خیر کی ملے نہ اک خبر
Kya mulk ki kahaniyan Burqoon taley insaniyan Bumbar ya asl pathaniyan Darhi bardar mardaniyan Bhi shamiley shataniyan Jamaatein aur nooraniyan Andheroon ki nishaniyan Sub Zia ki karastaniyan	کیا ملک کی کہانیاں برقوں تلے انسانیاں بمبار یا اصل پٹھانیاں داڑھی بردار مردانیاں بھی شامل شیطانیاں جماعتیں اور نورانیاں اندھروں کی نشانیاں سب ضیا کی کارستانیاں
Zara suno to sheikh ji Bhole baney ho aap bhi Bhala nawaz o maulvi Juda huwe bhi thay kabhi Aur "Bhutto" ki surkh pi pi pi Bhi ab "Zard" bun ke reh gayi	ذرا سنو تو شیخ جی بھولے بنے ہو آپ بھی بھلا نواز و مولوی جدا ہوئے بھی تھے کبھی؟ اور بھٹو کی سرخ پی پی پی اب "زرد" بن کے رہ گئ
Bood ka na hast ka Na dum qalandar mast ka Daur daulat parast ka Kuch na raha ab sast ka Ghar tak bacha na past ka	بود کا نہ حست کا نہ دم قاندر مست کا دور دولت پرست کا کچہ نا راھا اب سست کا گھر تک بچا نا پست کا

Umeed aur yaas gum Hoosh gum, hawaas gum Adal gum, insaaf gum Lehaz gum, bardasht gum Badhali ka ahsaas gum Taleem gum, ustaad gum	عمید اور یاس گم ہوش گم حواس گم عدل گم انصاف گم لحاظ گم برداشت گم بدحالی کا احساس گم تعلیم گم استاد گم
Tablighi jalwa khaiz hoon Fizain "ithar" raize hoan Tarareeq shar angaiz hoan Nafratain kyon na taiz hoan	تبلیغی جلوا خیز ہوں فضایں اِتر ریز ہوں تقاریر شر انگیز ہوں نفرتین کیون نہ تیز ہوں
Muslim League hazaar hai Garm sayasi byopaar hai Sub se "sood" mand to Ab "Sharai" karobar hai Jinnah ka naam lewa to Bas us ka hi mazaar hai Sub America zimedaar hai	مسلم لیگ ہزار ہے گرم سیاسی بیوپار ہے سب سے 'سود' مند تو اب شرعی کاروبار ہے جناح کا نام لیوا تو بس اُس کا ہی مزار ہے سب امریکہ زمیدار ہے
Baazar banein hein qatal gah Kahan so rahi hai adliya Tarameem ka pyala piya Kaum ko kis baat ki saza Insan aisa behiss hua Kal najaney ho ga kya	بازار بنے ہیں قتل گاہ کہاں سو رہی ہے عدلیا ترامیم کا پیالا پیا قوم کو کس بات کی سزا؟ انساں ایسا بے حس ہوا کل نجانے ہو گا کیا؟
Koi Fiqar-e-farda kyon karey Yuhein hama hami rahey Nishat younhi jami rahey Daulat mein na kami rahey Insaan marey, mara karey	کوئ فکر فردا کیوں کرے یوں‌ہی ہما ہمی رہے نشست یوں‌ہی جمی رہے دولت میں نہ کمی رھے انساں مرے، مرا کرے
Ab bhi mein nadaan kyon? Ab bhi mein hairan kyon?	اب بھی میں نادان کیوں؟ اب بھی میں ہیران کیوں؟

4

Decrypting the medieval mind set

Social persona & shadow archetype

Persona

Quite literally, the word persona means a mask. The role playing part is drawn from the ancient Greek theatre where actors would wear different facial masks to portray different characters. In its true social role, persona allows the dynamics of social interaction to run smoothly or at least run without violence and chaos. By way of an instant crude example, one may want to slap another person misbehaving in the city centre but his social persona tells him that is not advisable and certainly not without consequences. It may be a silent wish that someone at my work place just drops dead but my professional persona may still lead me to greet that person with a "Good Morning" instead. When a stranger says "How are you today?" one would normally say he is fine. With very intimate friends the response can be far more intimate or on the subject of chronic constipation. Persona navigates us through daily life behind a mask with a package of responses based on individual experience or upbringing in a way that keeps us and other people safe and functional.

Another familiar example is the different nature of conversations that are used for instance at stag dinners compared to kitty parties or mixed gatherings, those between parents and children, bosses and subordinates, members of a competitive sports team as compared to a team of management experts. Each role playing has a different set of expectations and behavioural types; each is carried out wearing a virtual mask that is referred to as persona in Analytical Psychology terminology.

Shadow

In Jungian psychology, the shadow or "shadow archetype" is a part of the unconscious mind consisting of repressed weaknesses, shortcomings, and instincts. "*Everyone carries a shadow*" Jung wrote, "*and the less it is embodied in the individual's conscious life, the blacker and denser it is*".

Just as the ego represents who we believe we are, the shadow represents who we believe we are not. Over a period of time it becomes a database of denied wants, temptations, wishes and impulses. Shadow is just as important as ego in defining individual personalities and inter-personal relationships. The proportion of shadow control in an individual will be greater, if the incumbent pretends to be more pious or totally non-indulgent in trivial or persuasive temptations.

While shadow content is inherent in human nature, the larger it grows in scope and suppression, the more imbalances it creates in such personality types. Personalities closer to well-adjusted and productive social creatures will be those with a good balance between the persona and shadow proportions. Lots of individuals find it very difficult to own shadow characteristics as part of their existence and externalise those characteristics as being in others; the evil ones in society. Very often an adult indulging in immoral activities tends to act more strictly with his family members, especially female members in relation to their outdoor activities. The rationale in their mind is that the evil in their life and conduct is because of inherent evil in the other party involved in their activities. In doing so, they off-load their shadow personality to someone else and in their perverted mind, retain their pious existence only.

Reverting to the issue of nature's rule of balance, a healthy mind is one that creates a good proportional mix of persona and shadow criteria but more importantly is reasonably aware and in control of his possessions, both positive and negative. When a society tries to create artificially, overly pious human beings burdened under the weight of their handed out personas, the end product is Taliban like, no longer able to neither adjust to normal societies nor relate to them in a two way communication. On the other hand, societies which are excessively permissive end up losing a good percentage of social control and moral codes. We all know which route we have gone down and what an unbearably hot and spicy meal has been cooked in the end. The control freak obsession is a logical outcome of the compulsive promotion and perpetuation of medieval submissive demeanour that holds back creative thinking and healthy competition. By now, the country almost has exactly the kind of society that our political and military doctors alternately ordered over decades except that it is no longer obedient and compliant in the manner inscribed in the original blueprint.

"Games People Play"

Psychiatrist *Dr. Eric Berne* in his book "*Games People Play*" defined mind games as, **"A game is an on-going series of complementary ulterior transactions progressing to a well-defined, predictable outcome. Descriptively, it is a recurring set of transactions... with a concealed motivation... or gimmick"** Most examples quoted by Dr. Berne may be very relevant to his society but some that are in common with what other groups and societies all play at times. But let us start with a very indigenous example. We will all have heard and even said at times phrases like *"mein is kabil nahein" or "nacheez ki rai mein" [I am not worth this OR in the opinion of this insignificant being]*, etc. The reality is that the speaker does not mean a word of what he says. On the contrary, his mind is begging for a compliment or reassurance and invariably he gets it in return and gets away with his game of fishing for a reassuring compliment. The standard response one would normally get is like "*no sir, you are being humble*" and so on. Try this check-it-out game of your own next time when someone says something similar by saying, "Y*es, I fully agree. I always thought you were a complete dud or a pseudo-intellectual*" and watch his eyes bulge out in horror!

These are relatively innocent games in social context but there are far more complex mind games that are regularly played out in every society. In societies or even families where the ratio of persona roles is far greater than expression of the real spontaneous self of individuals, these games will be more frequent because each game serves to support and sustain a particular role or a social expectation.

Ardeshir Cowasjee, a very senior and outspoken journalist whose articles I read with interest in newspaper columns recently provided some very insightful information of the mind games played out by politicians and military rulers in their international relations in real life dealings and the very different persona roles that they play out for domestic public consumption. Irrespective of some serious security issues that may be involved through the *WikiLeaks* exposure, there is one overwhelming positive aspect of the information in that the hypocrisy of civil and military leaders worldwide has been exposed. The information may be limited to a few names only but the hard reality is that the world is run in a different way to what the average human being thinks or is actually led to believe. The Leaks have shown in many cases the real faces of those leaders and military men down on their knees before their foreign counterparts from the big powers in private but demonising them while in their dirty public roles in front of local media and audiences. It is a thief's pride they say that he is not a hypocrite! Most political leaders and military generals know deep down the importance of military and economic aid and as soon as they come to power, their first port of call is on western embassies to offer reassurances of support and compliance but the public stance is shamelessly different for domestic audiences. According to one document, even the pious politician *Maulana Fazl-ur-Rehman*, while hosting a dinner for the US ambassador to Islamabad in 2007 conveyed to her that all his votes in the legislature were available for sale. He then pleaded with the ambassador to support his candidature for the post of prime minister of the country. There has not been a single denial by any accused party so far. Maulana Fazl and his brand of holy followers now lead the campaign in support of the blasphemy law in the country!

A web site with a very uncomplimentary and seemingly deliberately offensive name contains a video that spells out details of various similar statements and conversation of various leading characters listed in WikiLeak documents. It would be unfair to quote the uncultured website name because the sentiment, especially its intensity will almost certainly be lost in translation but it does reflect with some degree of accuracy the angry image in the public mind about those who are in positions of control of the destiny of the nation. It is a very worrying and confidence eroding thought indeed.

Playing mind games

The human mind as developed from childhood in societies dominated by feudal controls manifests itself in some typically archetypal behavioural patterns. The dominating undertone in these types of personality packages is one which is conditioned to be easily intimidated and overawed by those perceived to be stronger or more influential members of society. At the same time, in turn it has the tendency to attempt to dominate those below themselves or less likely to be able to retaliate in a harmful way. It may seem odd that someone should mete out to others the same treatment that he considers exploitative and inequitable for himself. Let us refer to it as the medieval or feudal mind set for purposes of our analysis. This is a much broader concept than the physical structures of political or economic feudal system of governance in medieval societies; this is about an archetypal state of mind that operates in society, in offices, business dealings and even within family relationships.

Given the very significant role religion plays in our daily life, there is not surprisingly, one exception to this rule. If someone manages to carve out for himself by any means whatsoever, a reputation of being someone close to God such as a saint or faith healer, etc. his social deprivation takes a back seat. People in much higher positions of power and influence will suddenly ignore his socio-economic status to extend the same kind of respect that they would extend to those with more power or influence. Unconsciously, it is the same mental process that schemes the attitude. That imposter in demonstrating his feigned religiously privileged position and divine contacts is seen as someone useful and gifted with more influence than ordinary mortals. It makes sense for the medieval mind set to stay on the right side of someone capable of causing damage through his spiritual powers. The driving emotion, even if not displayed overtly is one of fear of divine influence and consequences through a chosen one "*poncha hua*". The appended emotion is that potential benefits could accrue from keeping such pious ones on side. For the religious actor, the mind-set weakened by culturally induced insecurity is tailor made for his cunning trap of religious deception to grow and in some cases prosper into a fortune.

Such is the psychic stranglehold in this set up that even those in full time unlawful activities and illegal professions aspire to keep the pseudo saint or faith healer on their side just in case, for him to pray in their favour, use his successfully sold proximity with God in promoting their cases and causes, including success in such businesses as smuggling or fake medicines and caste his spell in protecting them from the application of law. That is the feudal or the medieval mind set mind set at work for you. The local feudal chief operates in his archetypical intimidating way so as to preserve his status quo; the ordinary citizen installed with that kind of mind-set goes along pragmatically to navigate his way through life with some degree of socially protected influence that in turn will bring along collateral benefits like career progression and financial rewards, comfort and a protective umbrella. Successfully laid out social equations take precedence over reliance on rule of law and organised society for the protectors and the protected. The results are there for all to see.

Freudian test analysis

Despite my recorded reservations about the theory of Psychology propounded by Freud, not only was his contribution not totally without merit, it was a great service to mankind. In fact, it was the foundation stone on which later understanding of human behaviour was developed. In Freudian theory the human personality is believed to be an aggregate of three segments; the Id, the Ego, and the Superego. The Id consists of instincts; the storage tank of every individual's psychic energy. In Freud's view, the Id bears no relationship with reality. As a child passes through the demands and boundaries of reality, a new structure of personality emerges called "Ego", the segment of personality that relates and tutors Id impulses through the demands of reality. The ego is sometimes referred to the executive branch of personality for adding reasoning to decision making. The Id and the Ego have no inherent morality. The superego is the Freudian structure of personality that is the virtual moral ombudsman. The Superego dictates to the individual whether something is right or wrong, the moral package with input from parents, teachers, society and other influences.

Freud's view of personality was like that of an iceberg, most of which existed below the level of awareness, almost like that massive part of icebergs that exists hidden from view beneath the surface of the water. Freud believed that most of the important personality processes operated below the level of consciousness. However, the observable behaviour of human beings is a product of both conscious and unconscious processes; it is very reflective of the likely nature and content of the hidden personality. It is therefore important to understand the interaction of the three personality components. The entire Freudian theory is a very vast pool of knowledge. For present purposes, let us take just one aspect of it. It should be obvious by now that for a stable personality, the Ego has to be stronger than the other two components in order to enable every person to conduct life in a rational way. In complete insanity or as it is referred to in technical terminology Psychosis, the ego is non-existent. The Id and Super-ego are in direct conflict. It is as if the Ego walks away from two extremely uncompromising warring parties, conceding defeat and metaphorically telling Id and Super-ego go the Hell and settle it between themselves. There being no agent of realism left to play any role, the psychotic personality is left in tatters, continually at internal strife, split from within and delinked with the real external world of ground realities.

In very much the same way, one can say that societies are structured along similar lines of interaction being the collective reflection of individual personalities that constitute any given society. In societies where there is a suffocating control through moral codes, whether based on reasonable or perverted assumptions, the collective social ego becomes weak and in extreme cases non-existent. It is a mirror image of the individual mental processes. Basic human needs and desires cannot be eliminated. They can only be channelled constructively or suppressed through controls and coercion. If suppressed wants and instincts are blocked completely from expression, they either surface in a different manner or regress into the "underwater" unconscious. As a result many consequent activities are carried out through a range of behaviours from direct defiance to doing forbidden things in secret. Where alcohol is banned in societies, drinking still goes on but in the invisible privacy of secure environments such as the Wikileaks story of booze activity in Saudi royalty beyond the reach of the social Super-ego. In fact, in this case it is the social Super-ego hiding from itself to satisfy a desire that it's public stance or social persona does not allow it to associate with. Put it differently, and the social ego, the sense of balance and reality unable to broker a workable deal proceeds on leave. As a result, the remaining personality splits itself conveniently into the other two segments that perform the roles of Id and Super-ego independent of each other, typical symptoms of the imbalanced individual mind and its consequent collective equivalent.

In everyday life terms, the absence or existence of a very weak ego is like the breakdown of governance between two extreme and uncompromising group positions. Basic instincts including pleasure seeking behaviour, desire for control and dominance, greed, freedom of thought and expression are denied outlets because of socio-cultural and religious controls. The state or government failing to find realistic solutions between extreme positions loses control. The two extreme segments, one seeking expression for socially suppressed desires and instincts and the other represented by the very rigid moral codes therefore get involved in a direct conflict in which governance is reluctant to or afraid of taking sides. Ineffective governance in societies or countries with extreme polarisation of thinking processes and religious positions is partly explainable as a gradual weakening of the Ego in relation to the strength of the Id and Superego. There is no other solution than diluting the extremities in the Id and Superego in individual personalities or extreme polarisation in societies, reverting to nature's law of balance.

Power, authority & influence

In the day to day operations and activities of average citizens and in matters of state governance, three factors are operationally very fundamental and all three are inter-related. The extent of impact or ratio in which each of the three interact or influence the lives of citizens and those in power varies from society to society and the level of development of each country. These three are power, authority and influence. Power is represented by those who are in a position to govern, political masters such as presidents, prime ministers, cabinet members, governors, etc. covering both federal and regional levels depending on the system of governance in operation in each country. Those covered under "authority" would include members of judiciary, executive and various enforcement arms of governance at various levels. To clarify the point, the prime minister or governor in a country may approve the case for the lawful arrest of a citizen for whatever reason under powers lawfully vested in him. To get his decision implemented, someone vested with specific authority by virtue of his official position such as a magistrate or police chief etc. will not only pass a specific order to that effect but carry out the physical act of implementing that decision. That is the general pattern of relationship between power and authority.

So what is influence then? That is a far more flexible concept. The Pope represents neither power nor authority but for those who respect him and his position, he can be a source of considerable psychological influence. The media is another example of influence, with neither power nor authority at its disposal it has extensive work tools to influence public opinion in a way that can either customise decision making or play a role in justifying wrong doings in governance through spin and distortion of facts. The role that media played or was acted out through it by those in power at the time through their respective media controlled or patronised channels in selling the non-existent weapons of mass destruction fairy tales to millions all over the world is a well-documented example of influence and much better understood now for what it was actually worth.

In societies where purposeful education and economic development levels are high or relatively higher, the roles of power and authority are better defined and understood. The role and dynamics of influence, however, are far more complicated in terms of the number of sources of influence and the nature of such sources. For instance the Royal family as a whole or a specific member of it in the United Kingdom can be a big influence on specific aspects of social life such as fashion or even shaping public opinion on a particular subject. The late Lady Diana represented neither power nor authority but the response to her tragic death all over the world is an example of the kind of influence I am talking about.

In developing countries, the role and ratio of influence in the troika of factors is far higher than in developed countries in general. That is the direct result of the lesser arm twisting role that influence plays in developed economies with more stable state institutions and public awareness. Stronger and more stable state institutions such as the judiciary and executive leave citizens less vulnerable to informal socio-political influences. Even big businesses use their financial clout to contribute their share of governance chaos in developing economies. Throw into this mix another complicating variable that dominates our demographic mix; the highly skewed rural to urban population ratio. With roughly 70 per cent of the population based in agricultural activity in far flung and backward areas, fair and effective governance is not only difficult, it is even more vulnerable to the pressures and intrigues of rural politics. It is not without foundation therefore that derogatory stories about field revenue officials like *patwaris, tehsildars* and local magistrates influenced by local power brokers and elders become the subject of comedy and disgust in television and stage plays, and local literature.

Mind games of the unanchored and insecure

Staying on the right side of power and authority is perceived as a practical prudence because it brings along in the baggage, real or wishful protection & security in a society where it is not necessarily guaranteed by rule of law. It also unfortunately gives the operating psyche a bit of boldness, even a slimy audacity to try to employ the same tactics on those below an individual himself in socio-economic status. There is an underlying suggestion that if one were to get into any sort of trouble, their patrons will bail them out as one of them or my man or as the expression goes in Punjabi; "*Sadha banda*" [*our man*]! This is how the feudal mind set of the subjugated positions itself for self-preservation and progression in life, based on support rather than ability or fair competition. It is worth observing how people rush to their envisaged patron saints or local feudal heads in positions of power and influence on special occasions like Eid. As soon as Eid prayers end, before returning home to be with their families, those trapped in this psychic setup will try to be the first to register calls to anyone who could be useful and fruitful in future navigation through life. The more committed ones even include their spouses in this mind game in attempting to cast the same magic spell on the women folk in the patron household; then return home to compare notes as to whether all went well as was planned and required.

Applied to religion, the mind-set positions itself in almost the same way, i.e. being on the right side of religion provides such mind sets protection and mentally privileged zones. Therefore the deluded believe that by behaving overtly and expressly in that way, they enlist themselves as being the divinely chosen and compliant ones. Heaven for them then becomes an exclusively chartered territory; for them alone. With the kind of a logic chain, what other outcome could there possibly be? God has been referred to by 99 attributes throughout the Quran. Unless we are missing big time, favouritism is not one of them! It has nothing to do with religion. It is a delusional extension of same medieval mind set. Appearing to be on God's side must bring about the fruits of guaranteed rewards and protection in the life hereafter, irrespective of what cunning standards of morals and integrity have driven them through their otherwise sorry lives. It is not uncommon to hear in an average Friday prayer sermon that Muslims have been guaranteed a place in Heaven merely because of reciting the first *Kalima [Islamic declaration of faith in God and the Prophet Mohammad].* That assurance puts them in a kind of comfort zone where a few excesses here and there will not matter in the end.

In this case too, the performance of an act or requirement takes precedence over the substance of that submission. What has been commanded as essential codes of conduct for individuals and society as a consequence of taking that oath of *Kalima* takes a back seat. By saying the *Kalima* aloud, enough has been done in their way of thinking by way of a verbal confirmation of loyalty and submission to God to guarantee or at least expect future protection and eternal favours. The attitude is a mirror image of the mental process at work in daily mundane earthly matters. Check it out at next Eid sitting quietly in a corner of a sitting room as the game is played out. For some it will have become an involuntary habit compulsion conditioned by the stimulus and response patterns of past experience or having seen the social and economic benefits others may have derived from this successful mind game. For the hardened criminals, it is a usually very well programmed and artistically delivered performance; one that several leading Bollywood actors can learn from. The frequency and intensity of switch between different emotions and moods to adjust to the stimuli from the patron host by the more talented con-artists defies belief. At times one can wonder whether a human frame installed with a decent heart and a healthy mind can be capable of such artificial control. The mind-set so hypnotises all thinking and body language that the individual degrades himself in his performance from a rational thinking mind to the reactions of an automaton, like the moth which makes an automated dash for the nearest source of light. It is the moth's destiny and sadly in the end, it burns itself with the obsession. Is there a lesson to be learnt by human beings? Yes it is, but only for a healthy, thinking and rational mind. For the feudal mind set already having surrendered itself into unconditional capitulation, the thinking process is like navigating through predetermined one way narrow lanes; no stopping, no slowing down and no turning back options.

Religious actors

Religious actors playing various roles programmed to cater to the requirements of the indigenous medieval mind sets are another source of influence in most matters. While the majority operate locally, there are some bigger operators who combine feudalism with religious patronage. This group consists of such social actors like the "*ruhani peshwas*" or "*gadi nasheens*", [*spiritual; elders*] some even play or claim to play the role of king makers through their dedicated followers and contacts within important state institutions. As to what precisely the followers see in some of their spiritual leaders is a separate subject in itself but for present purposes, the fact remains that they do exercise a considerable amount of influence on every important matter through sheer veiled intimidation and ancestral precedents of painful consequences for non-conformity. That kind of local influence coordinated through informal feudal networks aggregate to far more than an internationally iconic figure like the Pope could possibly exercise in any developed and educated society.

Conversely it follows that as state governance institutions develop and become more disciplined, the role of socio-cultural and religious influence starts to shrink correspondingly. It is therefore not surprising that where tribal and feudal structures are well entrenched, forces are always at work trying to destabilise state organs of governance; wherever and whenever possible, getting them into conflict with each other. In our country there is now public evidence in abundance that the forces of conflict and status quo have successfully implemented the strategy of keeping the army, executive, judiciary and politically elected people perpetually entangled enough to keep their attention away from the real issues that hold back the average citizen so that life remains rosy for them without competition. Public awareness and education is the only way to reduce influences that hinge on ignorance, illiteracy and lack of awareness. No wonder one of the primary targets for demolition by the *Talibans* are schools in general and girls schools in particular; schools that threaten to illuminate the lives of human beings and in doing so, threaten to put them out of business.

Loudness & exaggeration

In the feudal environment, normal healthy arm's length relationships between interacting individuals or groups normally do not fit in. There are two main parties in the set ups; the controlling chief or influential ones on the one hand; the insulted and intimidated large numbers on the other. The only way a third party emerges in this plot is the frustrated rebel who takes up arms or becomes a rogue element out of desperation to rough it out with his out of control master. Both roles are loud and abrasive; one seeking to retain control and supremacy at all costs, the other seeking to demonstrate his physical ability to disobey and revolt. Almost all plots and dialogues in Punjabi movies set in rural contexts are based on this role playing. In the absence of literacy, logical conversation and reasoning are excluded from screen play, partly because they do not convey the message loud enough or as the target audience is used to comprehending and appreciating. In dramatized roles seen in movies and local theatre, display being the dominant behavioural trait, characters do not often address each other through eye to eye contact. That honour is reserved for the camera. The loudest villain in a Punjabi movie is usually the most sought after and highest paid actor. It may be the same for movies made in the Sindhi or Pashto languages but I have never had the pleasure of watching one. That form of theatre has now extended itself to political talk shows on television channels, where civilised conversation has given way to high volume trading of insults. Anchors try to be louder than genetically loud guests as the sole criteria for winning all arguments. All this is an extension of the same mind games that are at the very foundation of individual and group relationships in feudal and medieval environments. In contrast, movies made on urban themes are less loud but still louder than real life.

Most one off plays and drama serials on television networks are a lot closer to real life situations. Everyone seems to understand and accept that but there is too much inertia and mental paralysis for changing a horribly failed and artificial way of life.

Apart from loudness, emphasis on exaggerated intensity of expression is also part of the same package. Let us take one example of a popular saying or idiom on both sides of the border. In the Hindi context or generally speaking in Indian culture, when a metaphorical reference is made for someone who has caused a major disaster, the relevant idiom is "*Lutya dubo di*" [*Sinking the boat*]. In the context of the part of province of Punjab that falls in Pakistan, that reference to sinking a small boat will simply not do. The corresponding saying is, "*Beera ghark*" [*Destruction of the whole fleet*]. Both are meant to convey exactly the same sentiment but in the loud feudal mind set, the message is ineffective unless the whole Armada is removed from the scene. The idea behind this illustration is not to pass value judgement but to demonstrate that individual and group behaviour is influenced and shaped by the totality of the environment in which both co-exist and operate. Is the lesser noise on the other side of the border fence just a coincidence or has it something to do with the lack of feudal relationships in rural and urban society in India? It is certainly worth a closer look at for better understanding of socio-cultural relationships.

The same unconscious psychic pattern is noticeable in most of the indigenous music compositions and the physical placement of musicians in recordings of background music. The "*Tabla*" [*drum*] which is essentially an instrument for tempo or rhythm in music compositions is invariably placed right under the microphone to maximise its impact. For musically sensitive ears, the end product is rather unpleasant. If we try to experiment by listening to our standard recordings of film music with most of those from Bollywood at the same pre-set volume levels, the listener will notice, firstly that our volume is discordantly louder and secondly, within that total impact of a composition, the beat usually has the loudest impact of all other music instruments. There is no attempt, perhaps not even a realisation that a muffled beat of a heavy drum placed at the right distance from recording equipment is more enjoyable than the direct beat of a small *tabla* shoved under the nostrils of a mike. Is this specific emphasis on beat too just a coincidence? Not in my analysis. Loudness is a symbolic manifestation of intimidation by the stronger over the weaker. Unless the loud beat is set in, many composers might feel a deficiency in the effectiveness of their compositions. Compare this to the mastery of our composers from the past, the likes of *Khawaja Khurshid Anwar*, *Firoze Nizami* and others. Their compositions had softness, melody, a calmness and tranquillity that touched the soul of the listener. That is why those compositions remain a pleasure to listen too even today. That is also why there is reason to be very concerned about deterioration of professional standards in performing arts.

In the first two decades, our music culture was also loaded with melody and softness in instrumental and vocal volumes because that generation was part of the broader sub-continental style. Anyone fond of music and who has been witness to the deterioration in singing style and quality of the nation's best known female singer *Madam Noor Jehan* from her renderings in the 1950s and 1960s to those in 1990s and onwards will not struggle to understand this point. As the political culture started to deteriorate and drift away from moderation and democratic values almost immediately after independence and into the lap of largely uneducated but influential stake holders, the cultural equivalent changed accordingly. Every change for better or worse must have its causal triggers. Understanding them is fundamental to undertaking reform and progress. We have certainly not done enough in this way and that carelessness born out of ignorance is the primary cause of our present poor standards in many disciplines.

Keeping education out of reach is the key to success for the *Talibans,* feudal and tribal heads; providing educational access and affordability is the state's most effective weapon for combating exploitation at the hands of the medieval systems and inculcating respect for law. In making the right choice, there is hardly a case for not opting in favour of universal education. When it comes to ground realities and a policy choice between allocating funds for a new primary school or for buying an extra battle tank, the scales have always been and will continue to tilt in favour of the latter. That national tragedy with flawed and heavily skewed priorities, attending to the well-off ahead of the large numbers at the bottom of the economic pyramid, survival of the fattest ahead of the fittest is at the very foundation of our present horror show.

As I was in the process of finding an appropriate practical example to illustrate influence at work, the pursuit was assisted by a very timely scandal in a media report in the form of a recorded tape of conversation between a judge of a High Court and then Chief Minister of the provincial government in Lahore in which the chief minister makes a clandestine private call to the judge giving him directions on how to proceed in two specific cases. The allegedly taped conversation ran regularly for days on many TV channels and was covered by many print media houses. There was no denial or protest from the parties involved, including by the ex-judge because the tape was already part of an official record of some previous litigation in the Supreme Court of the country. The learned judge, who incidentally acquired international limelight for having investigated match fixing claims of Pakistan's cricketers, responds to the call in the most timid and voluntarily yielding manner imaginable. This level of wielded and accepted informal influence permeates down to the lowest levels of governance and leaves very little room for the rule of law. It is a tailor made illustration of the medieval mind set implanted centuries ago and which lives on prosperously till today.

For local and regional political bosses and other influential presences, the local administration and police officials posted in their respective fiefdoms are assumed to be stationed there to protect them and their interests against any mischief or misdemeanour of the general population. They are expected, if not ordered or pressured into applying law in all its might on the common man. The influential actors meanwhile arrogate to themselves an aura of not being subservient to the same laws by which the average citizen is governed. That would be too equal a treatment for the rulers and the ruled, and against the very fundamentals of such relationships!

The concept of equality in law is inherently at war with feudal or tribal chiefdoms and survival of such systems of exploitation. Maintaining status quo is fundamental to ensuring political and economic territorial dominance. Education has the potential to undo all the hard work. It was kept out as long as possible but when matters seemed to be getting somewhat out of control, a second tier of lesser education was conceived to produce an educated class that was incapable of providing qualifications to make it to the top tiers but good enough to fill in clerical and low cadre jobs, that provided static career prospects without any influence on governance and decision making. Helpful concepts of fate and destiny were regularly endorsed to pacify those who did not do too well in life. Destiny implied that they were so positioned in perpetual disadvantage because they were willed by higher powers to be so and should reconcile to their fate instead of challenging God's will. That inequality was devilishly propagated as a divine policy is something that such people alone were capable of audaciously preaching with the singular objective of self-preservation.

Manipulators manipulated

In the first two decades, successful politicians used to have dodgy characters and local hooligans on their payrolls to do their proxy dirty work for them on the quiet. Some modicum of public decency was considered a useful trait or a political necessity. The local mullah or other religiously influential individuals were also listed on side to do the supplementary religious services including issuance of the now dreaded Fatwa to counter any status quo threatening possibility or to preach the importance of destiny such as that land belonged to God alone and if He had bestowed land on His chosen ones, no individual nor state authority including a sitting government had the right to take that divine gift off them in the name of land reforms or other legal pretexts.

With the passage of time, both the hooligans and mullahs manipulated by top level politicians started to realise that they could arrogate to themselves a higher independent role than play to the selfish controlling melodies of the local chiefs, feudal lords or tribal elders turned politicians. They decided to enter into politics directly by-passing their traditional patrons and the political cauldron became increasingly a mix of the generic local privileged class, those with notoriously rich criminal records and the religious politician. As the latter two classes entered the political corridors, educational and moral standards started to continually drop leading to sad tales of transgressions and uncivilized on-goings in the corridors of power. The drop was so glaring that it could no longer be wallpapered in any manner. In response to calls from common citizens and civil society organisations, a minimum academic qualification was introduced. Some questioned the motives and timing of the move. My concern is apolitical. How can a group of legislators, totally alien to education frame effective and complicated laws of governance, fiscal and monetary policy while not being able to in some extreme cases, even read let alone comprehend the intricacies of complicated legislation? Whether the graduation degree condition was introduced with noble or mala-fide intentions is irrelevant to the point in hand, it nevertheless brought to a head the present sorry state where a substantial percentage of legislators entered parliament riding on the back of fake degrees! Even the persona of fake piousness in the name of religious politics did not stop many of them from making dishonest declarations of academic accomplishments.

As has been the national tragedy, religious teachings and values have generally borne no correlation to practical life of the preaching ones. Putting on the religious role is more to do with structuralism compulsions, not honest intentions. In fact, the greater the pretence, the more likely it is that the performer will be more devoid of honesty and integrity in private life and public dealings.

Military self invasions

In between these brief and chaotic periods of politically elected governance, military generals gunning themselves for illegitimate takeovers as soon as one manages his way to the top position in the army, have contributed their share in the current mayhem. That was in addition to disrupting any semblance of a political process that had the potential to weed out some percentage of accidentally exposed and unpopular elected persons. When it comes to political corruption as well as financial and intellectual dishonesty, it is a very close contest between competing opponents, whether with or without uniform, very risky for a betting man to place money on in advance. Until a few decades ago, both sides lived happily together, peaceful co-existence by rotation. Following the Mughal Emperor *Aurengzeb* style period of power of Zia, the rivalry transformed from one of non-violent confrontation to intense hatred and bloodshed over a period of time. Zia introduced the tradition of violence in politics by the execution of Bhutto following an embarrassingly fake trial that had the outcome written all over the walls in the country even before the trial started. That hatred and revenge is now so deeply entrenched in the political set up that rational thinking, tolerance, objectivity, impartiality in judgement of moral and socio-cultural matters has been completely laid to rest; peace be upon all of those virtues. The hatred and intense confrontation that Zia sowed amongst various political and religious parties or groups with differing sectarian viewpoints served Zia very well and ensured the continuation of his devilish stranglehold on power. He had no other consideration or objective in life and the multiple waves of hatred that he set in motion during his period of existence have only intensified in frequency and intensity ever since.

There could have been no other causal outcome of the intrigues he set in motion. The regular incidents of violence between political parties, sectarian groups and their militant wings, attitudes of intolerance leading to blood stained confrontations between various factions of student representative bodies, attacks on minorities on one pretext or another, Talibanisation of some regions or segments of society and of course culminating in the senseless suicide bombings, are the produce of the crop cultivated by the deranged military dictator. The blame for this current mess lies squarely on the shoulders of Zia and his political and religious witchcraft. It was ill-intentioned from the start, its consequences relentlessly ill-fated and destructive. It will remain so until a quantum change in fundamental thought processes can be brought about. Change does not come about without a realisation first that all is not well, that the current thinking and drift can only lead to getting more of what we have always got. Thus far there is no sign, not the slightest hint of acceptance of flawed dogmas. On the contrary the evidence on the ground reflects the opposite. Many in the country continue to blame everyone, from the White House to the local cockroach for all the present ills except ourselves and plead guilty to no offences and no wrong doings either.

The dynamics of political inheritance

Very often, media talk shows are very critical of the ancestral nature of our political leadership. This becomes particularly important when all other political arguments against opponents are exhausted or cease to be effective. Third parties hoping to make their passage to power through back doors or trying habitually to destabilise those already elected to power are particularly fond of this argument. In reality, it has always been the case and is not likely to change in the foreseeable future. In a society that is driven by form and structure, political structuring cannot be expected to remain excluded. Leaving behind a well-educated family is not something that makes people stand up and take notice. It requires an educated population to appreciate knowledge and education in others. As a society and a nation, we have kept ourselves meticulously free of that burden. Feudal set ups breed on widespread ignorance and lack of awareness of civil rights. That being the case, it is surprising that some feel surprised that power is rotated within a privileged group.

What is, however, more damaging than the physiological symptom is the widespread psychological mind set in society as a whole. When a well-established doctor insists that his son should also become a doctor, a film maker demands similar loyalty from his son and so too many other professionals, these are extension applications of the same inheritance propelled feudal mind set. Even top media houses and business empires are structured on hereditary lines. The media dynasties in our country; the *Nizamis*, *Mirs* and others; are they not structured along hereditary lines even though their chat show anchors run themselves into fits of breathlessness in maligning the ancestral nature of political parties? Is there any system of leadership succession amongst top media empires? Like in most matters, the feudal mind desires bendable judgement tools for its case and a rigid application of laws for others. While having no pangs of conscience flushes for their own massive loot and plunder of incalculable proportions for decades, the social control freaks invariably sympathise if not openly support their version of "sharia" punishments of chopping off hands for the theft of a loaf of bread even if made in desperation.

Other manifestations of this mind-set that are widespread in society include many social practices such as judging people by castes and parochial loyalties, seating people at different dining tables at social events or family ceremonies in accordance with social standings, serving dinner by service grades, jumping queues as a matter of right and feeling offended if queried and so on. Social stratification is inherent in these types of societies at all levels, so how could it not be the case at the pinnacle of feudalism? Individuals and societies are not assessed by the presence or absence of traits and values. It is the degree to which most characteristics dominate or are missing that becomes the basis for comparison. The Kennedy family had a strong element of ancestral participation but the main difference was the exceptional ability, political ideology and personal charisma of the Kennedy family members. In our political power family strangleholds, inheritance is the sole criteria for passing the power baton. It is similar to a business inheritance because for most top politicians, power politics is nothing more than a lucrative business when in power and an insurance policy for protection of ill-gotten wealth during opposition stints. Even men in uniform turned politicians eventually end up passing their huge financial empires of ill-gotten wealth to their next generation to protect by staying in power politics. In comparison to our situation, Indian politics has a somewhat different matrix. Ancestral political dynasties are limited to a few families only. In large measure that is due to the fact that after independence, one of the earliest measures taken by India was the abolition of the "*jagirdari*" system with the stroke of a pen. We failed to do that and the consequences are there for all to see. This is not to suggest that Indian politics is free from corruption and exploitation but in their case, the causes and explanations have to be different and it is not for us to analyse their problems. We have an abundance of our own to deal with before making audit calls on others.

Imran is one of the most vocal critics of inheritance in party politics. In theory, his objections are valid but in the society's given context, it has to be the logical and natural arrangement. What will become of Imran's own party should he decide to step away from politics today? Will one of his followers with a lesser profile be elected in his place and the party still expected to carry on business as usual? No chance of that happening in the socio-cultural cocktail we have brewed over decades, if not centuries. Objective realities do not change because a leader or a group of politicians suddenly or temporarily feel inconvenienced by an incumbent in power. They themselves are products of the same modular processes. Either their sons, brothers or more recently wives will inherit whatever is there to be inherited or the chapter will come to a close.

The Nawaz League will end up the same way one day. After Nawaz, the party will be attacked from within like a mob let loose on relief goods in a devastated area. In all likelihood, 3 or 4 splinter Muslim League parties will allocate to themselves the remaining alphabets of Urdu and English languages. There are no other dynamics at work that could lead to a different conclusion. All roads lead to the same frequented city centres.

That is why the original ML disintegrated as soon as Jinnah passed away. If he had a son or daughter to follow him, history might have been different. After all, Ms Fatima Jinnah did emerge as the united choice candidate to challenge Ayub Khan! Even the mullah at that point side stepped his intrinsic aversion for Jinnah whom they had referred to as "*Kafir-e-Azam*" more than once; even forgot that Ms Jinnah was a female candidate who in their traditional pious thinking was not allowed to be the leader of an Islamic state!

The role of inheritance in our political party system is a direct product of the hypnotic and captive hold of the feudal mind set on our collective unconscious. An occasional protest that is more an exercise in cognitive cleansing of one's conscience or scoring a political point than a sustained and committed effort to change the socio-cultural equations will not bring about any desirable change.

Jinnah, Bhutto and Mian Sahib!

Here is a great example of how the dominance of feudal bent of mind directs thinking and perception of instant and closer influence over those that merit far higher respect and consideration but pose no immediate danger. I have seen at least two political chat shows on Pakistani television channels in the United Kingdom fought out with great intensity and certainly not as role playing examples for any watching youngster. By any independent measure of political judgement, the political statures and visionary potentials of both Jinnah and Bhutto would leave Nawaz Sharif running breathlessly for cover.

However, during comparisons or references to the three of them, Nawaz's representatives repeatedly referred to the former two as "*Jinnah*" and "*Bhutto*" but Nawaz was referred to each time as "*Mian sahib*"! It would be a cruel joke to suggest that Nawaz could be held in higher esteem in any comparison, but by virtue of him being alive and in business, references to him by his political followers were shaped by an air of cautiously padded reverence. The other too, long gone posed no instant physical or political threat and could be referred to more "*frankly*" than the still alive and kicking man of steel! In our rural context, there is a popular saying in the Punjabi language; "*Khuda neray ke khosun*?" [*Is God nearer or a punch to the face*]?" It is the rustic archetypal expression for the same socially and culturally intimidated mind. Immediate threats and dangers take precedence over long term considerations.

A friend from college days had seen plenty of life in military cantonments because his father was a career army officer. While posted in one of the army garrison towns of the northern province of *Pakhtoonkhwa*, he once narrated a rather funny anecdote, a quote from a pre-Friday prayer sermon in which the *Imam [priest]* leading the prayer referred to a quote from God in the Quran. The point he was making is not relevant but it was the manner in which the priest expressed himself that exemplifies a thoroughly tamed mind. Addressing his gathering in unconvincing Urdu as an ethnic *Pathan*, he said "*Allah mian bolta hai, aur general sahib bhi pharmata hai*" *[God says and the respected General says too]!*That is in no way a reflection of the priest's love and devotion towards God but his commanding General, being present amongst the gathering constituted a physically closer intimidation for him at that point in time; too overbearing to be disregarded and the priest's mind felt compelled to refer to him with added respect in the choice of his verbal expression.

This type and level of unquestioned obedience and mental subservience has deluded many men in uniform into believing that the rest of society also operates in the same way and that if they were to take over power and issue commandments of the kind that make human beings in army garrisons stand to attention or disperse by one loud shout from the commanding officer, those inferior "*bloody civilians*" as some rejoice in contemptuously calling civilians, would also respond with equally obedient and collectively promptness. A few months after martial law was declared by Zia, I was called by my boss at the time, the Commissioner of Income Tax in Lahore and told to report to the martial law authorities as early 5 a.m. next morning as a representative of the tax department. The nature of the mission was secret but my boss discreetly advised me to maintain equanimity in dealing with any overzealous young officer in uniform. It was bitterly cold by Lahore standards when I reported to the officer in-charge even before the sun had emerged fully. Let us name that officer as *Colonel Chaudhry Ramzan Khan*. There were representatives of other civilian departments too such as the local police, excise and health department and even a magistrate. I enquired about the mission but was told it was still a secret! Half an hour later, four open military jeeps rolled up in front of the main door to the building, each with a driver and a soldier in combat uniform. Two of us as representatives of various civilian departments were summoned to join each jeep for the operation. At that time we were informed that this was indeed a raid on the wholesale vegetable market in Lahore which is at its peak operation in the early hours of the day.

Off we went into relative darkness in a convoy of four jeeps. If it was cold indoors it was sheer torture in an open jeep carrying civilian passenger not fully aware of what was in store next. As the convoy entered the chaotic wholesale market unannounced, panic set in and there were shouts from each jeep for the crowd to behave itself and stay put. To cut the story short, a few shops were raided to find irregularities or breaches of any kind. The magistrate and excise staff got down to collecting cash fines for offenses like lack of cleanliness. I was asked to check the accounts in two shops and not surprisingly there was nothing available to check at the premises. When we returned to the martial law headquarters housed in the then local Gymkhana Club building in the serene surroundings of the Lawrence Gardens in Lahore, *Colonel Chaudhry Ramzan* asked all civilian officers to put their achievements on his office table. Cash collections from fines imposed on the spot, charge-sheets issued etc. were hurriedly deposited on the table and *Colonel Chaudhry Ramzan* seemed fairly satisfied with the instant outcome. Then he turned to me and asked for my contribution. I tried to explain that income tax operations do not take in place in real time. People do business during a financial year and maintain records, then have another period of 3 months to finalise their accounts and submit their returns of income for scrutiny. Before that, there is nothing to check because the businessman himself does not know whether he is earning or losing money before his accounting period ends? He was not pleased with my explanation and clarified to me in no uncertain terms that I was operating under martial law, not income tax law. I pleaded that I had been sent by my department as a representative of tax laws and therefore could only advise on tax matters. "*You have a single track mind*" I was told promptly for failing to understand that I was a martial law staff member in that operation! As a way out I requested for a copy of martial regulations in force at the time and conceded to being a complete moron on those military regulations and needed to be educated before any advice could be offered. That fortunately went down well with the Colonel, may be partly because a civilian had confessed to being a moron and a copy of martial law regulations was promptly handed over which I immediately started to browse through to find myself a point of anchorage. Eventually profiteering was the closest we came to an agreement on.

So off we went in open jeeps again next day searching for evidence of wrong doings in the wholesale paper market in Lahore on this occasion. We found some record in a shop that showed the dealer was a defaulter of taxes due from him for previous years. I told the army escort, a Major by rank that this case was ripe for action on income tax matters because tax due from him for previous years had not been paid. The Major got down to business with the paper dealer in his own commanding way. The recipient seemed fairly stunned and traumatised by his fate for the day. Both sides agreed that the inspecting team would return next morning and the dealer would wait for our arrival with cash on table to clear his tax dues. As we settled back into the army jeep for return to headquarters, the Major turned to me and told me triumphantly that this was how good administration was run. As agreed, we turned up at the market next morning to collect the waiting cash and I was again reminded on the way to wait and watch for effective collection of taxes. On reaching the market, to his horror and embarrassment the market was deserted and all shutters pulled down; there was no cash, not even a trace of the defaulter! Nothing was added verbally by the Major but I must confess I had a very quiet and private giggle at how his misconceived notions lead him into believing that all jobs can be done and results achieved simply through verbal commandments as in army garrisons; not to mention his premature celebration. To be fair that attitude is conditioned by the effectiveness of such commands on the home grounds of army operations. In away games, the "bloody civilians" are far more skilled in evasion, avoidance and in commitments serially never honoured.

It is precisely this mind set of command and unquestioned immediate compliance that got President Pervaiz Musharaf into his tangle with Chief Justice Iftikhar Chaudhry. The latter, an inferior civilian summoned to the intimidating environment of presidential palace and given some orders. Unfortunately, the response was reportedly one of non-compliance and the rest is history.

When war broke out at the *Wagah* border next to Lahore between Pakistan and India in 1965, we used to live in the staff colony of the University of Engineering in Lahore which was a proverbial stone throwing distance from the international border with India. Night sky in that direction could be seen lit up from time to time and the booming sound of guns fired from both sides was unending all through the night. Army personnel up to that point in history were held in high regard. We had some agricultural land even closer to the border and that was under army control. People would line up along the Grand Trunk Road on which the University was located to offer cooked and uncooked food, drinks, flowers etc. to troops using the road in both directions. Radio and a very newly introduced television service were full of patriotic songs that praised the fighting soldiers and paying tributes to those martyred in action. There was no other sentiment towards the armed forces in those days.

The eleven years of military misrule under Zia changed even that. In sharp contrast to earlier sentiments, the misrule reversed the public psyche almost completely. A widespread feeling of animosity towards military adventurers took over. Though those amongst civilians very perturbed at the development went into rationalisation for a long time, shifting their perception to positions like, "*Not all of them are bad*" or "*Zia is bringing the military reputation into disrepute*", etc. But the longer the rule continued, the feelings became increasingly universal because of intervention on issues and at levels simply not warranted at all, like the tax recovery attempt.

The concept of command and compliance is an integral part of military culture and rightly so. It serves military interests very well but civilian and democratic environment has no place for that type of blind and unconditional obedience to dictates from the top. When military personnel started to infiltrate unwelcoming civilian territory, even more so in the manner of their interventions, perception of and attitudes towards the armed forces took a sharp negative plunge. The damage may now have de-intensified to some extent especially after the happenings in the tribal belt in the north but the unconditional admiration and respect until the 1960s in no longer part of the civil-military relationship. The reality is that those who join the army are part of the broader indigenous culture before they join. By that time behavioural patterns, social values and attitudes are well integrated in individual personalities. While the command and compliance equation is part of the military culture, the desire to explicitly and forcefully demonstrate power and authority once military rule sets in is the product of the feudal or medieval mind wrapped in military uniform. Those young army officers seeking to stamp their authority on civilian wholesale vegetable and paper markets or on defaulting taxpayers were most graphic illustrations of those in position of power demonstrating their privilege disproportionately and well beyond a mandate, not lawfully conferred on them but self-arrogated in the darkness of the night.

To end the subject on a lighter note, I will narrate a joke in circulation during Zia's time then shared with a lot of people, including some from the armed forces; some of the more reasonable ones even enjoyed it at their own expense, partly because by that time public feedback reactions had already reached them. The story goes that three civilians were produced before a military court, charged with assault on an army officer while in uniform. The first defendant tells the court that the accused officer entered his residential premises unsolicited and started to misbehave. Out of sheer anger he retaliated and was sorry for his actions. The second witness explains that he is the neighbour of the principal accused. He heard commotion in his neighbour's home and rushed to his assistance. Seeing the army officer misbehave and threaten the family, he got involved and threw in a punch too but that he too was regretful about his conduct. The military court then addressed the third accused to ask about his involvement? "*Nothing whatsoever your honour*" he submitted. "*I just happened to pass by when I saw these two gentlemen beating up a military officer in uniform. I wrongly concluded that martial law must have been lifted and in celebration I threw in a few punches too; simply for that wrong assumption*!"

Despite all this, it wasn't too long ago that another civilian government was sent home in the military takeover of *Gen.Pervaiz Musharaf.* Very recently, information circulated through " *Wikileaks*" confirms that even that was not the last time military takeovers were contemplated. Insanity, as explained by Einstein has not been cured in generically irresponsible and greedy bent of minds. The childish desire to try the same old methods yet again and hope for different outcomes continues to burn in over-ambitious minds in which respect for law and rule of the majority struggle to find a safe haven.

5

Moving to the "right", getting it horribly "wrong"

From Sanity to Hysteria

Those who do not learn from history are condemned to repeat it!
George Santayana

From fanaticism to barbarism is only one step
Denis Diderot

There is a saying in statistics that if your head is in the oven and your feet in the refrigerator, then on average you are comfortable. Not exactly true if it were to be tried in practice and somewhat like the fake American wrestling which comes with a health warning for viewers not to try the visual trickery at home, it is strongly recommended that the cold and hot balancing act should not be tried out of curiosity. However, it does offer food for thought. The human body seeks a physiological balance and the mind seeks cognitive consonance at all times too. When feeling cold, there in an involuntary act of rubbing hands to generate warmth even before the performer may realise what he is up to. If one were to accidentally touch a very hot object, the hand is withdrawn automatically before the conscious mind can figure out what had actually happened. This is a reflex action in response to a sharp sensation. It is devoid of perception. Perception can be defined as sensation plus meaning. A new born child does not have any perception but is loaded with sensation receptors only. If a new born baby were to be pinched gently, the baby would register the discomfort and respond to the sensation without being able understand what happened. An infant left under an open sky may try to grasp the moon because it has the visual sensation but not the perception to understand the distance involved.

As growth process proceeds, meanings begin to be added to sensation and the understanding phase of life begins to develop. If a child sees an unpleasant scene, he will have a tendency to shut his eyes. Even as adults we sometimes do that. It is a defence mechanism of the mind, a state of denial of external events as if a difficult or unpleasant external situation is made to vanish by closing one's eyes or looking the other way. For a mind upset at an unpleasant stimulus, the act is a natural reaction to restoring mental consonance, something that the mind always inherently seeks to do, restore balance and achieve relaxation or as we say in Urdu "*sakoon*". As long as that psychic balance is not achieved, the mind will carry on craving to achieve it somehow. Whether it succeeds or not is a different matter and depends on the total external context. When consonance is not achieved over a period of time, frustration, anxiety, anger, bitterness, etc. set in. However, even with the same external situation or stimulus, different minds will react differently depending on the sum total of their previous experiences. That is why even real siblings will behave differently when faced with the same threat or entertaining situations.

Natural Equilibriums

When Woodrow Wilson was elected President of the United States in 1912 on behalf of the Democratic Party he implemented a series of progressive economic policies. It was in this context that he made a profound statement on economic justice and progressive thinking at a time of severe economic downturn. He said that if capitalism was to survive, it must socialise itself. The concept of a modern welfare state is spiralled around this premise; a socially responsible state that is run along free enterprise principles but one that does not let the disadvantaged, disabled and the worst off to rot in neglect and deprivation. It is essentially a move away from "one extreme" in classical capitalism towards a more central and socially responsible positioning. The principle of moderation has indeed now infiltrated into many ideological, social, cultural and economic excesses and exaggerations of times gone by. We see in present Russia and China, varying degrees of sprinkling of capitalism or free enterprise and that has at least for now helped in resuscitating their traditional ideological positions. Any reverse move away from the dilution of previous extreme positions in both countries will amount to swimming against contemporary currents and that is both exhausting and doomed to end unhappily.

Almost the same way, religious attitudes with post codes in extreme ideological and faith frontiers invariably leave all parties concerned in tears and that surely cannot be the objective and purpose of any religion. Very much the same way, societies that discriminate on the basis of castes, race, colour or any other lowly basis hardly ever enjoy enduring harmony, prosperity and respect of international communities. Extreme positions can never be the basis of accommodation, cooperation, mutual respect and lasting peace. For international communities to come closer, all stake holders need to sacrifice something to get something else in return. Until that can happen, international peace and collective wellbeing will remain just an elusive dream. But before this giant step by mankind can even be contemplated, domestic situations will have to be sorted out because they constitute the essential raw materials around which that wishful dream has to be interlaced.

Even when a new born baby cannot understand anything around it, the instinctive tendency of the infant to achieve balance is still visible in its reactions. If not covered appropriately with warm clothing when in cold weather or if covered too much in hot weather, it will struggle to sleep until nature's required balance is restored. These physical manifestations of life also have corresponding psychological connotations. Swallowing whatever feels tasteful and spitting out whatever is distasteful is exactly the equivalent of the mental process of acceptance and rejection of anything. The normal mind will automatically own or embrace (*swallow*) whatever it considers a source of joy or comfort and spit, reject or distance itself (*spit out*) all that it feels uncomfortable with. In very much the same pattern, human beings automatically hug each other when happy or in friendly mode and nudge others away when annoyed or angry, without being formally taught to behave in these ways.

These are very basic and fundamental illustrations of primary emotions. More complex behaviour that is considered normal or acceptable is also based on the balance benchmark. In societies where drinking alcohol is part of the culture, those who drink in moderation usually cause no harm to themselves or others. Those who defiantly or carelessly wander beyond the limits of moderation end up putting themselves and those around them in discomfort, if not at risk. In extreme cases of excessive drinking, physical violence and damage to life and property is common knowledge. On the other hand, in societies where religion plays a lead role, those who are moderately religious and carry out their religious activities without display or impeding on the privacy of others, are usually at peace with themselves and those around them. Those who go a step further and try to force their views and brand of religion on others get more involved in confrontational activities, which in turn leaves them agitated most of the time and they get labelled as unwelcome company in most social circles. Those who go even a step further into extremity become fanatics or suicide bombers. They neither do any good to themselves nor to the people around them but inflict only pain and miseries on others. In both cases, it is nature's rule of moderation that reflects normal behaviour and leads to tolerant and peaceful outcomes.

It therefore follows that whatever the nature of societies, their legal, moral, socio-cultural and religious values, the fundamentals of human behaviour will not change and the basic universal laws of natures will always apply.

Cosmic balance

If any further evidence is needed, it is to be found in perfection of the cosmic balance. When a cosmic body is exposed to a communicable energy in space it moves in the direction of the force. The entire system of the cosmos is a spectacle of interactions between body masses and interacting forces. These synchronized forces keep the entire cosmic system into predictable and continual movements that keep the universe in balance.

The principle of nature's law of moderation has been used by many civilisations in dealing with various issues of existence and prosperity. A full-spectrum of medicine is based by the Chinese on moderation and nature's balancing acts and principles. The *Bahá'í* approach led by Bahá'u'lláh warned long ago about the hazards to the planet of too much material civilization. "*Civilization, so often vaunted by the learned exponents of arts and sciences, will, if allowed to overleap the bounds of moderation, bring great evil upon men. If carried to excess, civilization will prove as prolific a source of evil as it had been of goodness when kept within the restraints of moderation*". Very well put indeed and makes me feel grateful to the author for the assist in support of my contentions.

Claims of divine guidance

جو بُتوں نے ڈالے ھیں وسوسے کے دلوں سے خوفِ خدا گیا
وہ پڑی ہیں روز قیامتیں کے خیالِ روز جزا گیا

Jo butoon ne daley hein waswasey ke diloon se khauf-e-khuda gaya
Wo pari hein rooz kiyamatein keh khayal-e-rooz-jaza gaya
Faiz

In recent years we have had Al-Qaeda and Zia-ul-Haq acting on God's will, and on the other hand Israel & Bush also acting on God's will in exactly the opposite direction. Or do Sunnis and Shias fight each other in compliance of God's will? If not, where do we draw the line? If we accept this hypothesis, then logically both sides claim to be fighting against each other in compliance of God's will! Not everyone on both sides is fighting or wants to fight against each other in any case or for any real or imaginary cause. In fact, those wanting to live in peace constitute the overwhelming silent majority in every society. If in any society, this is not so, there is something seriously wrong within that society.

Normally those claiming to be more religious than their fellow citizens and other extreme right wing members of society are the ones at the forefront of conflicts driven by notions of higher moral pretensions, whether in the name of God or religion. This crazy confrontation again has nothing to do with any religion. Perverted or unstable minds skewed towards anger and hatred use a defence mechanism of the mind called "*rationalisation*" that seeks to justify normally unjustifiable behavioural patterns or uncontrollable psychic urges to ride on the back of socio-culturally acceptable justifications, both for themselves and society or the nation as a whole. For them there is no better sanctuary for a dissonant mind to pacify it with a holy cover that camouflages their unholy and ill-conceived pursuits.

Jung's analytical approach

This is where *Jung* comes in again. His approach was that the very existence of God has been and will continue to remain a subject of disagreement and contention between various divides based on religion, science, logic, tribal and mythological beliefs since times immemorial. Irrespective of where any person stands today or stood in his time in history on the subject, the fact remains that his adopted position either way impacted significantly on his life, self-image and his attitude towards others. So the important question for *Jung* was not who was right or wrong but to study and try to understand how any and every human mind is influenced by any or all religions without taking sides or passing moral judgments on positions taken or expected to be taken. It was in this context that Jung concluded that in his practical experience of treating his patients or clients with troubled minds, it was easier for him to heal believing Christians than non-believers. There is an identifiable and fixed centre of gravity for a religious personality around which problems can be searched and resolved. That is the real and honest answer to the question.

Men have understood the potency of the use of not only religion, but even witchcraft or black magic, etc. over centuries to either use religion to good effect or to exploit the human mind, control it, redirect it towards their goals and objectives without the experimental subjects knowing that they are pawns in a wider agenda. When used positively for noble objectives and without coercion, there is never a problem or conflict based on religion.

In a tolerant society, followers of different religions do not mind participating in each other's religious festivities and other practices. Hindus and I believe even Sikhs visit the sacred burial places "*mazaars*" of Muslims Sufi saints in India. In Pakistan, before the Zia bewitchment cast its shadow over society at large, Muslims in Lahore frequently visited the burial place of *Madhu Lal Hussain* who embodied a rare Hindu-Muslim combined name. Not only that, the *Mela Charaghaan* or "*Festival of Lights*" was celebrated by *Lahorites* (*citizens of Lahore*) of all social and economic classes of citizens. It even used to be a local public holiday up to one point in time. Then Zia sprinkled his poison and the event first became controversial, then died the kind of tragic death that Zia's name eventually became a brand for. We will revisit *Mela Charaghan* later because it was an event worth retaining in our calendar of festivities.

If we try to establish a single differentiating factor in the development of different attitudes towards the religiously revered historical personalities on both sides of the timeline between the pre-Zia and post-Zia eras, the only answer that pops up is social and cultural freedom. If there is another explanation, I would love to be educated about it. Is there a lesson to be learnt from this, if one really wants to learn? Obviously again, we need to return to the older and now almost discarded socio-cultural values that served us so well and try to throw the free flowing hatred out of our systems that has taken us to the brink of disaster, domestically as well as internationally. Without implying that there are no conservative or influences or agents of hatred in Indian society, fortunately, for India they have rarely had the backing or encouragement of the establishment or governments in power. Despite this lack of state backing, they will still have managed to exercise some "*influence*" on relatively vulnerable segments of their society but without "*power*" and consequently "*authority*" aiding and abetting them. India succeeded in ensuring that the fires ignited during one of the greatest human tragedies in the form of undoubtedly the largest ever mass migration of mankind in opposite directions did not continue to burn. Divisive forces therefore, did not succeeded in creating a durable sentiment of divide between the majority Hindus and other religious groups. They could not have done so, because elected governments need support and votes from all sides in order to govern effectively. Dictators like Zia needed divisive tools to prolong their profane grip on power. It did not matter whether the divide was inter-religious or intra-religious such as between *Sunnis* and *Shias, Wahabis, Ahmadies* or between rural and urban Sind.

It is most interesting that each of these conflicts emerged in different eras of Zia's evil rule to cover the longest possible period of his total stay in power. Stretching a promised period of 90 days for a re-poll into intended infinity required a constant supply of conjuring tools that could keep the populace continually embroiled in issues that distracted them as far away as possible from the simple real issue; an allegedly rigged election which required a re-poll under the constitution and his moral commitment. Had his long term strategic plan not been "*rudely*" interrupted to a miserly period of 11 years, God knows what other additional evil tools he and his team of God fearing imposters in crime had stockpiled in their closet to torment a helpless, flogged, jailed and brutalised population.

As it is, his contribution in his cut short period has been enough to decimate a peaceful and overwhelmingly religiously moderate and balanced society into one that seems to have no shortage of blood thirsty creatures, the products of his deliberate policy of creating a parallel system of education in the name of religion. Did he or his associates send their own kids to one of these? Not in a million years. Why would he do that, because who would have carried on his evil agenda except his equally unscrupulous son *Ejaz-ul-Haq*, perfectly encoded to carry on his ancestral brand of family hypocrisy? He is the one who allegedly helped to bail out the imam of *Lal Masjid* [*Red Mosque*] in Islamabad when the former was reported in the media to have been apprehended in possession of a large stock of weapons in his car a couple of years before the violence was unleashed from within and outside the premises of a place of worship! How did he manage to do this? Surprise, surprise; he happened to be the Minister for Religious Affairs. Had he been the Minister for Labour instead of religious affairs at the time, and a labour union leader had been arrested for possession of large quantities of unlawfully obtained ammunition, would Ejaz have come in such clandestine and secretive manner to the rescue of a union leader or a student leader of a formal university? Never again in a million years. Could this have happened in any developed and civilised society which he and his fellow thinkers fail to quote ad-nauseous in their arguments about the inefficiency of subsequently elected governments? Does he have any followers especially when out of power other than those churned out of "*deeni madrassas*" (*religious schools*) to fill in the numbers for their long time patrons? We all know what the answers are.

Remembering lost traditions

Even before Zia came to power, Pakistan was a predominantly Muslim country with a Muslim majority population. But the fundamentals of the social-cultural relationships in society were unrecognizably different. Compared to the hate filled version of today, there was not just tolerance between all religions sects, there was also a reasonable degree of mutual respect.

"Mela Charaghaan" [Festival of Lights]

Shah Hussain (1538–1599) was a Punjabi Sufi poet, also regarded as a Sufi saint. He was the son of Sheikh Usman, a weaver, and belonged to a clan of Rajputs. Born in Lahore, he was considered a pioneer of the Kafi form of Punjabi poetry. Shah Hussain's love for a Brahmin boy called "*Madho*" or "*Madho Lal*" is famous, and they are often referred to as a single person with the composite name of

"*Madho Lal Hussain*". Madho's tomb lies next to Hussain's in the shrine, adjacent to the famous Shalimar Gardens built by the Mughal Emperor, *Shah Jehan*, better known for his architectural masterpiece, the famous Taj Mahal in Agra. His annual death anniversary "*Urs*" used to be celebrated every year during the "*Mela Chiraghan*" [*festival of lights*]. People would light up candles on roof tops all over the city. Religious and race distinctions never entered the equation of celebrations for all citizens of the city.

The parochial madness unleashed during Zia's period added yet causality to his catalogue of divisive policies, this time because a Hindu name was part of that celebration. How could such an all-incorporating, non-divisive activity be allowed under a fundamentalist military regime and fit into its way of thinking? The move also contributed to the more time procurement schedule of Zia in that it did generate some degree of controversy by disgruntled supporters of the event but such was the scale of other national disasters and worries faced by the nation, this one was lost in the wider mayhem that the country was engulfed in.

Given a choice, would any mentally balanced average citizen hesitate for a minute in going back to that period of our existence compared to the present hate dominated atmosphere? Was that more open and tolerant pre-Zia society better or the present one in which no one is encouraged or allowed to join others even in any innocuous celebration?

Minority Festivals

Pakistan is a diverse society of different religious, ethnic, sectarian and communal groups living under one umbrella. Muslims, Christians, Sikhs, Hindus, Bahais and other groups celebrate their religious festivals, such as *Eidul Fitr, Eidul Azha, Diwali, Christmas* and birth anniversaries of *Baba Guru Nanak* with full moral and spiritual fibre and received reasonable coverage in the media.

We used to witness joint celebrations by the people of different religions, and families used to exchange gifts on these occasions, while children used to arrange joint recreational activities and programmes, including quiz acts and games. The growth of intolerance in society has severely dented that culture and with each passing day society appears to become more hostile, aggressive and antagonistic towards the religions of others. Extremist elements and the right-wing media, particularly some TV channels of the country, often portray other religions as profanely exotic and obscurantist. On the other hand, a handful of corresponding extreme right-wing media in the West increasingly calls Islam a backward and extremist form of faith. Both are manifestations of unproductive negative sentiments.

Religious festivals are more than simply a compliance of religious dictates. They provide an offering for followers and sometimes followers of other beliefs too to receive, radiate and benefit from the collective essence of life. They offer a festive catharsis for people to get together for a shared joy, a voluntary temporary escape from the stresses and strains of daily burdensome lives. The annual "*Urs*" at the shrines of famous Muslim *Sufi* saints of the sub-continent are the best examples of such collective experiences of togetherness that embraced followers of other religions too, in contrast to today's cerebral approach of excluding people from different sects within Muslims, let alone other religions. Once festivities are over, average minds may recess again into petty prejudices but while the festivities last, individual minds are temporarily consumed by the overbearing collective festive atmosphere and experience. Even the normally rigid economic and social stratifications are drowned in the festive rituals as long as they last. Which trend or practice appears to be a healthier and richer experience, having everyone joining in the festivity or looking over shoulders to ensure no one else comes near? Why would someone want to join any such unwelcoming bunch anyway?

Although *Diwali* is a minority festival in the Hindu calendar, it is celebrated in some parts of Pakistan too, especially in the province of Sindh more than others. It is celebrated by both Hindus and Muslims with similar zeal and joy. There is no better way than religious festivals in bringing people together but that can only happen when firstly, individuals show respect towards other faiths and secondly, when society and the state have the vision to promote inter-religious and intra-religious harmony. Where governance and religious political parties bank on divisions and confrontations as an aid to loot and plunder, there is no chance.

"Moharram" processions

Until the mid-1970s, standing by the road sides to watch the *Zuljina* procession taken out by the Shia members of society pass by on the 10th day of the month of Muharram was another routine practice. The timing and routes for the procession were known to anyone who had interest or involvement in the annual ritual. Thousands of citizens of all sects and ages would line up in the streets in advance on both sides to watch in silence and reverence. Like other school going children, I watched the procession on the 10th of Muharram with family members including my mother and grandmother on more than one occasion. Both were extremely religious and practicing Sunni Muslims but would never speak a word against Shia Zuljina procession.

Amongst the mourning processionists would be many friends and acquaintances, with whom we would return to normal activities after the *Ashura* event. That was the kind of society that we were brought up in. That is not all! This is not a scene from Karachi or Lahore. This was the ground reality in the city of Quetta, which is now amongst the hub of Taliban activities. It was inconceivable, at the time that the city and indeed the rest of the country would be so negatively transformed that no one would even consider being in respectful attendance at an *Ashura* event out of mortal fear or that the procession itself would be impossible to take out without heavy security and close vigilance by well-armed security services.

Kabul & Quetta festivals

In international media today, the cities of Kabul in Afghanistan and Quetta in Pakistan are seen as belonging to the stone ages. Until around the same time, the mid-1970s both cities were known in the region for their annual summer celebratory festivals which even attracted cross border participants from India, Iran and Afghanistan! Quetta was considered to be an attractive hill station that provided relief from the intense heat in the plains of the provinces of Punjab and Sind. I used to spend my school and college summer vacations in my birthplace town of Quetta to beat the punishing heat of Lahore. The Quetta festival spanned over a period of about a month during the hot and humid season and was attended by visitors from all over the country, even by short term visitors from Afghanistan and Iran. My wife went to Kabul as a student in the company of her parents and siblings to participate in then popular Kabul festival where a lot of Indian citizens were in attendance. Both these examples based on personal experience have been quoted to confirm that these are not fairy tales or hearsay. These were the ground reality at the time!

Even outside of the festival period, life in Quetta had several healthy cultural practices. The main commercial street known as Jinnah Road and other leading shopping streets were littered with small cafes and restaurants that offered tea, snacks and regular food. At the entrance to most of these, was a reception counter. The counter top usually had a high pile of the black large music records that were the only means of music playing in those days. As regular customers, people would generally know the range of music collection at each café and we would choose our visit for the day based on the kind of music we would want to enjoy along with our cup of tea or whatever else was on the menu. Cafes were obliged to keep updating and improving their music libraries to retain customers or attract new ones. Before placing any food order, customers would state their choice of songs at the entrance counter to go with the food. Music would then be played on a first come first served basis. It was just a healthy, decent, and harmless method of relaxation and social interaction amongst people of different cultures, sects and racial backgrounds. It was also an exercise in discipline and customers waited patiently for their turn of selected music while having food and drink. No one demanded or expected an out of turn treatment. Would anyone in his senses prefer the present radicalised society over the one which has been sacrificed in the name of religion to get nothing in return except hatred and intolerance?

Opportunities for relaxation and social interaction, so essential to resting stressed minds and bodily fatigue have become non-existent.

Thousands if not millions employed in that kind of service sector have lost their livelihoods from the grisly transformation of society today. Is it not time to reconsider the reversal of the fatal choices made by those in power and inflicted upon the common man? Those who destroyed the socio-cultural fabric of society still have options to travel abroad and have a good time. Those who were never part of the decision making are left with no options. They have no opportunities to socialise with their fellow citizens. All they are left with is insecurity that leads them to continually look over their shoulders with suspicion at other follow citizens.

Security concerns

It would be an exaggeration to suggest that personal security and safety of belongings were never an issue. But the way of life then assisted in better security and collective vigilance. Violence was rare in normal times. The city of Lahore and most others in the Punjab have always been known for their punishing hot climates during the summers. A large proportion of the internal city of Lahore was characterised by wall to wall residential construction and terraced houses. During summers, most family members would take to roof tops where rows of beds were laid out at night. After a good night's rest under an open sky, all would disappear indoors as soon as the sun appeared on the horizon having made best use of healthy fresh air, often aided by large pedestal fans when required. People were less fussy about their visibility to their neighbours because there was an unwritten reciprocal memorandum of understanding about the levels of privacy.

Any mischief by an intruder would automatically arouse the whole neighbourhood into collective action or reprimand. Armed robberies were rare. Firearms were hardly ever displayed in public. Just imagine the amount of energy that was conserved during the summers by simply using nature's own resources during the darkness of the night. It was all down to mutual respect and trust in society. There was not a single window in our house in Lahore at the time fitted with strong protective steel grills to guard against forced intrusion.

In comparison to that, today people sleep indoors, with multiple chains and bolts on entrance doors, extra security installations on windows, armed night watchmen at the main gates, consuming costly electricity through high voltage air conditioners with many households resorting to power theft to afford that luxury and still do not sleep in peace and security! To reduce the cost of energy bills, households that resort to power theft do so either through their own ingenuous methods or in connivance with corrupt elements amongst power sector officials. Many even offer their prayers five times a day in the comfort of stolen electricity! How much further can moral values deteriorate before the structure of a civilised society as mankind has known for centuries will collapse all together?

Exemplary impromptu organisation

When Bhutto was temporarily bailed out of Zia's protective custody in 1977 following the imposition of martial law, it was a calculated move to test the political waters. By the time Bhutto was scheduled to arrive at the venue for a political address, there was a sea of humanity around Punjab University and surrounding areas in Lahore. I have never seen a gathering anywhere close to the mammoth crowd that gathered that day to give their verdict on what they thought about Zia's treacherous and unconstitutional intervention. That was to be the day that Zia and his evil kitchen cabinet decided that they could neither afford a re-poll not let Bhutto live on to return to power one day. Even worse perhaps was the realisation that the huge body of citizens in disagreement of the military intervention had to be divided and sub-divided along whatever lines was possible.

That was the beginning of the splinter groups of political and religious parties and the emergence of MQM as a counter-balancing force that could divide the province of Sind along urban and rural lines. Segmentation of religious groups had to be along radicalised lines so that they would never even offer prayers together, let alone think of unifying at any later stage. For present purposes, my focus is only on the impromptu organisation and discipline in that mammoth gathering. There seemed no central leadership to guide them. People could be seen voluntarily clearing the way to allow families especially those with kids smoothly navigate through voluntary narrow corridors without any hindrance. Not for a second did anyone who attended with their families felt threatened or intimidated. That is how group feelings develop amongst people with common causes. A political worker from any party in the extreme north of the country will have an automatic bond or sympathy for his fellow worker in the extreme south.

In the kind of society designed in 1977 and delivered in the last few years, political leaders speak to their own followers from behind bullet proof glasses, have security sweep through venues for political gatherings, families stay away, even grown up male students are advised by parents to stay away from today's political gatherings. Leaders and legislators who pass laws in parliament against carrying armed weapons in public only turn up at gatherings surrounded by a dozen private bodyguards equipped with everything short of nuclear weapons and still feel insecure. Far from concealing their own violation of law, the weapons are showcased as visibly as possible to maximise intimidation and as a show of force. No guesses anymore for when did it all change? Which society would we all prefer if we had a choice; that which existed just over three decades ago or the present pious one?

International CATA conference in 1993

In 1993, the Federal Board of Revenue hosted the annual international Commonwealth Tax Conference in Islamabad. By that time Karachi had lost its standing as the leading city for socio-cultural and official events, as well as being the known hub for evening and late evening social activity following long periods of violence. Islamabad was still comparatively very safe from where we all stand today. I was appointed coordinator for the national organising committee. The conference was attended by delegates from 33 countries including those from UK, Canada, Australia, etc.

Commonwealth tax conference hosted by Pakistan in 1973 and inaugurated by the then President, Mr. Wasim Sajjad

Almost everyone reported in the feedback at the end of the event that their weeklong stay in Pakistan had been most enjoyable and full of fond memories. We hardly put any curbs around their movements except to advise that they visit local markets in groups only. In one of the feedbacks several years later, one delegate who attended the conference remarked as follows; *"The 1993 CATA technical conference, was hosted in Islamabad. That conference, which was opened by the then President of Pakistan, was attended by over 100 senior level delegates from more than 30 member countries. The arrangements made for this important and prestigious event received unqualified praise from all participants, and it subsequently served as a model for all later CATA annual conferences. In my opinion few of those reached quite the same very high standard and none surpassed it".*

All that is needed to influence or change people's attitudes towards oneself and to make friends is to extend a warm welcome, a hand of friendship and hospitality at home, let them feel comfortable and ensure they enjoy their stay with freedom of movement and a feeling of security. Today, no visitor looks forward to come to Pakistan unless it is absolutely essential. Even the Sri Lankan cricket team invited with assurances of security levels matching those reserved for visiting head of states was left to rough it out as sitting ducks when attacked.

Notwithstanding the security lapse at the time, the real issue is the level of drop from a reputation for being excellent and generous hosts, a traditional strength and icon of our one time society, to ones who cannot look after guests despite assurances? Indeed how has the social environment deteriorated so much that we first need to talk about security for anyone we intend to invite from abroad? Is anyone in our ranks still happy with where we stand today? Yes of course, only those who consider it best to keep "*evil foreign visitors*" out of our holy land! The least we can do is not to be double minded about what should be our attitude towards guests. Doing that now is simply not good enough. We need to be proactive in restoring our previous image and reputation for hospitality and to completely reject those who have dragged our names in dust. These are just a few examples of how far we have fallen or deteriorated from our once proud international ratings. Unless we accept these blunders and appalling deterioration in socio-cultural values and practices from being continually misled in the name of religion, our present afflictions will only multiply and matters get even worse.

Reaction formation

Another common form of defence mechanism employed by the mind to handle anxiety or dissonance is called "*Reaction Formation*". Through this mechanism a person defends against painfully unacceptable and persistent thoughts, impulses or situations by migrating to their opposite and counter viewpoints. There is one recent example that comes to mind that illustrates this mental process. In almost six decades of existence, it was difficult to imagine that anyone could ever muster the courage to suggest changing the name of the country without fear of getting lynched, if not physically, at least by virtual socio-cultural flogging. So what could have changed the national ethos to an extent that the suggestion put forward by the traditionally secular *Awami National Party* to rename the "*Islamic Republic*" to "*Democratic Republic*" has not only not drawn that kind of public reaction, it has prompted some other parties to openly come out in support of the suggestion?

Many movements and noble causes throughout history have been damaged or discarded as a result of their own internal exaggerations and extremes. The way religion has been used as a tool for policy formulation and general intimidation of political opponents, it was natural that at some stage people were bound to say that it was no longer acceptable. If suggestions for changing the official constitutional name of Pakistan had come from abroad, even under extreme pressure, that would have never been acceptable in any way. But continual internal misuse and exploitation to the extent that has been reached today has only led to fast forwarding of thinking along these lines and a lot of this move in the opposite direction can be attributed to a collective reaction formation. This reaction essentially seeks to bring about a change in the opposite direction; an unspoken statement of "*enough is enough*".

Bhutto's economic slogan of socialism did not really mean socialism in the traditional sense but more of a tilt towards left leaning economic policies within a broader democratic set up. That in itself was welcomed by masses as a reaction to the previous domination of a select group of influential families or groups then universally referred to in society as the "*22 families*". However, the *Socialist Party in Pakistan* never aligned themselves with Bhutto's socialism claims. They felt that Bhutto in adopting socialism as an economic slogan had hijacked their manifesto and in their view that it would eventually lend adverse publicity to socialism. If any good may eventually come out of the blood bath let lose by extremist forces, it may be bringing about a positive quantum change in the direction that Jinnah always wanted us to go. It is as if traumatised children run back to the security of their parents in the hope of guidance and solace! Extreme actions generate extreme reactions and if radicalisation of society continues at the present rate, calls for changing the name in a secular direction will increase with time. The only way to not open up another divisive debate is to deal with the problem of misuse of religion for political and power agendas directly and honestly. Problems can either be resolved by dealing with them directly or we face the causal consequences of our neglect, as indeed we are doing at the moment. Problems cannot be simply wished away, except in dreams and child fantasies.

Historical parallels

Brutal dictators script their own tragedies, having to look over their shoulders all the time in a paranoid like symptom. The real paranoid can well argue in self-defence that just because someone is paranoid is no guarantee that he cannot be actually followed, but in the real lives of ruthless rulers, it is a professional hazard. When Zia was in power, one of his security strategies was that every time he travelled in his military plane, every technician who touched his aircraft had to travel with him on board the same aircraft. That practice was also reportedly followed in his fatal journey back from Bahawalpur to Islamabad but it did not prove enough insurance against whoever was determined to get to him. That inclusion of all technical staff explained the high casualty count in that crash.

Looking back at the history of the great Mughal Empire, parallels and lessons can be drawn between the approaches of Emperors Akbar & Aurangzeb. The third Mughal Emperor Akbar is also referred to as *Akbar the Great* or "*Mughal-e-Azam*" in local languages. When his reign terminated in 1605, the Mughal Empire encompassed most of northern and central India, becoming one of the most powerful empires of its age. Akbar was thirteen years of age when he was seated on throne in Delhi. It took him two decades to consolidate his power. Akbar's reign had a major bearing on art and culture, encouraging development of the Mughal School as well as patronising European styles of painting. He enjoyed literary activities. Several Sanskrit works were translated into Persian; and Persian authoritative books in turn translated in Sanskrit. His administration involved Hindu influential individuals and military generals. He regularly organised religious debates whereby Muslim scholars debated religious matters with Hindus, Jains, Sikhs, atheists, Jews, Roman Catholic and others. He treated all religious leaders with respect, irrespective of their faith. In a way it could be said that he lived before his time in history.

His great grandson Aurangzeb was a bigoted extremist who let loose serial killings of his own brothers and all else in his way to usurping power using a religious persona to justify his brutal pursuit of the throne. Once in power, his guilt and mistrust of others never allowed him to associate with anyone except those limited few he thought he could trust a little bit. Aurangzeb's policy of exclusion and rewarding parochial loyalties over an all-inclusive governance approach eventually led to his own demise and the fall of the might Mughal Empire. While history refers to the grandfather as Akbar the Great, most references to Aurangzeb relate to his role in the eventual downfall of the great empire. Religious parties and right wing historians have always had a soft corner for him simply because of his external appearance and religious pretentions, conveniently ignoring his political murders and the fact that he had his father's eyes removed to nullify any threat from him to his power. Hardly deeds worthy of pride for any man irrespective of his beliefs!

Having not learnt from history, are we now in the process of repeating it? Was Zia the contemporary version of Aurangzeb? Let us hope that the outcome of Zia's insane lust for power will not have as damaging an outcome as Aurangzeb brought upon the Mughal Empire. We have a harsh lesson from history to guide us. Whether we learn from it or repeat it, will decide our fate and the decision is entirely in our hands.

We can look at more recent history too. Is it just a coincidence that Muslims countries with moderate and tolerant societies like Malaysia and Turkey are far ahead of others? Those in persistent internal turmoil are the ones with extremist tendencies like Pakistan, Afghanistan, Sudan, etc. Iran may be a different case as far as internal security is concerned but we cannot talk about today's Iran, tolerance and democracy in the same breath.

The first signs of someone ridiculing or basing jokes on religious practices started in Zia's period. Any surprises there? When suppression or fear of intimidation crosses a certain bearable threshold, one of the manifestations of frustration and pent up aggression is through jokes that are widely quoted, even at social gathering because no one owns up to being the author. The stand-up comedian can get away with a bit more latitude than ordinary citizens. In our rural environment and even urban family events, the traditional "*Bhaands*" [*local entertainers*] started to narrate jokes about religious practices and symbols. Given the general atmosphere of intense intimidation, the audiences would respond with a disproportionately high volume of laughter which served as a safe catharsis for accumulated hostility and frustration under a brutal dictatorship.

Suppression through "Fatwas"

The dangerous and painful tool of "*Fatwas*" (*religious verdicts*) is limited to religious issues only. It has been a very hazardous tool of exploitation and oppression for centuries because it is not clearly understood who can or cannot issue one. A local mullah can on his own or prompted by local influence virtually pass a death sentence for stoning or lashing for an offence never actually committed. The use of Fatwas on minorities in recent times leading to lengthy imprisonments or even a couple of fatal mob attacks on their localities demonstrates how easily the instrument of a Fatwa can be abused by the agents of animosity and divisiveness. It has invariably been applied on the weakest and most underprivileged segments of the population, minorities, persecuted groups and those fighting for human rights and liberties. It is worth checking when was the last time a Fatwa was issued and implemented against a powerful group within our national boundaries, especially for a noble cause? Who has the lawful right or authority to issue one? Finally who decides which prevails if two conflicting ones are issues simultaneously?

De-educating the populace

Education has never really been an area of priority for Muslims in the sub-continent. Actual facts make an interesting reading. In 1872, out of 300 students on the rolls of the *Hoogly College*, maintained by the East-India Company out of the income of a Muslim Educational Trust, only three were Muslims! It can be interpreted in two ways. Either they were denied easy or equal access to education or that even more than well over a century ago, Muslims in the sub-continent did not consider education a subject of high priority. Those amongst us who are willing to accept past mistakes will agree that our current attitude towards education is not of recent origin but is well entrenched in our historical determination of priorities.

Another perceptible inclination at the time was the existence and dependence on trusts and charitable institutions amongst Muslims. This practice too is still very evident today and both are indicative of an inherent psychic resistance to institutional development. That is also consistent with the underlining vital thrust that the medieval thinking apparatus is controlled in as many ways as possible and having being intimidated into submission, lacks the psychic energy to break through that mental barrier.

At the risk of repetition, both propensities are symbolic of unhealthy minds. Lack of emphasis on education has never been a wise approach in any religion, culture or society and there is no evidence on record that sustained progress and effective nation building has ever been achieved where education has been a lesser priority compared to non-education sectors. On the contrary, there is a lot of supporting evidence that countries that have achieved substantive progress have invested reasonably well, if not heavily in human resource development. That would include education and related fields of health and hygiene too, another area of undeniable neglect in our case.

Private benevolence over state welfare

The trend of trust and charity is comparatively easier to explain and relate to in the over-all theme. Feudal set ups being basically inherently exploitative in nature, need a social persona of some sort to numb the impact of politics of intimidation. What can be more deceptively offered than in a persona of economic patronage of the exploited classes? It also serves the secondary objectives of perpetuating dependence and through it a system of control; the destined "*have nots*" being generously looked after by those destined to be their naturally appointed saviours. It is also a good strategic advert of piousness and generosity in the governing class over their less fortunate fellow citizens; a win-win situation from start to finish.

This can only be sustained by ensuring that state institutions that should ordinarily be the custodians of economic and social welfare remain weak and ineffective. If instead of manipulating a system of private generosity for social welfare, those economically privileged in society performed their national duties under law and constitution such as paying their right amount of taxes and duties to the state exchequer, supplementary private support networks would not really be required in the first place, at least not quite to the same extent. That, however, would be a more socially just arrangement whereby individuals would not be required to mortgage their souls in exchange for private patronage, thinking patterns would be positively different and recipients would get whatever was due to them as a matter of right or on merit instead of as acts of private favours.

It would be harsh to imply that all charities and trusts live a fraudulent existence. Some do a wonderful job but those are a mere handful and those names are generally on the fingertips of average citizens. But the brutal reality is that tax avoidance and evasion as well as corruption in general is rampant and widespread in the society leaving a massive public expenditure hole for socially noble causes. That vacuum is filled in by private charities funded mostly through tax evaded money or ill-gotten wealth, a fraction of which is siphoned back to charities as a conscience cleansing act. Several years ago, there was a very well-known charitable foundation, run by a famous bank which does not exist anymore. In one particular year, it declared a profit of Rs280 million out of which only Rs20 million of the earnings were offered for taxation and the remaining diverted to its own charitable foundation, liberated from taxation! During investigations, massive irregularities were found in the way tax free donations were distributed and the fraudulent manner in which funds were reinvested to generate more income on which tax could be avoided in turn. Much to the bewilderment of some of us, the chairman of the then Central Board of Revenue would either over-rule or side step proposals for initiating prosecution proceedings for tax evasion against that foundation. After retiring from public service he ended up becoming a top office holder in that juvenile charity foundation!

Agents of exploitation and status quo impede development of state institutions to leave a vacuum where personal or party influences can flourish. Those pursuits later either become stepping stones for career or party progression or serve as a good camouflage for sanitisation of tax evaded income and ill-gotten wealth; another very effective "*get out*" clause from potential financial hazard. Placing a higher value on private privileges and individual discretion over principles and service institutions is a matter of choice. The tragic reality, however, is that societies that end up placing a higher value on individual or private privilege over long standing principles eventually end up losing both!

Zia –Wicked spirit in holy persona

"When men are pure, laws are useless; when men are corrupt, laws are broken".
Benjamin Disraeli

Zia once said on national television that the country's constitution was just another book which he could through out of the window! That said it all about him and represented his true depraved self. He came to power on the back of deceitful campaign that was to be the beginning of our downward spiral. He then promised to hold elections within 90 days and return to his hole in the ground. If some believed a word of whatever he said, then they fully deserved any ill-effects on them of his period of misrule. If he could, he would have hung around for 90 years, even if the state of Pakistan had shrunk to the size of the city of Lahore by the time he was finished. That reality is now dawning on unsuspecting citizens in the most painful, if not fatal outcomes in many cases. He represented that breed of freedom molesters in history whose only chance of survival depends on the total silence and subjugation of those under governance. Punishments are deliberately dished out early and with disproportionate force and consequences to ensure that the message is seen and heard loud and clear.

While our rot set in the day we abandoned Jinnah and his political principles of governance to fall into the greedy laps of those that he stood against, no single person or factor has contributed to our current miseries by even a fraction of the damage inflicted by Zia alone on the nation, its institutions, society, the education system, culture, interracial relations and harmony, not to forget the promotion of corruption, religious bigotry and intolerance, gun running, state donations as political bribes in the name of development funds and so on. It is enough subject matter for an entire book in itself.

Ever expanding "Shadow" proportions

Structural society emphasis is focused on external appearance of face and body covering, irrespective of what is stored inside the skull. In real life, what really matters and affects a human being's relations with others is the stuff inside the head, not how it is presented externally to society or the world.

I remember having attended an end of academic year function at a private school in Islamabad. Young boys and girls ranging 5 to 8 years of age performed well rehearsed cultural acts such as short plays and group dances. Parents enjoyed watching their children and those of others enjoy themselves and make other parents feel proud too. A few days later I read a letter from a disgruntled parent, a *Ramzan Chaudhry*, who felt embarrassed and ashamed watching his own daughter join a group of class fellows in a perfectly decent cultural dance! How did he manage to see an evil which was not there for any other parent to see and moan about? The answer obviously is that the imaginary filth was inside his perverse head, not in the external act; "*a blind man, in a dark room, looking for a black cat, which was not there*"!

He was symbolic of the increasingly perverted mind-set that has been the product of promotion of fabricated and deceptive values programmed to keep a stifling control on society so that the de-educating agenda is facilitated and sustained. Many such characters are often themselves involved in dubious activities in private life.

They do so out of uncontrolled impulses for short term pleasures or material gains but fail to shake off the feeling of guilt. The flash back imagery of their own misdeeds leads them to project their deeds and wild imagination onto all other human beings and a display of hypocritical contempt for those in performing arts in particular. They will sit and watch television entertainment programmes and movies for as long as they can spare time to do so, listen to music of all kinds, even sign along with those who they publicly proclaim to be the carriers of social evils and therefore Hell bound. By watching and paying for that entertainment whether on TV or at movie theatres, they provide the finances and the viewing numbers that promote the career prospects of producers, actors, dancers, singers, etc. but that is all private craving. Publicly, a manifestation, an outer shell and a persona of fake piousness has to be maintained to rationalise their own guilt and to present a different and socially correct image to society. In reality it does them no good and does no favours to society through promotion of blatant hypocrisy.

This malaise of double standards spreads like a creeping disease in the whole personality. They could be deep into earning income through clandestine means, production of fake or substandard goods, theft of energy charges by monthly bribery of lowly paid officials, evasion of taxes by maintaining false books of accounts and legally payable duties, by dealing in smuggled goods, making bogus applications for plots of land or other assets when the applicable procedure explicitly prohibits or restricts an individual's claim to a single or other specified number of units, and so on. None of that will bother them in the least because that is rationalised by the self-deceit of overt holiness. They will pull down their shop shutters on Fridays afternoons to offer Friday prayers and return an hour later to resume their deceitful life. The visit to the mosque does not leave an iota of impact on their practical life. In fact, should that ever cause any psychological dissonance, the conflict is perished through the most common rationalisation device to restore mental peace and consonance; religious and material life are independent of each other. A man insincere to himself cannot be expected to be sincere to anything else in life.

The healthy human psyche is designed to work at its most creative and productive peak in a state of balance. Once moral controls and punitive codes reach a level that almost completely destroys the balance, the suppressed share of natural balance is not nipped in the bud so to speak but re-assembles in all its might in the unconscious hideouts of the mind. Some of the brutal actions of the militants and Talibans are tailor made examples of this process. Every suppressed instinct trickles down from consciousness and takes up a sniper position in the unconscious for an outlet, hidden from the conscious mind. No balanced healthy mind can carry out beheadings and stoning to death of women and infants in peace time. It is the overwhelming simmering shadow proportion covered with an artificial and weak holy persona that takes over completely in those moments to carry out acts of inhuman violence not normally associated with average human behaviour.

Sanctity of national passports

بیزار فضا، درپۓ آزار صبا ہے
یوں ہے کہ ہر اک ہمدم دیرینہ خفا ہے

اُمڈی ہے ہر اک سمت سے الزام کی برسات
چھائی ہوئی ہر دانگ ملامت کی گھٹا ہے

تعزیر سیاست ہے نہ غیروں کی خطا ہے
وہ ظلم جو ہم نے دل وحشی پہ کیا ہے

Bezaar faza, darpa-i aazaar saba hai
Yun hai ke har ik hamdam-i dairina khafa hai

Umdi hai har ik simt se ilzaam ki barsaat
Chhaai hui har daang malaamat ki ghata hai

Ta'zeer-i siyasat hai na ghairon ki khata hai
Voh zulm jo ham ne dil-i vehshi pe kiya hai
Faiz

Morning breeze irked, the atmosphere stress laden;
Seems as if every age old friend is disillusioned

Rainstorms of accusations rising from all directions;
The clouds of censure spread in all directions

It is neither in the ethos of politics, nor the fault of others
The kind of cruelty, self-inflicted on our own heart

It is a standard drill now for immigration officers at entry points at airports across the globe to exchange cheeky glances amongst themselves if not to fall off their chairs at the mere sight of our green national passport. A lengthy process of scrutiny then follows. It does not matter where the port of call is. In recent years I have been stopped, investigated, even not allowed to board the aircraft at places ranging from Ottawa in Canada, to other locations like Bulgaria, Spain, Tanzania, Cameroon, Malawi, Mauritius and many others. This is not while holding the ultimate document of suspicion, the green passport but even as a holder of an Official [Gratis] passport and mostly as a business class passenger.

Compare this to a scene back in 1985. While at the University of Bath, my family joined me during the school summer vacations in Islamabad and we took an affordable guided tour to four countries in Europe with a well-known tour organising company. No visa was required for entry to the United Kingdom on a Gratis Pakistani passport in those times. None was required for three of the four target countries in Europe on that trip. On return to the seaport of Dover in the United Kingdom and presentation of the passport to the immigration officer, it appeared he was looking for an entry visa. I enquired politely from him if there was a problem? He said he could not find the entry visa. So I asked if one was required on a Gratis passport? He immediately apologised and added that it was the first thing he should have noticed. That was it! No problem whatsoever. Not only that, a polite apology too for the extra scrutiny. That international image today has been so manhandled by a group of our own unrepentant fanatics that everyone gets brushed aside on arrival for multiple cross checks.

In addition to the extremism related scourge, the sanctity of the gratis and diplomatic passports has been left in tatters by the misdeeds of a few influential persons back home. According to media reports one well publicised example is that of a judge of the Lahore High Court, *Justice Chaudhry Ramnzan Khan* insisting upon being issued a diplomatic passport for travel abroad in exchange for a favourable judgement and actually being granted his wish! His Lordship later became a global brand for his well-publicised investigations into scandals of match fixing and unlawful money making by national sportsmen. How could that document of national identity retain the same degree of international recognition and sanctity when the internal house was in such disorder, ironically even at the hands of some of those who were there to ensure the rule of law?

6

Tax me if you can

Taxation is not the most popular topic for discussion at social gatherings or private family events. Those who pay taxes and those who avoid paying their share are equally reluctant to bring it up for discussion. However, ridiculing the subject and those associated with tax policy and administration is indeed a popular past time. So let us introduce an element of light hearted humour in the subject before going into really serious stuff. I came across this poem by someone I have not been able to identify despite effort. So with utmost gratitude and appreciation for our anonymous poet for the brilliance and graphic imagery of his contempt for and annoyance with the subject, it is hoped that most readers will find it engaging. Many extreme right wing politicians might find useful leads for their favourite fiscal pursuit of broadening the tax base through indirect taxes.

Tax his land, tax his wage
Tax his bed in which he lays.
Tax his tractor, tax his mule
Teach him taxes is the rule

Tax his cow, tax his goat
Tax his pants, tax his coat.
Tax his ties, tax his shirts
Tax his work, tax his dirt

Tax his chew, tax his smoke
Teach him taxes are no joke.
Tax his car, tax his grass
Tax the roads he must pass

Tax his food, tax his drink
Tax him if he tries to think.
Tax his sodas, tax his beers
If he cries, tax his tears

Tax his bills, tax his gas
Tax his notes, tax his cash.
Tax him good and let him know
That after taxes, he has no dough

If he hollers, tax him more
Tax him until he's good and sore.
Tax his coffin, tax his grave
Tax the sod in which he lays

Put these words upon his tomb
"Taxes drove me to my doom!"
And when he's gone, we won't relax
We'll still be after inheritance tax!

The expenditure estimation approach

Most developing societies share a common problem in lack of documentation of the economic activities. Except for the formal corporate sector, most businesses claim to maintain no regular set of business accounts. Many taxpayers, who do so in practice, take the opposite stance before tax authorities because determination of income in the absence of documentary evidence is far more difficult, and evading taxes a lot easier. We have already discussed how emphasis in our society on accountability in general is very low. When it comes to checking tax evasion, the level of accountability is virtually non-existent. So is social disapproval because tax evasion is not considered to be a serious crime; some even considering it an act of defiant chivalry. In support of this is contention a stark and staggering statistical fact. In our entire history, there has not been a single case of successful prosecution for tax evasion in any court of law!

Given the lack of documentation in support of economic and commercial activity, aided and encouraged by absence of social reprimand, the levels of tax avoidance and evasion must rank amongst the highest anywhere in the world. Instead of dealing with tax evasion menace head on, regularly repeated sideshows of tax reforms have been played out for public consumption. The matter is very simple and straight forward but like other attitudes in national politics, has never really been addressed honestly and sincerely. It is not likely to be addressed soon because it is not a priority, never has been. On the contrary, ensuring the protection of the worst offenders is a political necessity because they rampage the corridors of power in cyclical turns.

If tax evasion is pursued with honesty, strength of character and determination, it will probably never really be eliminated but the current levels of rampant evasion and corruption can be substantially reduced. There are additional ways of fighting tax evasion than those already incorporated in current tax statutes, but even in the current system the problem is one of honest implementation and not so much impotence of tax laws. It is a fact of life that nations and societies with higher levels of corruption also have more laws than others, there being more situations to cover. Sadly, most laws have a decorative purpose and implementation remains as weak as ever. When one of the richest businessman-cum-politician in the country like Nawaz Sharif pays less direct income tax than a moderately paid middle level civil servant, no one should be surprised that the country has a massive problem that gets more protection from state and society than serious attempts to get rid of it. Recent calls from foreign governments on Pakistan to increase its tax effort are not without foundation, especially when successive governments keep asking the international community to come to the assistance of millions affected by recurrent natural disasters.

Where documentation in support of most business and commercial activities is not available or claimed not to exist, determination of incomes for tax purposes becomes far more difficult. It is also a fact that where tax evasion is more common and widespread, the level of private expenses on standards of living and luxurious indulgences tend to be excessive and exaggerated because excess funds are available that are more difficult to reinvest without leaving risky trails of reinvestment that could lead to meaningful investigation later. However, earnings expended lavishly on private family events, or dowry investments, travels abroad including for Haj and Umra, etc. are more difficult to detect, even more difficult to back up with supporting evidence that can stand the test of prosecutions or judicial appeal proceedings. In such societies, a different approach to income determination is required. The best way to determine incomes is by using information about expenses incurred normally by individuals or households that can lead to more reliable estimates of individual or household incomes. One has to earn legally or obtain illegally before money can be spent. Details of a comprehensive system of income determination via expenditures cannot be abridged in part of a chapter. To give you a sneak preview of my drift, a person can claim not to have record or evidence in support of his earnings but no one can claim that his household expenses including payments of utility bills, rent on accommodation or property tax payments if the residential property is self-owned, even payment of educational fees at schools and colleges is not made by parents without obtaining a proper receipt for their record.

A very reliable and transparent system of expenditure based income determination can be developed in a relatively short period of time. However, the theoretical model is, as we all know far easier to design than setting up of an elaborate and fool proof operational structure that can really maximise revenue generation. The main obstacle is the absence of a strong political will and weak, if not dodgy moral social values in fiscal matters. A system that is transparent will inherently be more equitable and relatively more difficult to manipulate. Will society as a whole and more so the power brokers and stakeholders support that? Six decades of track record in fiscal priorities and discipline is shining evidence to the contrary. A feudal society has a strong undercurrent of the domination of personal influence over governance in general but in financial governance it is particular noticeable.

The scourge of tax exemptions

At the time I left the country to take over the prestigious job of Executive Director in the Commonwealth Association of Tax Administrators in 1996, the tax statute in force in Pakistan was the Income Tax Act 1979. There was a point in time where the Act had 187 charging sections and well over 350 exemption clauses! Each tax exemption is an indirect public expenditure to the extent that the tax that would have been collected is generously sacrificed even before it becomes legally collectable. As tax collectors, it is particularly more frustrating when the political masters twist arms and turn screws regularly into tax departments for collection of more taxes. No rocket science is needed to understand that the removal of 350 exemption clauses would in itself generate a huge amount of income tax. While the *mother of all exemptions*, incomes from agricultural activities gets all the attention, tax foregone through other exemptions is also colossal, if not potentially more in the aggregate.

It is universally accepted by tax experts and supported through studies in fiscal matters that there is no direct correlation between increased investment and tax exemptions alone. In addition to direct revenue losses, exemptions also provide a source of diversion of taxable incomes in the disguise of income from agricultural activity. Even barren lands on paper can be allocated substantial income by the owners giving legal cover to otherwise taxable income without payment of a single penny. In my estimation, if tax is eventually imposed on income from agriculture under the current taxation system, the net collection will be surprisingly and disappointingly low but the move would plug a massive loophole of tax avoidance and evasion.

If exemptions had been granted purely on merit, they could have been comparatively more bearable. However, like the rest of governance and exploitative opportunism, most have been granted under coercion of some sort or outright acts of favour to colleagues in power or even those in opposition when the iron is hot. Many people may not be aware that whereas the imposition of tax has to be approved the house of representatives [National Assembly], exemptions are granted by the Ministry of Finance, only after the explicit approval of the incumbent finance minister without having to refer the matter back to the representative body that imposed the tax in the first place. The political justification offered is always that the finance minister is under constant pressure from influential lobbies and that such pressure is too overbearing to resist. This is essentially nothing more than deceitful political spin. While posted in the board of revenue a very small group of officers including myself campaigned repeatedly for deletion of the enabling power in the tax statute under which tax exemptions or reductions in the rate of tax could be granted in specific cases through issuance of a notification or the now infamous SROs for indirect taxes. Our argument was very simple. If political actors found it difficult to resist pressure or the temptation of enlisting short term support from opposition benches, there could be no better solution than to abolish the exemption granting power altogether. That would imply anyone seeking tax exemption would have to get the approval of the majority in the National Assembly which was far more difficult than manipulative approval by an individual minister. It would also save the minister himself from undue pressure in the absence of the ability to lay a golden egg on demand.

That proposal was knocked down every year that it was included in the budgetary proposals. A couple of years after I left Pakistan, one of my former colleagues informed that something we had tried to be part of for so many years had finally been approved. The Finance Minister could no longer grant tax exemptions and in doing so had made life easier for himself and the tax system slightly less vulnerable to undue pressures from powerful individuals or lobbies. It was delightful news to hear because it is relatively rare for our tax policy makers to move in the right direction, more so for the right reasons. But a political system that is based on overbearing influences and pressures that stampede on principles and higher causes that stand in their way cannot afford the luxury of living by the rule of law and noble principles. If memory serves correctly, the amendment was undone within six months! Those born and bred on seeking favours simply could not afford the long and more transparent process of tax exemptions through an elected legislature. At the same time incumbent finance ministers feel severely disabled and disarmed from allocating favours to chosen ones or those from whom reciprocal favours are politically expedient. The position of a lame duck finance minister is severely undermined if he leaves home without his exemption granting card. It does not matter who is in power or opposition, this game of mutual benevolence and peaceful coexistence has never been interrupted for as long as one can remember because all sides are fully aware of their ancestrally allocated winning numbers in the "*national lootery*". The situation brings back memories of the famous English folk song and our school days nursery rhyme, **"Lavender's Blue"**. The bit that is particularly appropriate to this archetypal enactment is:

Lavender's blue, dilly dilly, lavender's green,
When I am king, dilly, dilly, you shall be queen,
Call up your men, dilly, dilly, set them to work,
Some with a rake, dilly, dilly, some with a fork,
Some to make hay, dilly, dilly, some to thresh corn,
While you and I, dilly, dilly, keep ourselves warm.

Let them be; smuggling is a way of life

The English national daily newspaper "Dawn" reported on 18 July 2010 that Federal Minister for Environment *Hamidullah Jan Afridi* said in relation to the famous tribal areas *"that as per the traditions of the area, the local elders would be assigned the responsibility of maintaining peace at Bara Bazaar and its surroundings under the Collective Territorial Responsibility clause of Frontier Crimes Regulation. He said that the continuous closure of markets had inflicted huge financial loses on the local traders while thousands had been rendered jobless. I had been personally taking up this matter with all officials concerned as closure of markets and imposition of curfew are creating mistrust between the ordinary residents of Bara and the security forces."*

For those not familiar with "*Bara markets*", these are properly structured sale outlets in regular commercial market areas, very well populated at all times by customers fully aware that all goods are smuggled, mainly through the porous Pakistan-Afghanistan border. We are not talking about hand carried stuff like watches or mobile phones. Refrigerators, air conditioners, washing machines, dish washers; you name it are all openly and proudly showcased like any other market dealing in lawfully imported or locally produced goods. It is a text book exhibition of supply and demand in action outside the ambit of law. The original Bara market was located in the bordering town in the control free tribal belt very close to the border with Afghanistan. That is what the minister was referring to. But there have now been Bara markets in operation for almost four decades in all major cities right up to the southernmost port city of Karachi; formal extensions or permanent establishments of the tribal belt in urban centres.

I remember a conference of the Commissioners of Income Tax and Collectors of Customs with the then Finance Minister, *Ghulam Ishaq Khan* around 1982 or 1983. During the meeting, the minister was particularly harsh on those tasked with prevention of smuggling. The then Director of Vigilance Wing, *Sheikh Sajjad Hassan* reminded the minister that he had requested the government several times that winding up all Bara markets was the only assured way of effectively tackling smuggling, but he was told that it would create a law and order situation. He should therefore "*catch the bird while it was flying*"! He added that it was therefore up to the government to sort out its priorities. If the government's fear of a law and order situation resulting from dealing firmly with a handful of dealers in smuggled goods was more important than dealing with smuggling itself, then why pretend to be concerned about that menace itself? The minister initially pretended that the Bara markets were not a big deal and then claimed before a stunned group that there was no Bara market in Rawalpindi; a twin city of seat of governance

Islamabad where the meeting was being held. The then finance secretary whispered discreetly in his minister's ear that the denial was a step too far for a fact of life known to even kids in both cities. We are talking about one of the most technically and administratively effective of finance ministers.

The narration highlights two very significant points. Firstly, that our political leadership has a history of compromising important principles of governance and ethics to buy comfort and avoid making difficult choices. Secondly, that policy makers are either horribly negligent and ignorant of ground realities or simply that staying in power is a far more noble cause in itself than opting for effective governance with any vision or concern for the long term future.

Smuggling has not just been an economic activity in the famous tribal belt that the British, Soviets in an earlier period of history and now NATO allies are struggling to tame. It is a way of living as reiterated in the afore-quoted statement of the minister. A study was once instituted to determine the cost of smuggling to smugglers. Smuggling is not a completely cost free activity as some seem to assume. There are costs associated with transportation, storage of smuggled goods, recruitment and arming of vigilance staff, pay-roll expenses of unscrupulous staff of governmental anti-smuggling departments and agencies, and so on. The idea behind the study was to determine the cost of smuggling and consequently lower the then very steep rates of import duties to levels closer to the cost of smuggling so that the attraction in smuggling as a lucrative form of business could be nullified. Smuggling is a cross border activity. The actions of one state alone cannot impact on partners in other countries and new anti-smuggling legislation alone certainly cannot change a way of life that is seen as a "*nothing wrong with it*" tradition.

Whatever the reasons for failure to arrest or control smuggling, the perpetuation and quantitative extension of smuggling as a way of life is now not just limited to the tribal belt. There is perhaps as much circulation of smuggled goods in Karachi as in the original small pocket of tribal territory. But it is not the economic aspect that has been most damaging. The psyche of a smuggler is one of revolt against authority and contempt for law. What is happening in Karachi at present is essentially the interaction of various lawless underground economic gangs aspiring for control and extension of their respective spheres of influence, all of it outside the ambit of lawful activity. It was only a question of when and not if matters would deteriorate to the present state. That prevalent mental state is germane to behavioural patterns exhibited in smuggling codes and practices.

Legal and financial accountability

Take the controversial Kerry-Lugar Bill for instance. I am not privy to the details of the legislation nor the allegedly mischievous string pulling in the background or build up and therefore have no comments to offer on the merits or otherwise, nor is value judgement of that Bill relevant to the current analysis. However, what is intriguing are the moral arguments of most politicians, mainly in opposition at the time about the financial aspects of the aid package. Most took offense to the Americans wanting some or total control over the use of the money to be provided by them to administrative authorities in Pakistan. The argument that was most fascinating as reported in the media was that a proud and "sovereign" nation could not be asked to explain the use of aid money by the donor country. Forget for a moment that Lugar and Pakistan were involved in the argument. Read "Sovereign A" for Lugar and "Sovereign B" for Pakistan and let us analyse the working relationship of "A" and "B". "A" lends money or provides aid to "B" for whatever reasons. In return "A" demands or insists on having the right to monitor or audit the use of that lending or grant. Does a lender of any description not have the right to ask for assurances from any borrower? In the commercial world, there is only one answer. In fact, most lenders will ensure repayment securities in addition to checking out the borrower's ability to pay back if repayment is involved, though political lending has a lower set of moral codes. So the financial equation is pretty much well defined in theory and in practice at domestic and international levels. In real life, the moment one country asks for financial assistance, especially from a country that is perceived or projected as unfriendly or hostile, the borrowing and even more so, aid seeking country surrenders a major part of its "sovereignty" status to a large extent. The first casualty of economic dependence for any nation is national pride.

Loans of no return

Our problem is that in the national psyche, a loan obtained through the use of influence or coercion is generally seen as a one-way transaction, depending on the clout or the lack of it that the borrower can muster. Even if not explicitly stated, in some remote corner of most borrowing minds, is a hopeful intent that circumstances will eventually turn borrowed money into a sort of permanent gift or donation. In the case of most top industrialists or politicians, this is not just a fuzzy desire, it is a definite plan that one way or another, the borrowed money will be naturalised by way of a manipulated write-off or bad debt. Hardly anyone has been held publicly accountable for the amount of or manner in which massive amounts of borrowings have been pocketed time and time again by those who have brought the country to its present financially anaemic state. Therefore how could someone from outside seek explanations on spending outlets and amounts involved once money comes into his coffers?

The average citizen should have been happy that somebody somewhere might be able to keep a check on those whom the nation has failed to keep under any control whatsoever. In fact these con artists have never been put beyond any polite probe, let alone any meaningful investigation. Remember the massive funds collected for the deadly earthquake in Azad Kashmir? Is there any publicly available record on how much was received in all and what was spent when, where and on whom? Does the nation not have a right to know how development money sent to the nation by others is spent or wasted? Civil society needs to play a more robust role in finding out the real figures. If not, are we as a nation justified in complaining about lack or absence of integrity in our national financial culture? Question time is now over. It is either decision time or the dustbins of history await us. This is the real "wake up Pakistan" call; an internal wake up not a hate campaign showcased by media channels against other countries which would simply not matter and would ordinarily be irrelevant if our own house was in order.

Who led the chorus of abuse for the Kerry-Lugar Bill? All opposition parties of course, supported by the clueless amongst the population so easily misled in the name of patriotism or a largely phantom nationalism. Those in power might just have been happy at yet another opportunity to enrich their coffers. When our rich class has never been accountable at home in money matters, who the hell were Kerry or Lugar to suggest they could intrude in our control free spending habits? That discomfort is understandable for the recipient stakeholders but why should the man on the street also be in alliance with those who have exploited them for 60 years? That is because he has been programmed to follow blindly; not to think analytically for himself. Control freak feudal set ups cannot afford the luxury of allowing stimulation of the thinking process because that is dangerous in that it leads to questions, and questions in turn lead to the truth which in turn can lead to a change! Change is an exorbitant indulgence because the edifice, the structure and the glittering interiors of feudalism and status quo are built on the perpetuation of ignorance and illiteracy.

The chorus of anti- accountability was sung largely by most opposition representatives for whom it seemed a definite vote winner. Accountability at home is a non-starter and accountability from abroad is an affront to national pride! Corruption without inhibition is not an affront but looking into it whether at home or by more independent sources is an affront. Can there be a better programme for a more conveniently organised life for stockpiling easy money? Interest earned by pensioners on petty accumulations of lifelong savings in fixed deposits of choice constitutes "*haraam*" interest earnings but "*Haraam*" earnings of life-long swindle, deceit, commissions and kickbacks, huge loans written off as bad debts or more courageous write-off constitute "*Allah ka fazl*" in the eyes of our pious religious and political leaders, feudal and industrial Brahmans! Having done all that they even look forward to an "*assured citizenship*" in Heaven by virtue of having performed all 5 essentials of the religion, most of all Haj and a catalogue of Umra visits by spending a fraction of their ill-gotten wealth whereas the starving daily wage earner can only dream about one chance.

When similar accusations or assessments are made from abroad whether by any formal, national or international transparency watchdog, accusations of bias, anti-Pakistan or anti-Muslim conspiracies begin to fly. If corruption, nepotism, out of turn benevolence have plagued our daily lives and the common man individually or collectively cannot do a damn thing about it, any supporting activity from the international community should be welcomed, not condemned. During periods of military rule in Pakistan in recent times, the Commonwealth suspended the country for variable periods of time in condemnation of the overthrowing of lawfully elected governments under the Harare Declaration. Politicians of all shades welcomed the move every time, even staged strategic protests in front of the Commonwealth headquarters at Marlborough House in London. Those protests were not against intervention by the Commonwealth but to encourage or persuade it to inflict bigger blows on domestic military rulers. If that did not tantamount to interference by the Commonwealth in our scared internal affairs, why should similar pressures against financial corruption in public and private life, especially by top political creatures of all shades, shapes and standings suddenly be deemed interference worthy of condemnation? Is this either another faceless display of deliberate double standards or simply an inability to decipher right from wrong?

Manifestations and consequences of ill-gotten wealth

The impact of tax evasion is not limited to loss of revenue to state exchequers only. There are several other wide ranging collateral damaging ripples. Disparities in wealth or incomes widen through evasion and there is indirect encouragement for corrupt practices in the knowledge that the probability of detection and punitive action by enforcement authorities is minimal. Wasteful expenditure habits are encouraged based on easily earned money which in turn creates inflationary pressures on the lower income earners in society. There are exclusive books on tax evasion alone.

Kidnappings for ransom: Kidnappings for ransom payments are known to happen in many countries. Where corruption and tax evasion is freely practiced, from reports in media and private conversations, such kidnappings seem to be conducted in the nature of established businesses. Kidnappers do proper homework in selecting their victims, who by most reports are well treated during captivity and handed back on payment of agreed ransoms. Nothing unusual there but the most intriguing part is the follow up conduct of ransom payers. Most do not lodge a proper report with the police and those who do conceal the real amount of ransom paid because their official worth in taxation records is usual a tiny fraction of reported one time ransom payments. It is a case of one thief, loaded with ill-gotten and tax evaded wealth being found out by interested parties and getting mugged in turn by another. Reporting the correct amount of money paid can result in investigations by tax authorities on unreported income and wealth resulting in more pain. Unfortunately, once in a while things go wrong or the kidnappers may get their investigations flawed. In some of such instances, kidnappings have resulted in horrible tragedies for undeserving families caught up in the consequences of greed and money driven unlawful activities in a near lawless society.

Loutish wealth display: One theoretical model on tax evasion behaviour supports the hypothesis that decisions on tax evasion are based on the perception of taxpayers about the probability of being caught by tax authorities. If the perception is that the probably of getting caught for tax evasion is very high, the temptation is muted considerably. When one feels that it is pretty safe and worth the gamble, taxpayers will avoid and evade tax without the slightest hesitation. The propensity to avoid taxes is another archetypal behaviour pattern and sentiments like patriotism do not seem relevant. A weak tax system anywhere will lead to evasion and avoidance. In our case, it is safe to say that taxpayers hardly seem to worry about the possibility of being found out for evasion of tax.

Being in that mental comfort zone, those with considerable accumulated wealth quite often shamelessly, if not defiantly display their wealth at private family events and social gatherings. Far from being condemned for doing so, many attendees confer compliments on hosts for the quality of hospitality. Sometimes these exhibitionist attitudes provide leads and temptations for kidnappings and armed robberies but the feudal mind set is so propelled with the craving for showcasing its status, irrespective of the manner of acquisition of that financial status that it cannot see the inherent dangers to its own best interests. Easy money is easily thrown away for display. Those with hard earned and tax paid income struggle to keep up and many social tragedies result from financial pressures. When that happens, a few people may pause for a second to clear their throats in faked sympathy and then it is business as usual.

Aggressive display of ill-gotten wealth: Wasteful expenditure that is arrogantly showcased at family weddings and other social events way beyond known or recorded means of income of the spending families is all too well documented to require supporting evidence. Easy money is so callously and audaciously thrown away for spectacles that satisfy recognition obsessed egos; sort of easy come, easy go syndrome. Hard earned tax paid income would never be thrown away without feeling the pain and without many questions to answer to authorities and the public. Instead of the guilty parties feeling guilty or embarrassed about their vulgar display of wealth, they seek to climb up a few positions in an imaginary social ranking system that is built on false and perverted values, if at all such pursuits can be insulted in the name of values. The following incident will highlight the point. The Islamabad to Lahore motorway is generally far better regulated and controlled for traffic discipline and speed controls compared to the traditional intercity roads. In a relatively recent drive from Lahore to Islamabad, there were signs that the effectiveness of highway police control had dropped a bit. As luck would have it, in a chance social meeting during that very trip with the officer in-charge of highway traffic control, the perception was conveyed to him. The explanation that followed was stunning and graphically demonstrates the dark side of ill-gotten incomes. A gentleman started his journey in a brand new four wheel drive social icon vehicle. He was stopped for speeding very early in his journey and asked to pay what would be a fairly deterrent amount for an average citizen and then warned to be careful for the rest of his journey. By the time he emerged at the other end, he had been stopped and fined 13 times to only push the accelerator into top speed after each fine. For his full to the brim with high denomination currency bank lockers, that level of fine was peanuts compared to the thrill of breaking the law and getting a perverted kick of satisfaction at his financial affluence and beyond the arms of law status!

The instinct of competition comes naturally to the human mind. In moderation, it channels the individual into healthy competitive pursuits. When it falls below the minimum threshold of moderation, it leaves him under-employed in mind and body. When it grows out of proportion, it is bad news for the owner and those who interact with him. The instinct of competition needs fuel or avenues to test itself against others. When skills are involved as in education, careers, sports, art and so on, they constitute the running tracks. When these are scarce, the instinct will still be there but have no stage to perform on. Where knowledge and education are the missing ingredients on the one hand and too much economic affluence keeps knocking on empty heads, the expression of the competitive instinct is usually in the kind of juvenile behaviour, such as of the afore-mentioned four wheel driver. Very few women in our society are actively involved in professions or vocations. Sitting at home, with no other skills to fall back on such as singing, painting, even quality cooking, the most common and popular past time is comparing prices of jewellery, clothing or even trading high brand retail stores as their respectively preferred shopping venues to feed the instinct of competition.

Membership of prestigious clubs: Far from effectively censuring behaviour that is etched in classical moulds of malpractices, some arrangements in social contracts actually reward ill-gotten wealth and tax evaded income. Whether such situations arise from design or default, is not important because the end result is the same. Where such arrangements or projects are well thought out, the rationalisation is, if we cannot catch them, let us use them. One illustration that comes to mind is membership of prestigious clubs. Known tax dodgers, those involved in illegal pursuits, even documented smugglers can become members provided they make hefty donations, sometimes with amounts arrived at through negotiations, while those with fixed or known levels of income can qualify to become members through reasonable fixed amounts of membership fees based on fairly transparent criteria.

This social contract provides a certification of honourable citizenship to unscrupulous members of society, rewards dishonesty and offers a very productive social stage to hobnob with the generally respected members of society. As if this were not enough, those assembled together complain about corruption in society; the aggrieved sharing their sorrows with the principal accused. It is a ticket for immunity they buy from carefully budgeted illegal wealth that lifts them above law in many situations. Two trends are at work simultaneously; conflicting values interacting without mental conflict, and opting in favour of easy choices that tide over current hurdles. Tomorrow will take care of itself. Has it? Regrettably it has not and never will in this way. We keep making the same fateful choices and keep getting what we have got for six decades and still discuss in media chat shows where and why have things gone wrong?

Tax amnesties

When tax exemptions were a popular tool of political and social favour games, there was no lack of opportunity for taxpayers to accumulate large chunks of legalised incomes under cover of exemptions. Huge amounts of investment money can be siphoned away in different ways. The most popular corrupt practice was that of over invoicing the cost of purchase of large plants and machinery against loans acquired for projects. If for instance, a loan of one billion rupees was obtained for import of a manufacturing unit, a cheaper version, even a used version of the plant was bought. If it was actually worth Rs600 million, it was invoiced at Rs 900 million and the excess amount was paid back to the buyer by the seller as a "kickback" or "commission" that ended up in a different bank account in a foreign land. These amounts were never declared. The national tragedy in this was that firstly, production units bought were naturally less efficient because they were not the latest and often discarded by users in developed countries under their respective modernisation schemes. Since these were not the latest version of machinery, their produce was of a lesser quality and quantity, the former making it less competitive in international markets. As a consequence, export earnings suffered and the local population was left to feed off crumb products that no one abroad would accept. Secondly, the investor having made a considerable amount of money through misappropriation of loans, couldn't care less about the fate of the project later because he too knew the real worth of his plant and its produce and in any case, profits had already been pocketed in advance. His project was virtually completed as soon as the commission or kickback reached his secret bank accounts.

If this surprises any reader, the average investor was not yet done with the national exchequer. The units were shown year after year to suffer losses. These losses were either carried forward to future years of tax assessment or set off against incomes of other businesses of the same investor where tax exemption was not available. This may really seem like "*this is too much*". But hang on; the plot does not end here either. Tax exemptions are usually time specific, such as five or ten years. As the tax holiday period would approach its lifeline and records showed that the business had been in losses all along, repayments of loans were not made and a well fabricated case would normally be ready to present to the bank for declaration of the business as a "*sick industry*" leading to a consequential write off of all outstanding loans and bad debts. Records show that getting the necessary approvals usually ended on a happy note.

This "*national lootery*" was restricted all along to the elite or ruling class while at the same time the quality of life of teeming millions gradually drifted away in the opposite direction. What is in evidence today is the proud product of the work that has been in progress for six decades. Whether things can improve before they hit rock bottom and decay sets in or there can be some miraculous realisation in time of the looming dangers is a decision for the nation itself, especially its leadership. Taking a corrective course of action might just set some kind of recovery in motion, going further down the wrong road will only end in tears for all concerned.

When so much wealth is put together and sits idle, something needs to be done about it to bring it back into circulation. If the desire is driven by genuine nationalism, good governance that has the welfare of the majority at heart, the way forward is for the government to take the initiative and set in motion serious and transparent investigations to unearth tax evaded income and wealth. Since those in governance also have stacks of skeletons in their closets, this option is a non-starter. The tool that has been repeated in our history time and time again is that of granting *tax amnesties*; an opportunity to bring untaxed money into the tax net through a sort of *fiscal sale*. When the top rate of income tax was around 50 per cent, taxpayers were invited to declare their untaxed earnings at rates as low as 10 per cent. The justification was that revenues were short, untaxed money was already in circulation but in non-revenue yielding underground economic activities. So let these honourable citizens contribute to the national exchequer in its hour of need and make a fresh start.

The question is a fresh start for what? For getting down to tax evasion all over again for another decade and wait for the next tax amnesty offer of discounted legalisation of illegal money? The approach has nothing positive about it from a moral or legal point of view.

- It is an insulting slap in the face of those who paid their taxes regularly in accordance with law and at the right rates of taxes. Through tax amnesties they are indirectly conveyed that they have been unimaginative and law abiding when easier and cheaper options could have been availed.
- That the state is happy to run its affairs by begging for part of tax evaded money and not by taking punitive action but offering an honourable "get out" clause.
- Finally that those with a propensity to by-pass the law should not lose hope. In fact, they will eventually be better off buying their social respect and legal protection on far easier terms.

Given these facts, tax amnesties have been used by various

governments almost in the manner of a "*Fiscal law of necessity*". The political version is a confession that we cannot get rid of a usurper of power, so why not give him a legal cover to carry on living in peace. The tax amnesty has a similar underlying admission. Catching tax thieves is beyond our capability and political will, so let us confer a legal hat while sharing a fraction of the loot which is subsequently spent on wasteful governmental expenditure in any case.

Sorting out revenue officials

When the government of Nawaz Sharif came to power for the first time, it took a new direction in fiscal management in the name efficiency and eradication of corruption. It moved to recruit a foreign company to carry out pre-shipping inspections of imported goods. This was to be in place of inspections normally carried out by the Customs Department and Federal Board of Revenue but they were considered to be too corrupt and inefficient for the government's liking. Two vital issues arose out of that approach and are still relevant today.

The first takes us back to the escape from responsibility and good governance approach. If the government of Nawaz Sharif was so aware of and annoyed with rampant corruption in revenue services and there is no question that it was not the case, the honest approach would have been to tackle the corruption head-on instead of outsourcing the fundamental state function of revenue generation. There are presently persistent and widespread allegations by the public, civil society and media of uncontrolled corruption by members of the elected assemblies and senate. Should people demand that candidates in the next general elections should be shipped in from abroad to improve matters? Why stop with revenue services only? Why not recruit security firms from abroad to do the policing duties in the country because the security situation is more alarming than other national concerns?

The move did not materialise for a number of reasons, including intense resentment from the staff in the customs service. I was privy to the technical discussions that were taking place with interested parties. The main contenders were repeatedly queried about what percentage of increase in revenue were they willing to guarantee to the state in return for a hefty fees? The answer was "no guarantees" at all but a more efficient alternate. There is no escape from honest and responsible governance if genuine progress is to be achieved in any field. Conversely, repeating the same deceitfully hopeful and responsibility ducking measures that have led the country to its current woes will end in nothing other than getting even more of what we have always been getting in return.

Summary dismissal

During the Zia era, a public scandal broke about acquisition of luxury cars by top politicians and some military generals without payment of import duty. The beneficiaries had managed legal cover of duty exemption via a kind of a confidential notification. News about those acquisitions was, however, leaked to the media and a list of beneficiaries was tabled before the national assembly in response to demands from public and some media sources. The released info included names of a number of retired and serving army generals, in addition to politicians and other privileged public life individuals. While the rest took a low key position, the military men named in the listed report conveyed their annoyance at the betrayal of their special privileges in high positions in uniform to Zia.

Dr. Mahboob-ul-Haq, was fondly referred to in taxation circles as "*Dr. Mukarjee*", the word "*mukar*" literally means "*denial*" in the Punjabi language. The title was a derivative of his uncomplimentary ability to take or approve decisions and then deny approval or responsibility at the slightest hint of a protest from any pressure group. He would do that with unerring regularity and without a hint of remorse for the lack of moral in this ritual. The list provided to the legislative body was done with his prior approval as was required under the rules of business. In this case too, he kept mum when put on the spot by Zia leaving the chairman of the revenue board to take the full brunt of the vindictive dictator's wrath. Zia promptly issued orders for the immediate dismissal from service of the tax boss without regard to the rules and procedures. A couple of days later, Zia proceeded on a one way journey to Bahawalpur and the rest is history. *Ishaq Khan* took over as President and the dismissal order was reversed. Is it any wonder then that people pay no taxes? The episode brings to mind one of the numerous witty lines from the famous television comedy serial "*Yes Prime Minister*". While discussing a leak to the press, the cabinet secretary unfolds the mystery to the questioner saying, "*The ship of state is the only ship that leaks at the top*". Let us add that information is not the only leak at the top, in our case, as with many developing countries, the ship of state also leaks revenue at the top!

Compensation for burnt properties

Recently some Asian television channels operating in the United Kingdom reported huge fires at a bombed market site in Karachi. Scores of shops and business premises were gutted. Affected shop keepers made immediate calls for compensation from the government. The question that arises is what would be the basis of working out compensation amounts? The recorded value of such business premises for tax purposes is a negligible fraction of their real worth. Since that gross undervaluation of fixed assets also applies to the stocks-in-trade and that itself is further compounded by the presence of a high percentage of smuggled goods that are obviously not backed by documented evidence. So a catch 22 situation arises when such tragedies strike. If compensation is paid on recorded values, compensation amounts would be peanuts in comparison to real worth of property destroyed. If compensation was to be demanded on real market worth of destroyed assets, the taxpayer can never explain how he managed to accumulate that kind of wealth.

There is yet another twist. The same businessman not only declares the real worth of his assets to his bank, at times he even overstates the value to obtain disproportionately high loans. Between the bank and tax authorities a true Christian spirit prevails; the left hand not aware of what the right hand holds! So the state is ripped off at both ends. In revenue collection, the lowest values are the only fair and acceptable standards. When it comes to seeking compensation, nothing short of market value is a fair treatment. The same holy spirits that cheated the state exchequer year after year of millions if not billions in revenue then come out arms waving, fists wrenching, throats flexing in confrontational rallies to demand state support without delay and on their demanded terms. It could be asked if there is any chance that some involved in this double bluff game might feel the slightest remorse about such blatant display of double standards? Well, what a silly question? An overwhelming majority of this category pretend to lead pious lives. Most of them in business premises and government offices, proudly hang selected verses from the holy book on the walls as evidence of their God fearing spirits but their practical lives are usually completely divorced from their decorative hangings.

In any society with respect for law and accountability, such blatant maintenance of two sets of accounts would get any businessman in trouble with authorities. But in the land of the pure, tax authorities and taxpayers feed off each other, both fully aware of each other's positioning in the game, unscrupulous tax officials salivating at the intake potential from each case of cheating taxpayers; on their side taxpayers aware of the extent of ability or lack of ability of their auditor to take their share of stolen incomes. Both sides live a life of peaceful co-existence like honourable citizens pretending to have the best national interests in their hearts. Honest operators on both sides watch in despair, frustration and helplessness as the business of the state and nation building is held hostage by a tiny percentage of those who control over 90 per cent the nation's wealth.

Zia & tax return theatric

There may be few better illustrations of why our tax payment culture and collection levels have been traditionally poor and will not improve unless there is a miraculous change in political and social honesty levels. It is part of a broader culture of non-compliance and financial indiscipline that includes non-repayment of loans, utility bills and even power theft, etc. At some stage of Zia's rule, tax collection fell more than expected. As is customary, a series of meetings were scheduled for review and for gathering fresh ideas to boost tax collection.

A final cabinet meeting was summoned by Zia to decide on solutions. Nothing concrete was on the table because there was no serious intention from the start. Then a grand media master plan was unfolded to encourage tax payment by exemplary lead. Zia declared various stages of his plan. First the chairman of the board of revenue would be shown on national television filing his return of income. Then the finance minister and some of his cabinet colleagues would follow similarly in front of television cameras. Finally the president himself would be seen by the nation filing his tax return. That would be enough incentive for the whole nation to follow such role model behaviour. Having said all that, he felt the need to make it clear that this was nothing more than a political stunt. So revenue officials present on the occasion were warned not to take this seriously with thoughts of any follow up proceedings!

Once a return of income is filed, it becomes a legal statement on oath of the financial status of the filer. The fake returns that were to be filed in front of cameras could have landed each of those imposters in trouble later if normal tax procedures of investigation and verifications had been carried out. That is why Zia did not file his return of income for a single year during his eleven years in power. There is a misconception that an incumbent head of state is not required to file a tax return. He was exempt from tax on his official salary but not on his other sources of income. Zia had about half a dozen reported or alleged properties in the twin cities of Islamabad and Rawalpindi alone. How could he afford to risk making a commitment about his financial empire for any reason or offend his wealthy urban and rural support base?

Those who supported him in the United States Senate and House of Representatives had little to argue in his support. But when cornered and put on the spot for supporting a brutal dictator, a media source reported that a top official informed one of the two houses that that the US was aware of the lack of general popular support for Zia but that it was important that Zia enjoyed the support of the economic constituency in Pakistan. That said it all about the man and his cronies. With continuation of that kind of attitude towards taxation and domestic resource utilisation, the country has always been and will remain dependent on foreign aid and support. So let us stop being pretentious about claims of sovereignty and self-respect, unless claims can be backed by practical deeds. Who is to blame for these fiscal theatrics? Cannot be the hundreds of millions who live below the poverty line or those devastated by floods and earthquakes. It is again that tiny minority that have owned the country since its creation.

It is for these reasons that we will have to remain reliant on foreign loans and aid for the foreseeable future. That being the case, our dependence on external support will continue to remain high. If the domestic situation worsens further as it might due to deterioration in law and order or social unrest because of the widening gap between the rich and poor, the fiscal situation will get worse, so will external dependence. Having served for two and a half decades in revenue services in the country, the only direction tax policy and administration has moved has been downhill. It was for these reasons and knowledge of ground realities that an offer to re-join the Federal Board of Revenue as its chairman in late 2008 had to be regretfully refused. It came from a finance minister whose own integrity and professional competence was never in doubt but the country's problems needs a total reform of collective social and economic mind sets and attitudes. It is not a problem that the best meaning finance minister can solve in his individual capacity. On the contrary, sincere and effective tax collection efforts would only isolate such an incumbent and make him the subject of media witch hunt through economic pressure groups.

Far from the evading crowds

Enough of exhausting tax matters for now. Let us end on a lighter note, just as we started. The currently popular taxation topic, especially with politicians is that of environmental taxes. The following poem from another anonymous poet paints a picture of how life might be affected by imposition of environment taxes. Enjoy the light hearted moment that ends with a big bang, before reverting to further mundane analyses in the subsequent chapters.

The flatulence tax

A flatulence tax on cattle and sheep
Another rip-off to make us all weep
Preserving the ozone at any expense
It's all propaganda that doesn't make sense

Abandon the flock and abolish the herd
When it comes to survival, then nothing's absurd
But what will we eat for daily protein?
The answer is simple, the mighty baked bean

So plough in the forage and pastures too
Put paid to the curse of the cattle pooh
Then plant all the land with navy beans
Belching out gasses from smoky machines

The resulting erosion will wipe any smiles
Make the Greenies appear they're suffering piles
With options so few when it comes to a meal
And the after affects still part of the deal

With the whole population gobbling baked beans
The potential was there for some horrid scenes
The worst of our fears were about to come true
The Follies were gobbling their baked beans too

And adding more fuel to their natural reserve
The electorate was poised to get its deserve
Their innards vibrated their faces contorted
The speaker collapsed and debate was aborted

Then rising as one from babes to old Granny
With timing so perfect was almost uncanny
The whole population let off a great fart
With a bloody big bang blew the ozone apart!

7

The divided self of several halves

Gautama Buddha, the spiritual leader of Buddhism was once asked by a devotee as to where did the lion gain its strength from. In the Buddhist tradition, the answer was, "*availability of the total self*". That meant that when the lion decides to do something, his total existence is in agreement and available to it in the execution of any act. When the lion decides to go after its prey, there are no if and buts in its mind. That available totality of its existence gives it the strength. That explanation was meant to illustrate a point in the context of human attributes too. Human beings who are not disintegrated intellectually and psychologically will be best equipped with inner strength that is not reliant on artificial support from others. The opposite of that is a mental state housing several splintered and incoherent processes that have the opposite effect of dissipating psychic energy. There is a common street wise saying in Lahore "***Soochi piya, tey banda giya***" [*When someone gets into a mental tangle, he becomes pretty much useless*].

The late ***Zameer Jafri***, one of the finest humorous poets of his generation once wrote a couplet about how the blending of various cultures in today's closely inter-related societies can give rise to problems of identity and adjustment in the human mind:

دو تمدنوں کے درمیاں هم اس طرح سے جیتے هیں
باجرے کی روٹی کے ساته سوپ پیتے هیں

Do tamadunoon ke darmeyan hum is tarah jitey hein
Baajrey ki roti ke saath soup peetey hein

Torn between two cultures, we compromise by
Mixing a meal of millet flour bread with soup

It is a subtle bit of humour in the local language though most of the spirit in the message is unfortunately "*lost in translation*". There is nothing wrong with making any combination of meals that suits our taste and excites our taste sensors' as long as we are aware that we are making a creative fusion and getting joy out it. When we do so out of false notions of our roots or reject an option because it represents an alien culture, that chain of logic is the emission of an unhealthy and disengaged mind.

Taking pride in one's past is one thing and a healthy attitude as long as it does not become an obsession for judging everything else in life; holding all other cultures and societies in contempt is definitely unhealthy and does that kind of person no good, neither for himself, nor for those he interacts with. Every mind will have blurred concepts of many aspects of cultural inheritance from time to time because there is a great deal of overlap in socio-cultural experiences otherwise the concepts of archetypal patterns of behaviour and collective unconscious would not exist. That overlap is bound to increase as time passes because of the easy mass mobility of mankind with advances in modern travel and communication.

Complicate and Rule

There is a wonderful quote attributed to ***Carl Sagan*** that illustrates the tragedy in the state of muddle of a confused mind. It goes as follows: **'One of the saddest lessons of history is this: If we've been Bamboozled long enough, we tend to reject any evidence of the Bamboozle. We're no longer interested in finding out the truth. The Bamboozle has captured us. It is simply too painful to acknowledge – even to ourselves – that we've been so credulous.'**

Individuals and societies that rely on physical appearance instead of the spirit or real purpose of most types of behaviour and values tend to have far more contradictory values and morals. When a mind is docked into well-defined objectives and goals in life, it is less preoccupied with how those can be achieved. That element of clarity in purpose and sense of direction is in itself an antidote for too many digressions away from principal pursuits in life. Try this simple experiment in your family or social circles. A lot of people like to hang beautifully *painted* and framed verses from the Quran on their home and office walls. Ask them the translation of all that is displayed. In most cases, the meaning will be lost on the person who owns and displays these paintings. That does not reflect any disrespect at all. Even where this is done with an intense level of devotion, the act of having it displayed on the wall is often an end in itself. If ours had been a society dominated by functionalism, most people would want to know the message or command in the quote and therefore can relate better with what the actual spirit and purpose of the verse is. That makes it a bit more difficult for such persons to knowingly disregard the message compared to someone who not knowing the message may be unwittingly acting out a lifestyle or an act that is the exact opposite right under the message he has hung up on the wall. The personality of the former is therefore more anchored than free floating, which then helps him to operate in life in a more cohesive manner.

Crisis of Identity

Far too frequently we hear debates about what exactly our socio-cultural origins and parameters are. Exaggerated emphasis and attention on the past is never healthy because it distances those involved not only with their own present but also away from those who co-exist in their times. Some confusion is the direct result of ignorance or lack of understanding of the relevance of cultures and illiteracy. However, a lot of confusion stems from deliberately induced attitudes that serve specific interests of different groups of power and influence such as the notion that Hindus and Muslims can never get along together. They certainly can but if they always did, a lot of those divisive forces would be out of business and careers that are built on conflict and adversarial pursuits would risk extinction. There are countless other vested interests that profit from sharp and artificial demarcations of culture for their survival and prosperity. Entertainment business is one such example. When competition in a level playing field is too demanding or unmanageable, concepts of protection of local industry are promoted as justification for eliminating competition threats.

That strategy has been raised to dizzy heights of perfection by interested parties throughout our short history. The result has been a continual downwards spiral in national educational, intellectual and artistic standards. Most alarmingly it has downgraded the general demeanour of human values. From a society with values to be proud of and respected for, present events have led to creation of a most uncomplimentary reputation in international circles. The crazy acts of extremist elements have destroyed the very fabric of society at home and left the nation's international image in tatters.

This seems the ideal time to introduce another proud son of the soil from our history. *Mir Bulleh Shah*, commonly referred to as Bulleh Shah lived in his time in what is today part of Pakistan. His family was very religious and with a long tradition of association with the famous and respected *Sufis* of the sub-continent. His father was especially known for his learning and devotion to God. Bulleh Shah himself became a respected scholar. He is considered to be one of the greatest mystic poets of the Punjab region. His tomb in the small town of *Qasur* in Pakistan is greatly revered even today. One of his better known and popular poems is captioned "**Bulleya ki janaan mein koun**?" [*Bulleya do I know who am I?*]. The entire text focuses on common denominators in the broad cultural diversity in the sub-continent and is expressed in exotic and captivating Punjabi expression that attracts and induces admiration in equal measure from every Punjabi speaking or understanding human being irrespective of religion or race and on both sides of the international border between Pakistan and India. The present socio-cultural milieu is just the other extreme, full of divisive and blood thirsty forces. I have tried to pay a humble tribute to the great Sufi poet by using the tone and rhyme of his masterpiece to depict our current religious and cultural deterioration; a disturbing development that has created a new brand of intolerant human beings who bear no relationship whatsoever to their forefathers in their behaviour and moral values.

بُلیا دس مینوں میں کون؟

تھماکے کر اُڈاواں مسیتاں
میں نہ مناں تیریاں ریتاں
چہرے پاکی اندروں پلیتاں
وسے میرے اندر فرعون

بُلیا دس مینوں میں کون؟

آگاں بال وچ سٹاں کتاباں
ونڈاں میں نفرتی شراباں
دل لگے بس خون خراباں
بد زُبانی بنا نہ ہوئے سون

بُلیا دس مینوں میں کون؟

شامل نہ کسے دی غمناکی
کُج ہوئے نہ میتھوں پاکی
بچی میتھوں آبی نہ خاکی
نہ میں آتش نہ میں پون

بُلیا دس مینوں میں کون؟

نہ بلوچی پسند نہ کوئی لاہوری
نہ ہندو نہ ترک نہ پشوری
نہ کالا نہ گورا نہ کوئی بلوری
فیر نال وسے میرے کون؟

بُلیا دس مینوں میں کون؟

مذب ناں دا پڑھا بڑھایا
آدم ذات دا مذاق بنایا
اپنا بخشیا نہ کوئی مترایا
خود وی نہ جاناں کی کمایا

بُلیا دس مینوں میں کون؟

دوست توں دشمن نہ پہچاناں
جہنمی باقی سب جگ مرجاناں
منزل کتھے میں کی جاناں؟
میتھوں نہ کوئی ہور سیاناں

بُلیا دس مینوں میں کون؟

Bulleya das meinoon mein koan?

Dhamakey kar udawan maseetaan
Mein na manain teriyan reetaan
Cheraay paaki, andaroon paleetan
Wasey mere andar phiraun

Bulleya das meinoon mein koan?

Agaan baal, vich suttaan kitabaan
Wanddan mein nafrati sharabaan
Dil lagey bus khoon kharaabaan
Badzubani bina na hovey saun

Bulleya das meinoon mein koan?

Shamil na kisey di ghamnaaki
Kucj howey na meinthoon paaki
Bachi meinthoon aabi na khaki
Na mein aatish na mein paun

Bulleya das meinoon mein koan?

Na baluchi pasand na koi lahori
Na hindu na turk, peshaowri
Na kala, na gora na koi bilauri
Pher naal wasey merey kaun?

Bulleya das meinoon mein koan?

Mazhab naan da patha bithaya
Adam zaad da mazaak banaya
Apna baskhya na koi matraya
Khood wi na janaan ki kamaya

Bulleya das meinoon mein koan?

Dost to dushman na pehchaanan
Jahanumi baki sub jug marjanan
Manzil kithey, mein ki jana?
Maethon na koi hor siyaana

Bulleya das meinoon mein koan?

Pre-partition mind-sets

During the run up to national independence in 1947, Hindu and Muslim communities faced somewhat different psyche shaping circumstances. While Hindus and Sikhs were fighting the British colonial rulers for independence as the majority community, the Muslim psyche was more siege laden viewing both the British as well as the local Sikh and Hindu majority community with suspicion and insecurity. That siege mentality has never ceased to linger in the vast majority post-independence Muslim population even though it may have diminished in intensity but is repeatedly manifested in exaggerated conspiracy theories about daily life at home and in the country's relations with the rest of the world.

Another significant factor was the difference in quality and capacity of the leadership of the Indian Congress and the Muslim League. Apart from the dynamic, visionary and educated stewardship of Jinnah as leader of Muslims, save a couple of others the rest of his early associates were quite a few steps down the intellectual ladder compared to him. More importantly most also differed quietly, if not deceitfully with Jinnah's vision of governance and value package for Pakistan. Unfortunately, he passed away too early after independence to stamp his vision for future prosperity and those longing for an opportunity to hijack the movement towards their particular pieces of the national cake got down to work straight away and that "*work in progress*" signboard of negative forces is still on display at present.

Muslim kings and emperors of India generally accepted as the successful or great ones were those who were the least bigoted. The worst were those who wore the persona of holiness and fanaticism such as Aurangzeb. The Mughal Empire's tragedy was that Aurangzeb won the war of succession at the time. The nation's more recent tragedy was that Zia cunningly managed to crawl his way to power. The similarities are striking, the outcomes one would hope can be different but the present direction of governance and social-cultural values and morals paint a picture that is more scary than promising.

Veiled mystery

The issue of Muslim women using a veil to cover their faces is a burning one, not surprising given the heat generated on both sides of the argument. In some European countries, it has become a matter of litigation and constitutional rights. Without getting into those foreign disputes, let us concentrate on our domestic situation.

In our society, the veil is used for a variety of reasons. Some are forced to wear for cultural or domestic compulsion; some use it because they feel comfortable and secure in specific parts of the country such as between various provinces or even when shuttling between urban and rural residences and a third category of women who use it to conceal identity in specific situations, especially those in entertainment industry. Sadly there is a fourth category these days, those known as suicide bombers, whether female or even males dressed as such to try to slip past security personal. Quite obviously this last category merits no attention or discussion. Amongst the others, those who volunteer to use it for social convenience by choice, there is no problem. The problem as always is the element of coercion in cases where females are veiled by compulsion or oppression.

In this day and age where equal rights are claimed by everyone, in quite a funny way it seems that the right to equality for men is violated in this situation! Fair enough, the female face is hidden fully by her *burqa* so she cannot be seen. But what about rights of men in this arrangement? Why should she have the freedom then to be able to make a full examination of men moving around without even their husbands or accompanying male family members having any control over her viewing options? One would just not want to be seen by those that the seen person himself cannot see! This "*visual activism*" is one sided and an unfair privilege collaterally created as a result of exaggerated protection. On a serious note, however, there are contradictions in practice that are quite annoying and hypocritical. I have for instance a particular case of a former colleague in mind. He never allowed his wife to attend a single official social event. That was fine and his rightful choice. However, he had not only no problem in participating in social gatherings where other spouses attended by invitation, he would insist on being invited! I once raised a serious objection to his participation even though he was considerably senior to me. He instead campaigned with his seniors to ensure his participation. That is where hypocrisy and double standards set in. If he had been sincere in his belief, he should have voluntarily stayed away from all mixed gatherings on principle. For him not missing out on an opportunity to hob nob with senior civil service bosses in mixed social gatherings to seek favourable relationships, meant far more than his proclaimed moral code. Later on during his career, he stage managed an elaborate set up of persecution to support his immigration case to another western country. These types of behavioural patterns symbolise the double standards that destroy trust and respect in society. It also smacks of a lack of understanding of social contracts and scarcity of clarity on adopted moral values. Either a specific belief or value is there to be followed or to be rejected as a matter of principle; slipping in and out of beliefs as and when advantageous is a deplorably double faced attitude.

Bollywood cultural invasion

A legislator pointed out in the National Assembly that Pakistani children were now incorporating Hindi words in their normal conversations. He should have been asked what about the dresses now proudly worn at weddings and parliamentary events and proceedings? Was this the dress code of *Mohammad bin Qasim* and his army when they first landed in the sub-continent? If the dress code now worn discarding the previous dress is okay, how is the use of words from other regional languages in social or private conversation any different in spirit and intake? He certainly did not express his disgust at the overwhelming influence of Urdu in Bollywood activities because following his argument that would amount to cultural counter-invasion from our side. Not to forget that the Urdu language itself is a derivative of many regional and international languages in the surrounding countries, including Persian, Turkish, Arabic, etc. The culture minister had his answer ready when quizzed on why were Indian films allowed and popular amongst viewers in Pakistan if they were seen as a cultural invasion:

Indian films, he clarified were shown in theatres in Pakistan to keep alive the cinema culture in the country.

Those who are the surviving few of our local movie industry themselves watch Indian movies at home and cinema houses all over the world. Indian films were not allowed to run in Pakistani theatres for decades though everyone who could afford still found the means to watch them in the privacy of their homes. The main beneficiaries of those artificial barriers were those running the illicit trade of banned movies at more than double the fair market value of watching movies in those days. It is the same today with banned alcohol. Anyone wanting to have a drink can get it but at three to four times arms-length prices. It was alleged at the time that people from the local film industry did not want the public exhibition of Indian movies because their trade and monopolies would collapse. The same charge can today be levied on those who run the underground trade in alcoholic drinks; making them available under a controlled but transparent mechanism would destroy many extremely lucrative underground businesses.

People cannot be redirected by emotional blackmail towards what they do not like, whether by way of movies, sports and entertainment in general, personal cars, mobile phone and even in choosing another airline of their choice for travel in preference to the national carrier. The out dated approach of creating artificial barriers now rests in peace internationally because that strategy takes hard work, acquisition of knowledge and skills, achieving excellence and a level playing field for all out of the equation.

Even while the Indian movies were banned, the average cinema goer would still listen to and run Indian music in the privacy of their living rooms. Those who could afford more, would travel to Afghanistan to watch the latest releases during the annual Kabul festival; yes, Kabul festival! That now sounds like a mis-statement or wishful thinking but the people of Afghanistan were not always drenched in blood from fratricidal conflicts. That came about with radicalisation of society. So which society would anyone in his senses now wish to be part of? The alleged anti-Islamic society of the 1960s and 70s or the current faith driven set ups dishing out beheadings and public floggings in the name of religion?

Identification with fictional characters; contempt for them in real life

Like the laws of natures, the fundamental traits of human behaviour are fairly consistent, as long as external forces or compulsions do not control, manipulate or condition behavioural display into specific moulds. Every now and then, media reports an adult boy and girl running away from family to live together as a married couple, only to be declared wanted dead or alive by their own parents and family. Quite often they are hunted down and murdered in the name of honour killings. It would be very interesting to see how those who run these vile vendettas in families react to neutral stimuli? The standard theme of movies, television plays and popular drama serials invariably contain stories that hinge on love affairs on the one hand and on the other hand, negative characters out to wreak relationships. It would be very surprising if these couriers of social intolerance did not identify and sympathise with every positive character in movies and plays as well as express hatred and contempt for the spoilsport or villainous characters, whether in inter-family or intra-family relationships. It should not surprise anyone if they even shed tears at harsh and petty treatments meted out on the good ones by the bad ones. When it comes to real life, the goal posts move in the blink of an eye. If someone in the family, especially a female member were to per chance end up in an identical situation to that in a fictional plot which aroused nothing but sympathy in such persons, the tables are turned instantly and violently. The explanation is that the reactions of a normal human mind to fictional characters, including the historical icons of romance like *Heer-Ranjha* or *Shireen-Farhad*, etc. is that of the natural, un-tampered and almost free of restrictive social persona minds. The diametrically opposite reaction in real life is that of a mind loaded with misconceived values and conditioned by socio-cultural boundaries of conformity and compliance. It is a potent tool of control in societies dominated by medieval mind sets. The more rigid and inflexible the cultural environment is, there will always be greater numbers of those torn between basic human instincts and the dictates of their artificially acquired social personas. When that happens, the shadow proportion of the personality grips the total being more forcefully bringing about what in common parlance is referred to as the animal in man. It is another example of tampering with nature's law of balance and moderation, in this case in the human mind's natural balance.

Another well documented socio-cultural reaction of such individuals is that towards babies born outside of formal marriage relationships and even new born infants abandoned by legitimate parents. The fact that a perfectly legitimate child could have been abandoned by a desperate parent or parents out of economic compulsions does not even come into consideration. In real life, there are countless reports of a newly born baby stoned to death by an impromptu crowd in response to an isolated call of insanity, even at the door steps of a mosque, in some cases by the imam of the mosque himself throwing the first stone! In fictional situations, reactions can be amazingly different. The viewing audience will invariable sympathise with unclaimed and abandoned infant in Urdu or Hindi movies, especially if that infant grows up to be the hero or lead character in the script. Popular reactions can go a step further in fictional situations in that the hero is not only admired for his heroics, all about his past is totally forgiven and erased from memory. In real life, this corresponding type may be taunted and rebuked all his life. That again is the distinction between the inherent positive instincts of man compared to the psychologically mutilated finished product that illiterate, rigid and intolerant societies produce.

Both attitudes can be gradually de-intensified, if not totally corrected through education and awareness, if that is an objective. Unfortunately, in the present messy socio-cultural hotpot, those who could possibly bring about a positive change by virtue of their positions in society are themselves agents of hatred, parochial thinking and double standards. Expecting them to trigger a change for the better will just remain wishful thinking.

To lash or not to lash; that is the question?

Last year a privately taken video of public flogging of a woman forcefully held to the ground by a group of able bodied males was telecast by a number of private channels. While it generated immense shock and disgust amongst the majority of the viewing population and civil society, those who silently sympathise if not openly support such draconian punishments let out frenzied allegations of a fake video. What difference does it make whether the video was fake or genuine? The vital and only question is whether they religiously own or disown a practice or contention in their code of religious beliefs or morality? Is public flogging allowed or not allowed in Islam? If it is not, then we need to condemn it even if the video is one hundred per cent fictional. If on the other hand, someone harbours a belief that flogging a woman forced to the ground in public is the Islamic way, then he should have the moral courage and integrity to say so face to face with the public and not be concerned about the veracity of evidence. The honest and honourable reaction in the latter case should be, yes this is what our interpretation of religion recommends and we offer no apologies for that; period. The fact of the matter is that most references to religion are either lip service till the position does not cause any discomfort or inconvenience. The moment these positions are put to scrutiny, schemes of deception and digression are set in motion because defending such manifestations in today's world is not easy, if at all possible. Most ill-considered rulings put up in the name of religion have been passed on from generation to generation without invoking the thought process at any stage. They thrive on the silence of those who do not agree, even more the role of those who simply do not apply their minds. It is time to borrow another piece of poetic magic from Faiz:

چشمِ نم جانِ شوریدا کافی نہیں
تہمتِ عشق پوشیدا کافی نہیں
آج بازار میں پابجولاں چلو

Chasmey num jaane shoorida kaafi nahein
Tohmate-e-Ishq poshida kaafi nahein
Aaj bazaar mein, pa bajolaan chalo

The incident recorded on video also raised another fundamental question. Under strict Islamic interpretation, women are not supposed to come in physical contact with unrelated male members of society, not even a social handshake is approved by advocates of that brand of religion. So why was it okay for those self-appointed male executioners of Shariat law to forcibly hold down an unrelated woman by physical contact in public? Why could that not have been done by lady enforcers? When and where the trial was held and did the accused have a lawyer to defend her or does their perverted interpretation of religion have no role for self-defence for any accused? The overwhelming majority of our population will not have considered these aspects. That is why we have reached our present state of affairs, letting our politicians get away with day light robberies and cruelties. Those who are generally referred to as religious leaders are only run of the mill politicians plying their trade under different concocted brands of religion. That has got nothing to do with religion itself which is strictly a private relationship between God and man, or so we were told when we grew up in a far better society than at present. In support of religion being a private matter between God and man, the relevant query is will any human being be held responsible for the wrong doings of another or be rewarded for the good deeds of someone else in life hereafter? If not, what right does one human being have to arrogate to himself a near divine role, to issue verdicts of right or wrong on behalf of God?

The video caused an international embarrassment, a PR disaster at home and abroad for the advocates of what they consider to be introduction of Islamic punishments in legal frameworks and society. The widespread condemnation home and abroad created a psychological dissonance for those who were inclined to be followers or at least sympathisers of that flawed thinking process. On the other hand, there was also the threat of loss of political standing and public support in the streets and homes of voters in owning up to such visually repulsive display in the name of religion. Causing a diversion was the safest way out of a difficult situation rather than being forced to confess where exactly they stood on the punishment itself. Challenging the authenticity of the video was the attempted diversion and for some people, it did get the desired result.

There is also sometimes a lack of perspective of the viciousness and intensity in the actual execution of these kinds of draconian punishments. An anecdote was once narrated by a superintendent of jails during Zia's period. It was common for military courts at the time to award sentences for 10 lashes after summary proceedings to every accused even on petty grounds such as wearing a black arm band in protest on any issue. It was then left to jail authorities to execute those sentences. The jail chief said that the lashing was so intense that invariably the skin would burst open after three or four lashes. The recipient of the sentence was clamped onto a special trap placed at an inclined posture and he was in no position to release his hands to attend to his own wounds until the sentence was completed or the victim passed out, whichever came earlier. Very few actually stayed conscious to be administered the full dose. So this jail superintendent made a courtesy call on the president of the local military court, someone in the rank of a major in the army and invited him to visit his jail to see for himself how effectively and loyally sentences passed by him were enforced by his counterparts in jail. The invitation was promptly and gleefully accepted. When the demonstration started, the jail superintendent noticed the first sign of discomfort on the face of the army major as the second of the 10 lashes sentenced by him was administered. The accused passed out half way through the sentence. The major quietly left the scene but never passed another sentence for flogging after that!

A lot of brutality that is carried out in the name of religion, martial laws, local customs and traditions is romanticised in a way that it can appear to be the natural way of dealing with crime in society. However, there are two fundamental problems that remain unaddressed. Firstly, punishment if rightly deserved can only be justified if the crime has been proven beyond doubt. The reality is that in the circumstances in which charges are levelled and mock trials adjudicated by local elders or summary military courts, both the charge and conviction have huge question marks, if they are not completely fraudulent or for political reasons. Secondly, even in urban towns, with far higher levels of literacy and awareness, a very common complaint is about fictional case registrations by police on any number of grounds such as personal vendetta, bribe, political victimisation, etc. These excesses are not just common but a part of the feudal or tribal control mechanism. So how can anyone in his senses condone or even ignore the execution of such sentences on helpless victims, involving the worst form of double jeopardy; firstly, being framed on fabricated charges and then be administered punishment in the most inhumane manner such as through beheading or stoning?

The myth of equal treatment

A romanticised theoretical version of law envisages equal rights and treatment for all members of society irrespective of circumstances, a similar treatment for those who are filthy rich and still steal as well as those who steal from starvation or for survival compulsions, as some might be doing amongst those without home and belongings followings from the devastating floods in 2010. In its majestic design, the law also states that the quantum of theft is irrelevant to the crime, whether the stolen amount is in billions or petty cash. On the ground, however, those guilty of petty crimes, once caught invariably face the law in all its might, fairness, magnificence and all else. But if the intake is huge or reasonably rewarding, the accused have an inherent "*buy out*" mechanism in their social contract. Therefore in our national history, hardly any big gun has ever faced the much trumpeted accountability for reasons of pure accountability only, though some may have spent considerable time behind bars in the name of accountability but in reality for other reasons. By inference, if and when heartless and inhuman punishments become part of common law, the only recipients will be the ill-fated and defenceless millions who only exist to decorate national statistics or vile causes like induced street agitation in numbers, lowering the national labour wage rate to eventually being transformed into deadly suicide bombers. The real problem has never been lack of legislation. On the contrary, there have been regular over doses of legislation to assist ad-hoc measures or to buy more time for maintaining status quo.

The tragedy has been in lack of or selective implementation of laws, discrimination based on class, influence, financial status and so on. So even if for the sake of argument, the Shariat laws were to be introduced, they will meet the same fate. The rich and powerful will still get away in the same way they do at present with existing legislation but those already at the receiving end will be in for more grief and suffering. That is exactly what Zia sought to do through his proposed Shariat laws, strengthen his hold on power in a way that dissent could be taken care off in a much more draconian way. Fortunately for the country, he did not live long enough to land that fatal punch. Not that the damage done in his time seems easily reversible in the near future. Had he then succeeded, our present state could have been far worse. We cannot continue to do what we have always done and hope for different outcomes. If we carry on, our future will move even more rapidly in the present direction. This can hardly be a sane choice.

In many Muslim countries, the system of governance and justice in Saudi Arabia, including beheadings and chopping off hands for various offences is romanticised in the conservative segments of society as model and exemplary governance, and closer to the reactionary version of Islamic justice. But is the practice in reality as pure and even handed as the theoretical model envisages? Very recently a document circulated by the controversial "Wiki-leaks" source included a real eye opener. An extract below highlights the point that societies where the concept of and respect for rule of law is selective and directed at the most vulnerable, it will not matter what changes are made to the laws of the land. Those who are above currently operative laws will carry on with their inherited immunity from the application of any law. The specific document captioned, "***Saudi princes throw parties boasting drink, drugs and sex***" was released and reported on 8th December 2010. Selected text from a lengthy document is as follows:

[***Quote***] "*Royals flout puritanical laws to throw parties for young elite while religious police are forced to turn a blind eye. In what may prove a particularly incendiary cable, US diplomats describe a world of* *sex, drugs and rock'n'roll behind the official pieties of Saudi Arabian royalty. Jeddah consulate officials described an underground Halloween party, thrown last year by a member of the royal family, which broke all the country's Islamic taboos. Liquor and prostitutes were present in abundance, according to leaked dispatches, behind the heavily-guarded villa gates. More than 150 Saudi men and women, most in their 20s and 30s, were at the party. The patronage of royalty meant the feared religious police kept a distance. Admission was controlled through a strict guest list.*" [***Unquote***]

While this may seem to be an anti-Saudi Arabia propaganda attempt, the real purpose is not to pick on a single country for a practice which is deeply entrenched and widespread in most developing countries, including non-Muslim ones. Since Saudi Arabia is seen by many Muslims the world over and particularly in Pakistan as the sacred Muslim land, it highlights the point even more forcefully that if the application of law in the holy land is as selective between those in positions of governance or influence and those not so privileged, what chance will similar Shariat laws have in Pakistan for a better fate for the downtrodden?

Lofty morals in perverted minds

The current level of social violence triggered by economic injustices and religious intolerance would definitely register vibrations close to 9 on the Richter scale, if there was one to measure violence in society. It has reached a sort of mental blindness that cannot differentiate between a human infant beheading from stamping on a cockroach. The irony is that those very people who remind us every day that life and death are in God's hand then proceed themselves to take a life in the most inhuman manner imaginable, only then to preach society again the same beliefs that they themselves violate through the crossed wires in their mental processes. This is just one more example of countless conflicting values resident in such split, if not splintered personalities.

A festive tragedy

The festival of "*Basant*" [*kite flying*] had become a flag ship social event in the calendar of citizens of Lahore until a few years ago. Even foreign diplomats based in Islamabad would get in touch with their local friends and contacts for an invitation from a celebrating family. The festival itself is a secular seasonal event to mark the end of winter and in anticipation of spring. The full expression is "*Basant; pala urandt*" [*basant; the disappearance of cold*]. With time the kite flying element was supplemented with loud music, great hospitality for friends and families on roof tops throughout the city but in particular the oldest parts of the town. The merchants of doom and divisiveness tried to undo the enjoyment through name calling such as it being a Hindu festival that was polluting the country's cultural sacred mix and so on. Their scattered noises were disregarded by and large by the society.

But where the mullah failed to cause a dent in the yearly celebration, a handful of newly rich but largely uncultured, selfish and illiterate morons turned what was inherently an occasion for joy and celebration into a tragic ending for many families. Instead of using the traditional chemically treated fabric cord to fly their kites for contest, they started to use very thin metallic wires which resulted in many slit throats on roof tops. They should have been given exemplary punishment for causing death through callousness. That would have been the fair but more practically cumbersome option. The authorities deemed it easier and more pragmatic to abandon the event itself! It has stayed banned for many years now because of abuse by a handful of citizens. There is neither the governing ability, political will nor the moral courage to set an example of those committing crime but the easy way out was just to ban the event itself. In doing so, another positive event was taken out of an already very thin social calendar thereby adding to the aggregate anger and hostility, general frustration in society. The fact that countless people depending for their livelihood from making and selling kites and kite flying strings, domestic catering and street vendors lost essential earnings because of the end of festivities and associated hospitalities that took place around the *basant* festival was a matter of no consequence. It was something the common citizen was a part of and so abolition of his entertainment did not matter. Excluding the interests, choices and rights of the common man from decision making has been the heartbreak all along.

Yes, we know him. No; we don't!

Kasaab, the only surviving person from the group that went on a killing rampage in Mumbai, was alleged by the Indian authorities to have been a Pakistani born and trained terrorist. The government and public representatives promptly disowned him then or at least tried to do so. Subsequently, when an Indian court passed judgement against him for murder and terrorism, there was a sudden chorus of "biased against us" in the judgement passed by an Indian court. If in our collective opinion or official position, he was not one of us when the crime took place in Mumbai, then logically the court in holding him guilty could not have been biased against him as a Pakistani? Or could it be that in all honesty we were not ourselves entirely convinced about his true identity. Those captivated by the current bamboozle could innocently have been unconsciously reluctant to add to our catalogue of allegations about being a safe haven for dodgy characters. It typifies the confusion and crises of identity, indecision or just embarrassment for being associated with another crazy act. If we do not make up our minds and firm up our opinions quickly, there could be more madness at home and abroad. Taking a decisive position based on reality, not on wishful thinking is always the key to overcoming a problem otherwise overcoming the problem will always remain a wish. The "*holy*" actions of the crazy gang of misguided youngsters led to punishing consequences for average Pakistani citizens in the form of visa cancellations, loss of financial contracts such as for cricketers or even a handful of very talented young singers who got the rare opportunity of representing the country on a global stage in live reality music contests in India. All that is nothing compared to the personal and family tragedies of those average Indians who were killed or severely wounded in that act of senseless bloodshed.

On the other hand and on the same Indian soil, *Rahat Fateh Ali*, a relatively young but exceptionally talented Pakistani singer was frequently involved in the unholy act of music and singing. How ironic is it then that what some holy cows at home usually refer to as *Satanical* activities in the form of music and singing, contributed to a lot of damage limitation, while the damage itself was done by the activities of religious extremists; those declared profane at home trying to clean up the mess and restore some respectability and credibility abroad. Which performance between the two would most of us prefer to be part of?

Criticism criticised

Following the events in Mumbai, the lucrative cricket circus in India popularly known as IPL decided to exclude Pakistani cricketers from its recruitment of overseas players. While the anger that prompted the action in India was understandable, the end result was a sort of victory for terrorism in the sense that they achieved what they set out to do; stop the people of the two countries from becoming too friendly. It may have been better to recruit a few cricketers purely on merit and then requiring them to publicly condemn acts of terrorism before signing contracts. It could have forced many to take a firm position against religious extremism. The payments involved in playing IPL tournaments are phenomenally higher than what cricketers traditionally get paid. Those looking forward to their share of generous pay cheques were obviously disappointed and some could not hide their disappointment in public. A few were invited to a private Pakistani television channel which operates in the United Kingdom too. The anchor of the show in his traditional aggressive style took them apart for allegedly thinking of money ahead of national pride, sermonising that they should not be running after Indian money like barefaced mercenaries. Before any could respond, he declared it was time for a commercial break.

Having laid into allegedly greedy cricketers for chasing money from India, the entire commercial break consisted of adverts of to be released Indian movies, juicy Bollywood film industry gossip and finally an advert for an Indian movie's first release in Pakistan for which that television channel itself was a partner promoter within the country! Quite oblivious to what transpired during the break, the chat show resumed with a continuation of the onslaught on cricketers and their pursuit of greed. This is an example of innumerable issues on which mental confusion prevails because of lack of conviction in causes, values and ethical issues. The totality of a consistent thought process is unmistakably conspicuous by its absence. That can come only with purposeful education and awareness, but those two are very dangerous tools in the hands of a general population that is kept well under control with regular doses of incessant bamboozle.

Why me syndrome

A common mind game is one in which at every unpleasant experience or set back, some people display a bit of paranoid reaction by questioning why does it have to be me every time? If someone is in continual misery the reaction is understandable and justified but this is often seen with people who otherwise enjoy a very comfortable and affluent life but will react in this manner in for instance failing to get another financially lucrative contract. Arthur Ashe, the legendary Wimbledon player died of AIDS contracted during a blood transfusion. From the world over, he received letters from his fans, one of which read: "*Why does GOD have to select you for such a bad disease*"?

To this Arthur Ashe replied:

"The world over – 50 million children start playing tennis, 5 million learn to play tennis, 5 hundred thousand learn professional tennis, 50,000 come to the circuit, 5,000 reach the grand slam, 50 reach Wimbledon, 4 to semi-final, 2 to the finals. When I was holding a cup, I never asked GOD, Why me? And today in pain I should not be asking GOD, Why me?"

That is a glorious illustration of clarity of thought with consistency. It is a profound statement and many can learn from that provided learning is on the agenda.

8

The art of serial blundering

The Learning curve

"Insanity: doing the same thing over and over again and expecting different results. We cannot solve our problems with the same thinking we used when we created them."
Albert Einstein

Some readers may not be aware that *Einstein* along with *Bernard Shaw* is regarded by psychologists as amongst those blessed with the highest IQs amongst the human race. There are more than one ways in which the human mind seeks to learn and solve problems from early childhood till the very end. In psychology, one of those methods is known as the "*Trial and error method*". Without delving into details, it is a process of gradual elimination of errors in favour of successful learning and solutions in a series of repeated trials. Some societies specialise in what can be called a slight variant of that well accepted principle. For want of a better expression, let us call it a "*Trial & constant error method*".

For quite some time I struggled to find an accurate expression to explain a commonly witnessed approach of staying put with a system or a way of thinking that has not worked for ages. Trial and constant error approach was the closest candidate for that vacancy in my chain of thought. It was a potential solution but one that never quite excited me. Some activities in life teach a lot more than what is generally thought to be the case. Modern sports in particular, especially those involving sport psychology, statistical and computer technology offer a lot to learn about life in general than just sporting situations. Top sports coaches are trained, programmed and under constant pressure to perform to the highest standards. In addition to trial and error, another method of learning is referred to as intuitive learning, wherein a solution suddenly pops up. Some psychologists call it the "*Ah ha*" experience, like when *Archimedes* proclaimed "*Eureka!*" as he stepped into a bath tub to accidentally unravel the mystery of specific gravity. When trial and error hit the buffers, "*Ah ha*" stepped in during a chance viewing of a game of cricket on television. *Nasser Hussain* of England was one of the expert commentators for that game. He was never one of my aesthetically favourite batsman but he was a fierce opponent and very effective for his team. On the basis of his usually honest evaluations of others, he may not have been his own strongest admirer of batting style but what he lacked in batting flair, he made up more than that through sheer grit, determination but above all else good reading of the game. As a commentator, however, he along with David Lloyd is in a different class both for the honesty of their analysis and the ability to spot the absence of a minor detail which may have made a significant difference to the outcome. The difference and the devil that impact on outcomes are always in the detail or the small print in many aspects of live. During that game, Nasser quoted a professional coach who is stated to have said, **"If you always do, what you always did; you will always get, what you always got"**. Hopefully this is exactly what was said because I heard it only once. Even Nasser may not have envisaged at the time the impact of this principle to the broader canvas of everyday life situations. These words of wisdom describe with perfection what I had been struggling to put together to elucidate my original intention. We will see how this hypothesis unfolds as an analytical tool in specific situations.

Nature's laws of universal application

Some rules of this universe are brutally direct and irreversible. Those who understand and respect them, get respect, prosperity and peace in return. Those who ignore nature's rules or knowingly make a different choice, do so at their peril. One such rule is that time never stops, will not even slow down for anyone or any nation. There is no turning back the proverbial clock. If there is an opportunity for possible redemption; it is always in a new beginning from that moment onwards. Every moment lost in thinking about change or a new start, makes the job that much harder, time that much scanter.

Sadly, the incidence of realisation amongst defaulters of time is on a considerably low side. It is perhaps the inherent propensity to default in the first place that inhibits a timely realisation of things not working or having gone wrong. Whatever the reason, the damage is irreversible and the aliment commonly terminal, if the ailment continues for a fatally long period. In the scales of history, 50 or 100 years of nationhood mean nothing. Even periods of prosperity for any length of time are by no means an accreditation for eternity. Getting into zones of mental comfort and security is an inviting prescription for trouble, if not eventual sorrow or disaster. Such pessimism may seem unusual but we are living in unusual times. Nothing short of an intensive dose of realism or virtual spanking of juvenile thought processes will stand the slightest chance of getting the message delivered effectively and in time.

Equally undesirable are intellectually confrontational trends like the famous provocative cartoons in the Danish media that drew an angry response in many countries. Like religion, the aim and role of liberty and freedom of expression is the pursuit of noble causes, of bringing peace, justice and equality in human life. Using liberty to pursue crazy acts of ridicule and provocation that can only lead to angry confrontation is as thoughtless an inclination as housing extreme views on any subject. That is precisely what came out of that deed, nothing positive for all parties involved. If there could have been any positive intent in opting for that kind pursuit, it must be a carefully preserved secret because nothing seemed to make sense on face value.

Idioms & popular quotes

Idioms and other indigenous words of wisdom referred to globally from time to time are not developed overnight. They represent the collective wisdom of mankind developed over long periods of time and if they are true enough, they survive the test of time and are passed on from generation to generation. They are symbols of the collective streetwise as well as intellectual wisdom of our forefathers. In modern terminology one could call them timeless best practices of mankind. These can be another useful basis for analysing how rationally or irrationally people perform in specific circumstances.

Quotes of wisdom from respected personalities, schools of thought, politics, media or show biz provide a lot of insight into human behaviour and thinking; sometimes much more than the author may have envisaged or intended in scope or application. Some specially selected illustrations of the collective wisdom of humanity can be employed to match against actual performance in specific situations, to analyse and judge whether good or poor sense of judgement was demonstrated at various times.

Choices made and opportunities missed

What we achieve or fail to achieve in life is overwhelmingly the sum total of choices made or opportunities ignored. The choices our leaders have made for the nation or society till now have been unfriendly, myopic and have delivered hardly any good. The choices they now make or fail to make will determine in which direction our future will lead us. The fact that a lot of people feel offended at suggestions of a potential cessation of existence as an ill-conceived offence will not change the causal development of events in the times to come. That state of mind is simply a defence mechanism that provides temporary amnesty from the stress of accepting ground realities. During our days at university, some of us would express comparable sentiments of apprehension about the future of then East Pakistan and get similar rebukes or name callings like unpatriotic nationals or foreign agents from most other students. But after the fall of Dhaka, a number of those accusing students were in tears at the outcome; too late then and of no remedial consequence. The country might well be heading into a bigger disaster if the leadership cannot not arrest the present free fall and mend its confrontational attitudes.

The fruits of excellence

Our education system has been the subject of many reports, reforms, reviews and analysis, most of them with no end product what so ever. Whatever qualitative shortcomings there may be and there are plenty, but in my opinion the biggest shortcoming is the percentage of population that is not and never has been part of any educational system at all.

Was that Jinnah's vision of Pakistan? This is a straight affront to governance by majority principle that was the basis for Pakistan, to consist of provinces with a Muslim majority. We turned the wrong road as soon as Jinnah left us. The faster we run now, the farther away we will keep putting ourselves from the nation's destiny that Jinnah had in mind. The only option is a U-turn, not even a slowing down or standing still. Can things get any worse than they are at present by changing our course and distancing ourselves as quickly as possible from the proximity of the mine-fields that we are standing next to? There is no time to waste, only instantly change track in shaping the nation towards one that once again welcomes everyone within its boundaries irrespective of religion, race and caste; an approach focused on common denominators, not highlighting differences that can only lead to friction and perpetuation of status quo.

Imaginatively crafted downgrade or sheer stupidity?

In my school days, during the summer vacations I used to go from Lahore to Quetta, my birth town. While in the eighth grade, during one such visit I accidentally met a gentleman who was the principal of the then Government Polytechnique Institute in Quetta and took the opportunity to ask him if I could visit his school for a day or two, just to get a feeling of what kind of education and skills were imparted?

He said he was a bit pleasantly surprised that a student wanted to attend classes during summer vacations and promptly agreed to offer a "*guest artist*" role. During the two days that I attended, we were taught how to set up electricity circuits with two bulbs and one switch or one light point controlled by two switches. We were also taught a bit on wood joinery; cutting two pieces of wood to join at right angles etc. Those skills still remain in my mind's databank. Think about those regular students who went the full distance coming out with enough skills to start self-employment opportunities instead of begging people for irrelevant jobs based on personal favours. Firstly, in the absence of opportunities, inherent skills and aptitudes are wasted when someone with painting skills is led to strike a hammer all his life. Secondly, such students are more likely to develop into self-confident human beings capable of independent opinion and to stand their ground against any injustice inflicted on them.

The starting point for any successful endeavour is a strong positive desire, not wild cries of desperation and revenge. It is said that with every problem comes an opportunity. Potentially disastrous failure is now providing us with an opportunity, even if a painfully costly and undesirable one to begin afresh but with a different and more intelligent approach, and certainly not anywhere near the same way as before that is prompting us into a restart. That requisite desire and motivation will not come from the tried, time tested and untrustworthy leaders in circulation. They are simply not capable of leading. It is now time for the average citizen to lead them. Any leader who tries his ancestral brand of greedy politics inconsistent with Jinnah's vision of Pakistan should not be given a single vote and that includes those more than others who use the name of Muslim League to hide their leadership shortcomings. For them the use of the name of Muslim League of Jinnah is not for guidance and illumination but for use as crutches to overcome their political, moral and intellectual disabilities. At the next opportunity we need to check the manifestos of each party against the direct sayings of Jinnah and to support only those who score the highest number of ticks. If we fail yet again to do that as a nation, no one else at home or abroad can be blamed.

Managers of de-education

Woody Allen in his typical style once said **"My education was dismal. I went to a series of schools for mentally disturbed teachers"**. Perhaps an apt description for those who train suicide bombers or nurture religious extremism that triggers senseless death and destruction, without discrimination for the scared and the profane, young and old, healthy and the sick.

So where do we go from here? With the present lot of teaching talent, the brutal truth is not too far from Woody's description of his teachers. In fact, there could have been no other logical outcome other than "*getting what we always got*". Time is not on our side. We watched it flit by. Retrieving the situation is a dim and distant bit of optimism; at least realigning ourselves in the right direction might just arrest the present free fall. But can that be accomplished through the medium of the current crop of tried and failed bandwagon? Can it come through in numbers by the sheer commitment and thrust of a tiny fleet of very competent and dedicated teachers and professors? Nothing has changed as yet in the national mind-set to signal a more promising future.

We are blessed that we live in this present age of human development and history. Even until the 1970s, war zones were forbidden territory unless limited prior approval for restricted access was granted by competent authorities. Today people watch, in fact demand to see "live" war action. The God fearing Bush even went to the extent of promoting his Wild West exhibition of "*shock and awe*" on a tormented and defenceless population to a global audience. On the positive side, modern standardised knowledge and education can be shared with large numbers through the use of information technology at affordable costs; education that adds to the quality of life and makes the individual an active and productive participant in society; not the helpless, unproductive and disgruntled onlooker that the average citizen has become today. A product of the average school or religious "*madrassah*" cannot even go to a medical store in the market and ask for a specific medicine for a common cold or fever. What good is that education that does not help the recipient to relate to daily life requirements? Developing countries do not need to reinvent every wheel. If we can cut the bias and contempt for others out of our lives anyone can gain from the fruits of toil and achievements of others. The *mullah* will naturally position himself against the idea of modern education because that will threaten to marginalise his role in society. He has to be by-passed if he tries to impede even now.

Wasted generation

The current generation is essentially one dispossessed off purposeful contemporary education by General Zia. When my generation joined public service in 1973, in the initial years, persons who worked as steno typists in government offices were competent enough to take dictation at a reasonable speed and emerge with a typed copy in decent time that was largely error free. As soon as Zia decreed that all education at school level was to be Urdu based, decay and decomposition set into our education system because the Urdu language was not equipped as a medium for technical and scientific subjects. Today, a person who has a graduation degree to wave in the air as evidence that he attended a bricks and mortar structure designated as educational institution for 14 years cannot take a single line of dictation without appearing to be in pain. This is no longer about English as a tool of western civilisation. This is about having a decent professional career with the likelihood of progression in the future. Zia lived on for 11 years too many for the good of the nation, had a jolly good time and now his next adopted generation continues to contribute its share of hypocrisy. Those children and young men at the time at whose expense this cruel joke was played out are the equivalent of a generation wasted, both for themselves, their families and the nation. Can their squandered lives ever be returned to them for a fresh start?

I happened to visit Hungary in 1991 when it was not yet completely free from Soviet stranglehold. During negotiations for a bilateral tax treaty, it was mentioned by a host delegate that English had been recently introduced as a compulsory language in Hungary.

As usual, my curiosity for understanding thinking involved pushed me into a polite query as to why that was deemed necessary. The response was most illuminating. English, he said was no longer the language of the English people only. It was a trading advantage! He elaborated that if he came to my country looking for business but could not communicate with me in a common language, he was likely to lose business even after a bilateral treaty for the avoidance of double taxation with Pakistan was signed. Sound and objective judgements cannot be made until dislikes and bias can be kept out of the thinking process.

The ability for a reasoned sneak preview into the foreseeable future is absolutely essential. The past is past and nothing can be done to change that. The present belongs to us, or so it should if we are aware of that. But it takes a blink of an eye for the present to become past. Every success is built in the moment people live in. No success has ever been built going back 50 years. No success can be had in the future, if the present is wasted. This is the basis of the approach of Existentialism. In *Nietzsche's* words **"Live as if life were here and now".** Think of the time we prepare for an academic examination. A few days before the D-day, anxiety starts to set in. This anxiety is a direct consequence of the discrepancy between the "here and now" and the time yet to come. As the examination starts, anxiety levels drop because we start to live in that moment; the present at that time. After the exams are over, we may start to feel nervous again thinking about the result. That again is a discrepancy between the present and future; while the body lives in the then present, the mind is either left behind in the then past or the possible future. Take yourself away from that and walk into an entertaining movie. If you enjoy it, anxiety will fade considerably because our whole existence lives those couple of hours in the "here and now". Such is the significance of living in the present. The great Sachin Tendulkar is famed for his approach of living in the moment; not thinking about the previous delivery that beat him or that another one might come soon. As long as one can stay in and handle the present, the rest will usually take care of itself.

We all have dreams, not those that visit us during our sleep but those dreams and aspirations that drive us forward through life. Dreams of our glorious ancestors, dreams about rosy futures are useful reference sources of inspiration. It is good to have promising but realistic dreams in living human beings. It is one of the features that separates us from animals. So letting dreams live in us is normal and even healthy. But us living in dreams most of the time is unhealthy. In increasing intensity the presence of dreams can shift a person's status from a creative individual to a state of neurosis and in more extreme cases the individual will drift into psychosis, a reference again to the saying in psychology that "*neurotics build castles in the air and psychotics live in them*". The last part is deliberately omitted. For the curious ones, it reads on to "*and the psychologists collect the rent*" but the last part is usually a well-guarded professional secret!

If we believe that man has been gifted with a free will, then he alone should be able to use it for his welfare or destruction, and that is the only way he will be held accountable in life hereinafter. Another Existentialist, ***Jean-Paul Sartre*** put forward the concept of "**existence precedes essence**". What he meant was that human beings, through their consciousness, create their own values and determine the meaning of their lives because to begin with human beings do not possess any identity or value.

Our possible redemption therefore will have to be a function of the ability to exclude our dislikes and prejudices, false vanities and the ability to think objectively for what is best now and whether it will have an ascending or descending bearing on the future. Can we transform ourselves enough and in time to configure our future with all forms of hatred and parochial prejudices completely excluded from our planning process? Have we even started to think along those lines? Can we afford to let more time go by? If we can change course immediately, we may stand a chance. If not, we will continue to get what we have always earned in the process. You think. You decide. No one else can, will or should do it for you.

A virtual write-off

If it were possible as in business practices, one might as well make a "virtual write-off" for the generation wasted by greed, ignorance and poverty. Their mind-sets cannot be reversed; a failed business that cannot be built upon and must be discarded in favour of a new, efficient and scientifically structured business. That is the theoretical model. Real life is far more complicated but nevertheless the secret to any potential success is identifying the causes of failure correctly with honesty and in our case with an urgent realisation of running out of time. Inaction and indecisions are not an option any more if disaster is to be avoided. It is time to get out of the false sense of security and comfort zones; give up the lunacy of sticking by out of time and tune decisions taken that have done no good to any nation. Looking at what was done differently by those who achieved success or are at least better off than us. Accepting our mistakes as an act of favour to ourselves without worrying first about who else might benefit or suffer from our progression. Thus far most of our energies have focused on how our real or perceived enemies can be harmed or set back. Just as it is said that democracy is the best revenge for dictators, the best blow one can land on those whom we dislike or think they dislike us is to do better than them. If some of us cannot overcome our deep rooted hatred and jealousies, then the positive line to pursue is to make more progress, to force others to look up to us, not look down upon us. There is no other way because everything exists in relativity.

For that to happen, our minds need to have a greater proportion of positive energy than destructive trends. The current equation is so terribly imbalanced that one cannot find a shred of positive thinking in the average mind. Those who are miserable because of the misdeeds of the successful villains in society now seem to have no inkling of what to do with their lives. The ability to think rationally and react proportionately has been taken away from them through degrading a once satisfactory education system so that a more obedient and subservient mass of citizens is produced. In the mid-1980s, Margaret Thatcher's strong arm actions against the once powerful labour unions in the United Kingdom, through the dubious concept of a "*natural rate of unemployment*" in society was borne out of somewhat similar considerations. Even though it was essentially from motives of corporate greed and private sector economic priorities in contrast to social welfare, there was at least a well-crafted method to that economic gluttony; the hypothesis being that if a generation was left to live a life on minimum state benefits, it would get used to a lower standard of living and therefore settle for lesser wages in the future. A detailed commentary on the success or long term negative impact of those policies is not relevant to the point in hand. The main purpose in bringing it up is to contrast that approach with the one our parasitical vested interests took through their respective economist stooges. If status quo was to be maintained and ensured, if feudal and tribal set ups were to be perpetuated through tools like basic democracies, full and partial martial laws, Shariat courts, etc. then it was imperative that meaningful education should be taken away from the masses to sustain such progress blocking buffers. The strategy was adopted without thinking of its long term consequences to the society and the nation. Technical and modern science based educational and vocational institutions were gradually marginalised, demonised as symbols of evil western education and replaced with so called religious schools which churned out the kind of devoid of thinking ability automatons that could be led by their noses for any deceptive and fraudulent causes. Are we better off now having taken this line? Should we carry on like this and still hope that things will change for the better? Has anything at all improved ever since we moved our focus away from a strategy of promoting self-help endeavours to faith healing? There is nothing to offer hope of a positive change away from current thinking. Indeed there is not even a sign of any thinking process left at all.

The human mind is like a flower in the garden. The more sunlight, fresh air and water it is offered, the fresher it grows, flourishes and fills its surroundings with fragrance. If you invert a bucket over it to cover it with darkness, protect it from the evil looks of others, not to let the neighbour enjoy the pretty sights of your hard labour, it will begin to decay, smell foul and perish. The overpowering obsession of thinking negatively about others before a positive thought can enter a person's head has lead us to our current mess, internationally, domestically and even within the confines of family relationships.

In the name of local industry protection

Like accountability, innovation and fair competition have rarely been important components in our upbringing as individuals and more importantly as a national pursuit. One particular experience I had was in buying a new 800cc car in Islamabad for the first time around 1992. The car was of Japanese origin but mostly assembled locally in Pakistan. A deletion programme was in full swing to allow local vendors to manufacture many parts instead of importing all from abroad, a very good principle in theory and policy. The excitement of a new car was soon to be drowned in shock and frustration. It had unbelievable flaws. The driver's door would swing open on its own when negotiating a sharp bend. There were problems with the dash board and lights. All this even before the car had a number plate on it! The matter was referred back to the company's showroom only to be told that there were many other aggrieved parties and that replacement parts could only be sent from Karachi. There were no apologies for the inconvenience, not an iota of embarrassment. On the contrary, the sales representative had an attitude loaded with arrogance. At the time that was the only car brand in local assembly. Monopoly breeds arrogance and unjustified security of livelihood, especially when not backed by proper education and professionalism. I had to drive to Lahore with a piece of rope that secured the juvenile car door to the fixed door column. The journey had all the ingredients of a comic thriller.

As luck would have it, a month later the owner of the company that assembled and marketed the car and its parts visited the then chairman of the Federal Board of Revenue to register a complaint. I had already been summoned to that office to discuss another case. The gentlemen delivered his complaint in my presence. At the time, the government of Nawaz Sharif had introduced the now universal "Green Channel" at Pakistani airports. The automobile tycoon's grievance was that people were bringing car spare parts in large quantities from abroad and walking through the Green Channel without any duties paid. As a result therefore the local vendor's business was being undermined, if not destroyed. I was not going to let the opportunity pass by and requested the chairman to allow me to share my experience before the matter was taken up formally. I said to the gentleman that I was delighted to hear that the local vendor's business was going down and hoped they all go out of business completely. What our indigenous producers have always wanted in the name of encouraging local manufacturing was elimination of all competition and an insulated protective wall built in high tariff mortar that forces the local consumer into buying whatever sub-standard trash is produced at home. The idea that consumers were helping themselves with quality imported parts in personal baggage was too much of a challenge. People could not be allowed to get used to better quality. That worked well in times when global communication travelled on camel back. It also served well in limited domestic markets but for selling abroad, quality has to be the sole criteria. That meant honest hard work which is in direct conflict with the *Chaudhry Ramzan Khan* mind-set. Hence our export earnings have remained pathetic there being little by way of real competitive quality to sell except non-value added nature's contribution of crops and fruit.

Absence of direction, a direction in itself

Ever since Mohammad Ali Jinnah's death, desires for an alternate leader with even a fraction of his ability but more so his integrity and vision for future direction have lingered in national hearts. But that is all they have remained; futile lingering desires. When we did find someone with internationally acknowledged brilliance and a vision for the future, the usual suspects managed to cook a curry burning hot in deceit, pure fabrication and as far divorced from the law of the land as can be conceived to pass a death sentence for a crime the accused was alleged to have committed but which under the law of the land did not carry the death sentence. He was guilty of talking about the plight of the poor and of the voting right of every citizen.

His followers considered him a saint of sorts. Those who hated him thought he was defrauding the nation and his followers in the name of "*roti, kapra aur makaan*" [*bread, clothing and housing*]. If the assertion of his opponents was to be accepted, it defies belief that even an allegedly fraudulent campaign that sought to focus on the plight of the common man was an unpardonable sin for it had the potential for a breakdown in the stranglehold of the piously preserved but out-dated medieval society.

What has the common man got to do with the affairs of the state? It was most important to set a horrible example of someone who dared to differ with the establishment. But the deep inroads that he made in the hearts of his followers by merely bringing up the subject of their rights and sorrows have been so intensely imbedded that subsequent martial law floggings, imprisonments, character assassination campaigns, attempts to demonise leading characters amongst his followers, exaggerated tales of corruption failed to convince his followers that they had made the wrong choice. This is mainly the cumulative feeling of deprivation amongst the masses for decades of repression and exploitation. The first time someone spoke to them directly, he managed to occupy vast empty spaces in their hearts that no one earlier had considered worth a visit. There was a fundamental lesson for others to learn from but we are not and never have been in the business of learning from history, our own or that of others. Since the days of unsponsored mammoth public gatherings in the days of Bhutto's period in power, there was hardly any development worth comparison, not until the spontaneous assembly of citizens that led to the restoration of the superior judiciary after Musharaf was forced to relinquish office. Tragically, the restored judiciary has been too obsessed with trying to settle political scores. From that negative mind-set approach, it failed to understand how much more it could have achieved by mobilisation the power of the people to ensure accountability, good governance and other noble objectives. That course of action would have required a hate free thought process, an awareness of how the collective power of the common citizens had not only led to its own restoration but brought about a fundamental change in our politics in the past; a change that included universal adult franchise for the first time in our history and framing of a representative constitution that still remains the only document of political consensus. The current vacuum was crying out for sane and visionary stewardship but like most flawed choices in the past, we have all seen how the opportunity came and went and how little has been achieved that impacts directly on the current miseries of daily life of the average citizen. For the judiciary to point out to a handful of cases in which corruption has been successfully blocked or challenged is not an achievement to be proud of. It is certification of a massive underachievement in a potentially hugely promising situation, while the hardships of mere survival continue to haunt those who saw possibilities come and wither away as always. If the current judiciary were to try to ask all those who braved the intense heat in Punjab to march all the way to the capital city to come out again and assist in the suggested manner, only a tiny percentage of those who campaigned at the time might consider it worth another repeat today.

For now the lingering and burning desire for a leader equipped with necessary knowledge and tools as well as the capability to lead with integrity and vision remains an elusive wish. *Faiz* as usual puts it better than other lesser mortals could have done.

کدھرے نہ پیندیاں دسّاں
وے پردیسیا تیریاں

Kidhray nan paindiyan dissaan
Pardesia vay tairian

[No sign of you anywhere
Long awaited stranger]

شام اُڈیکاں، فجر اُڈیکاں
آکھیں تے ساری عمراُڈیکاں
آہنڈ گوانڈی دیوے بلدے
ربّاً ساڈھا چانن گھلدے
جگ وَسدائے میں وی وسّاں
کدھرے نہ پیندیاں دسّاں
وے پردیسیا تیریاں

Shaam udikaan, fajar udikaan
Aakhain tay sari umar udikaan
Ahand gawandi, deevay baldey
Rabba sadha chanan ghal dey
Jug vasda aye, mein vi vassaan
Kidhray nan paindiyan dissaan
Pardesia vay tairian

[I wait all evenings and mornings
If need be, can wait all my life
Brightness lights up all neighbourhood
O God, send us our light too
The world lives on happily and I also wish to
But still no sign of you anywhere
You awaited stranger]

Absence of direction is the only visible direction at present and that is a definite non-starter in nation building. Nation building is about realistic dreams and visions not **building castles in the air and living in them**". That is the scheme of things in the world of many horribly disturbed minds. In the healthy and practical world, dreams still play a role but that role needs to be clearly understood. Visionary leaders like Jinnah, Martin Luther King, Mandela, Ataturk, Mahathir Mohammad and others had a dream to start with. We all know, however, that when a dream ends, eyes open and real life begins. Dreams have no predictable beginning and no ending either. When one runs its course, the next may be around the corner but guess what? It could be a nightmare, not a dream.

Two party system? Well almost

Without having any formal declaration, the country has been dominated by an informal two party system, at least since the mid-1970s. Those two parties are either the Pakistan Peoples Party [PPP] created by the late Zulfiqar Ali Bhutto and the Muslim League. The Muslim League itself has no political anchoring. During this period, anyone opposed to or possessed by hatred for the PPP or Bhutto found sanctuary in a Muslim League of some description.

There are some smaller splinter parties too but they have settled all along in the role of supporting actors. The cast of politics in this set up is therefore settled in a mould of intense dislike and intolerance, if not hatred. Policies and the practical conduct of politicians are driven by motives of bringing down the other side when in power rather than taking the country forward. That obsession is pursued with singular pig-headedness, through fair or foul means with the hope of delivering the final knockout punch well before set time frames. The pattern is all too familiar for any observer to miss out, the outcome for the nation equally visible even for those who can barely see. As for the common man, he looks on helplessly from a safe distance afraid to get too close and personal with two fearsome wrestlers dying to get the other side into a submission hold. It is never safe to interrupt two contestants when in that kind of intensive combat.

When military rulers take over, most of the time, it becomes a two party system of a different nature; military adventurers versus political parties as the opposing group but the confrontational nature of politics does not change, nor does the fate of the average citizen.

Eid fiasco

Every year, in every city of Pakistan and wherever Muslims now reside in any representative numbers, the issue of the selection of the right day for the month of Ramzan to commence and on which day Eid should be celebrated becomes a raging debate, especially if that city or locality has more than one mosque. Does it also happen with deciding the day for Haj? Not at all because the issue is beyond the jurisdiction of the local mosque imam nor is there a *Ruet-e-Hilal* [*moon sighting*] committee in Pakistan to decide that matter. All line up months in advance because of fear of consequences and exclusion by a foreign government from that holy pilgrimage for the slightest dissent. Back home, a different stance on every issue is the basis of a separate "*Derh eeinth ki masjid*" [*a tiny corner mosque*] run at the whims of the personnel in control.

Consensus on key issues would leave them jobless or without any vocation. Dissent is the foundation on which different schools of religious thought are constructed. On the face of it, there has to be a difference of opinion and the engine rooms run overtime to create and sustain with fierce momentum all possible differences, each claiming superiority and legitimacy over all competitors. All systems run on the same fuel; dissent, disagreement and conflict. If all sang the same song, individual noises would drown and that cannot be good for career progression and a handsome kitty of donation by specific followers! Could that possibly be in the national interests or the interests of Muslims in general? Having seen what has happened to the country since Zia the "*Mother of all hypocrites*" unleashed his devastating brand of bigotry for creating divisions to rule the nation, the seeds had been laid for a poisonous crop. The deeply religious Allama Iqbal bemoaned this ailment during his time, even though the intensity in confrontational attitudes then was a tiny fraction of current levels. No aspect of this chaotic practice has any element of religion about it but it is top heavy with motives of holy pretence that is simply a lucrative money spinning game.

This is neither a secular nor a recent complaint. It is important to highlight this because the first line of defence from the accused will be to ward off the arguments on grounds of anti-religion conspiracies. It is a frustrating experience for each and every Muslim, not having the assurance of a decent preparation for the biggest family celebration of the year, especially for those having to travel back home from places afar to be with their family in time. The fact is that the annual fiasco brings about widespread ridicule and projects a poor image of the ability of Muslims in general to operate with cohesion even once a year. It is a massive collateral damage to the image that is both completely unnecessary and fully avoidable. Should we be happy living with this self-inflicted stigma all our lives? If we continue to do the traditional way, we will always get the same confusion and ridicule that is earned each year. To get something different, we need to do something different from the existing arrangement if at all the present set up can be called an arrangement in any professional sense.

If by some divine miracle, it was decided that the celebration of Eid-ul-Fitr in Pakistan and/or other Muslim countries should be synchronised, what would happen to that white elephant known as the moon sighting committee, which enjoys the comfort of posh air conditioned offices in the heart of Islamabad, siphoning fat salaries out of taxpayers money only to meet once a month to sight the moon? The distasteful irony is that they take to the roof top and start the search with the most powerful binoculars and telescopes at their disposal. So why not let those professionals mandated to do the job at the metrological department do an independent professional job? After all we all accept the "*Sehr*" and "*Iftar*" timings announced by the same people for the full month of *Ramzan* well in advance without a question being asked. If they can tell us that a full or partial solar or lunar eclipse is destined for a particular time on a particular day of a particular month in the next year, that precision forecast goes completely unchallenged but they cannot be trusted with telling the nation with professional and scientific assurance whether the moon will appear or not in a day or two! Does it make any sense in any logic or language? Should this be allowed to go on so we continue to get the same confusion, uncertainty, embarrassment and hostile dissent on the eve of one of the biggest celebratory festivals in the Muslim calendar? Is a change not long overdue?

The chemistry of Muslim Leagues

Zia once summoned a meeting of all civil servants who had been involved with budget making. That was the time his fraudulently elected non-party assembly was about to become operative under Prime Minister Junejo. The meeting was a rather meaningless assembly of rubber stamps, myself included, because the budget dish was cooked in Zia's domestic kitchen and served in a plate that displayed the logo of the ministry of finance for public consumption. There seemed no point calling us all together to tell us what most already knew and had gone through the motions; politically obscene choreography delivered through the barrel of a gun. He delivered his usually senseless drivel for about 45 minutes. All gathered speculated as to what was the real purpose. My reading was that a seemingly benign statement he dropped into his sermon was the real message. He narrated a tale of the widow of a deceased civil servant stopping him somewhere to complain that she had lived a long time in government provided accommodation while her late husband was in service but after his death she was being pressurised to vacate the premises for re-allocation to another civil servant on the waiting list. He said that he had ordered the housing ministry staff to lay-off and added that he felt the widow might be concerned that following installation of the new government, his influence might drop. He therefore assured the widow by saying that she need not be worried about the elected government. He then added with a broad villainous grin that life and death were in God's hand but he had no intention of leaving. No occasion for the story except to tell the gathered assembly through a fairy tale, not to be under any illusion about his future controlling role in governance.

Elections for seats to the national assembly were held on a non-party basis because the official justification for the unconstitutional removal of an elected government was that governments elected on the basis of political party representations in the past were simply too corrupt. The real purpose was the fear that party based elections might sweep the Peoples Party of Bhutto back to power. Once the electoral process had been completed, the non-party deception lost its utility. Some mechanism was needed to retain the loyalties of elected members behind Zia's handpicked prime ministerial nominee. So someone suddenly remembered that Jinnah could again be useful after all. A new Muslim League was created to enlist the support of all members for confirming *Mohammad Khan Junejo* as Prime Minister. Given that sequence, there was a popular saying in official circles, "*This is not a government of the Muslim League. It is a Muslim League of the Government*"!

Infiltration of sectarian influences in state institutions

As part of career progression in civil service, attending various administrative training courses is a precondition for promotion to the next level in civil service. In the days relevant to my period, all these institutions were infiltrated and frequented by a number of self-appointed religious scholars. Some arrived with high reputations and expectancy, until they had spoken! Some of their preaching was offered in unapologetic and explicitly confrontational tones towards other Muslim sects that they did not represent. While at a training course in Lahore, one such gentleman pleaded the case for Sunnis to stage a "*Dharna*" [*sit in*] on the streets of Islamabad until they too were exempted from application of Zakat like their Shia counterparts. The reasoning was brutally straight forward and based on the numbers game. He said that if the Shias being a minority could stage a sit in and get themselves exempted from the application of Zakat on their bank accounts, why could the Sunnis being the majority not get their wish by staging a similar *Dharna* for days till the government caved in?

During the question-answer session that followed, he was first taken to task by a Shia participant for his biased and allegedly misleading position on Zakat. I asked him a question and made a dissenting comment on the short-sightedness of his pleadings. The question was that if Zakat was a sacred religious duty as he had emphasised during his sermon, why on earth would he want an exemption in the first place? The comment was that a large group of senior officers from various civil service departments had been taken off their current service positions with a view to participating in a mandatory administration and management enhancement programme that should build their skills for better service in the future. What he was preaching in place of better governance and administration was obstructing governance through anarchy and civil disobedience in numbers until a favourable decision could be blackmailed. What about other pressure groups? After the Sunnis finish, students from all over fill in the roads of Islamabad, then labourers and workers do the next shift, followed by lawyers and journalists. Could he then justify inviting a large population to stage a *Dharna* mainly because of his dislike for Shias but not support other pressure groups if they resorted to his preached tactics? Like almost always, straight answers did not come; none were expected anyway.

Rule of law

While he was Prime Minister of Britain, Tony Blair's son was once held by police at some club in central London for drinking when under 18 years of age. Blair needs no re-introduction as to his dubious character because of his contribution to human misery in Iraq. He has never once shown the slightest remorse that his actions have led to the senseless death of thousands of Iraqis who had nothing to do with Saddam Hussein and in fact could have been at the receiving end of Saddam's dictatorial brutalities. But when it came to his domestic institutions, he was forced to follow the law of the land in this incident. He had to go to the relevant police station, complete all legal police station formalities that any other fellow citizen would have had to do in order to get his son released. That is a huge compliment to the maturity of the system and state institutions that someone who had no hesitation in going for a senseless kill abroad without involving the United Nations had no room for manipulation in his domestic environment.

This is not a compliment to Blair for he deserves none, nor is this in condemnation of his son because many youngsters commit mistakes in early life. This is essentially a lesson in the importance of the effectiveness, equality of treatment, transparency of governmental institutions but above all respect for law as the generally accepted core value of society in general. Had Blair been a politician in Pakistan's present political infernal, firstly, no state official would have had the guts to even issue a notice for not having filed his tax return let alone arrest his son for breach of a petty law. Secondly, if some official out of his mind had taken action there would be plenty of his own colleagues who would have volunteered their services for a safe passage for the "*beqasoor*" [*innocent*] victim. Every citizen of the country, media anchors and reporters cry foul play and corruption from the top to grass root levels of society; the country is allegedly practically being run on crime, corruption and mafias of all shapes and descriptions but there is no criminal in the country. Individually, everyone is a "*beqasoor*"! Surely all this cannot be God's will or preordained state of affairs for if it was then logically there would be no justification for complaining about it. But we do complain all the time. This, however, fits in fully with the alternate belief that there is complete freedom of choice and action for a man or woman to do here as he pleases or elects to do but accountability will come in at the end, not half way through the crime. We need to change the whole attitude package to stand better chances for the future. If we cannot see even now that what we have got so far by doing what we have been doing so far, then time may run out faster than many may imagine. We have specialised in living in the past and that is where we risk being left behind as long as we manage to survive. You cannot even walk briskly when your head is turned around to look at how much distance you have already covered. That behind us is gone – for good. The important question is how much is still to be covered? That can only be done by looking in front of us. Only when we accept in our minds that there has never been nor will be any divine intervention or special favours from God to anyone that we might start to think about accountability in this life. Until we do that, those who have carefully navigated our thought process into believing into inaction and fatalism, will continue to have a field day and the country will incrementally edge its way towards complete disaster. Is there any other solution except to take control of our own destiny and to start now? That does not mean taking to the streets to cause destructive mayhem. All we need to start doing is the basics; identifying the law breakers, tax dodgers, chronic defaulters of state loans, manipulators of energy meters to rob the country of vital resources and so on. The electricity and gas my neighbour steals is at my expense because it makes the supply more expensive for me in the least and is one of the fundamental causes of massive load shedding in the country. We need to start doing that at every street level and forget about the next street. Let the next street take care of itself.

New judiciary; conventional priorities

It would be scant consolation to the victims of recent unprecedented floods staring into space in the hope of instant help to be informed that a full bench of the highest court in the land will be looking closely to see whether a constitutional amendment is intended to clip its own wings or to add more power to places already overloaded with power? These may be important matters of state governance but they certainly do not require the entire Supreme Court to sit for months to the exclusion of the misery of the common citizen. When foreign aid waited in the wings for the helpless but was allegedly not delivered for want of reliable guarantees, it would have made more sense for the superior court to step in and demand that aid distribution accounts and implementation be shown to a bench on a daily basis so that energies could be focused on the immediate human suffering, not in deciding for months who did or did not legitimately belong to the corridors of power. I am sure if in the punishing heavy downpours that caused the deadly flooding, there was a reported minor leakage in one of the residences of His Lordships official residence that could damage expensive carpets, it would have been reported immediately to the public works department and a team of obedient and exhausted technicians would have lined up immediately to do repair work before a judicial offense was caused. But the sufferings of millions in full view of live media coverage across the globe demanding immediate attention as matters of live and death were involved; those simply did not alter priorities. They never have and the consequences are there to see. This time round public expectations were somewhat different for those with relatively short memories, but the judicial track record is so heavily skewed towards embarrassment of judicial actions throughout history that expecting a qualitative miracle was bound to end in tears. These false dawns are summed up beautifully in Faiz's words:

لو سنی گیء ہے اپنی یوں پھرے ہیں دن کے پھر سے
وہی گوشاءے قفس ہے وہی فصل گل کا ماتم

Lo suni gayei hai apni, youn phirey hain din ke phir se
Wohi gosha-e-kafas hai, wohi fasley gul ka matam

For people who may have harboured any hope for an upturn in the fortunes of commoners within an unchanged set up, nothing can illustrate the futility of that optimism more than one recent court ruling. On 21 April 2011, the Supreme Court passed its very long awaited verdict in the case of Mukhtar Mai, a matter in which the apex court itself had taken "*Suo moto*" action once the hushed up matter became media headlines, at home and abroad. A female correspondent of the English daily aptly expressed her feelings of desperation at the judgement in the following manner; "*No words can describe the dejection, pain and anguish that many of us felt on hearing the Supreme Court's verdict on Mukhtar Mai's case. After nine arduous years of waiting for justice, five out of six accused in Mai's rape have been acquitted*".

On 22 June 2002, Mukhtar Mai, 30, from Meerawala village in southern Punjab, was ganged-raped on the orders of a local Jirga, a **village council of elders traditionally entrusted with the role of rural judiciary.** The jirga was convened to seek punishment for Mai's 12-year-old brother, Shakoor, accused of adultery with a woman from the Mastoi clan. Mai insisted her brother was innocent and the charges were fabricated. Mai's brother was then arrested by the police on charges of adultery. Mukhtar Mai appeared before the Jirga and was gang-raped by six men in front onlookers and forced to parade naked on the streets!

Almost contrary to customary roles in recent times, a certain *Maulana Abdul Razzaq*, an imam of the village mosque, protested the decision of the jirga and Mai's rape. He urged the villagers to report the matter, declaring it a grievous sin and a crime. He then proceeded to inform a local journalist by the name of Murad Abbas, who is said to be the first who reported the case in a local newspaper. The imam also reportedly convinced Mai's family to report the case which was then filed on June 30, 2002. In **August of 2002, a** Court sentenced six of the fourteen men to death, under the anti-terrorism provision. An appeal was filed in the Lahore High Court against the release of the eight men. The Lahore High Court reversed the trial court's decision, acquitting five out of the six and reversing the death penalty for the sixth man, to life imprisonment. "*Lack of evidence*" was cited as the reason for the decision reversal for a crime which media reports claimed was committed in full view of onlookers and allegedly explicitly ordered by local judicial elders!

The "*azaad adaliya*" Supreme Court's three-judge bench upheld the decision of the Lahore High Court and acquitted five out of six suspects in the Mukhtar Mai's case. The remaining eight have also been released. Justice they say is blind. In this case it appears that this was not the only disability it suffered from. So what has changed for the suffering common citizen?

There are a few key notes and lessons from this ghastly and shameful tragedy. Firstly, this horribly outdated system of *jirgas* and *punchayets* is not only a symbolic throwback to pre-medieval ages of civilisation, it continues to survive on a support service it provides to those in positions of power, authority and influence. The superior judiciary invests so much energy almost on a daily basis through large benches in chasing well concealed bank accounts in foreign banks where billions have no doubt been swindled, it took the judicial system nine long years to deny justice to a humiliated female citizen in a society wrapped from head to toe in a deceptive persona of holiness. Thirdly, a single dedicated Maulana Razzak can play a role with the help of civil society and media men with integrity in at least bringing such incidents into the public domain. He must qualify for acknowledgement as another unsung hero surrounded by generic villains. Fourthly, about the judgement itself, the less said the better.

Is there any other reliable evidence of reduction in corruption in society or various tiers of judiciary itself, especially at grass root levels? Will our judiciary have ever had a better chance to redeem itself in public estimation or in leaving a durable impact on society in general? In view of a reasonable impression about too much attention on the ruling party only, will even its findings be accepted as fair and proportionate in public opinion given the intense politicisation on most issues? Unfortunately, some incumbents in judiciary's own ranks do not help their cause by their own irresponsible statements of loyalty towards specific political parties or individuals. A former Chief Justice of Lahore High Court was recently famously quoted in the media making political statements and public display of loyalty and indebtedness towards a particular chief minister in office. It may be a social blessing to have good relations in top judiciary while being in private life, but public proclamation of love affairs between judges and politicians amounts to as stupid as it gets. But remember, this is a quote from a feudal mind-set judge. Two overbearing states of mind were operating in tandem, perceived immediate benefits collectively trampling over good judgement and long term consequences of words and deeds; a weak mind seeking to anchor with power of immediate consequence and making a loud and audible expression of rewardable loyalty. Was any rule violated by his lordship in taking pride in his political association over the essential judicial criteria of neutrality? If it was, then how did he get away from internal cognisance by the highest relevant disciplinary judicial forum? If not, the public has the right to ask whether their lordships themselves are above the application of law. It is incidents like this that have gone without the same reaction from the judiciary that would have almost certainly invoked, perhaps even *suo moto* action, if another state functionary were to be involved. Taking immediate and effective action against anyone else exceeding his power or authority, or involved in corruption is perfectly justified but ignoring a grave violation of propriety by a judge himself is the kind of uneven treatment that is the subject of regular media discussion. It is an example of why a glorious opportunity to write a new chapter of judicial conduct in an otherwise inglorious record has been adulterated if not put aside altogether.

It is common for people, especially businessmen to demand strict application of law in a particular situation. But most of time they all want strict rules only for application on others. The nation was presented with a rare golden opportunity after an unprecedented movement to establish some semblance of independence of the judiciary in Pakistan. Even those who toiled for months on the streets and motorways in unbearable heat to sustain the movement may not have envisaged how little forward their movement would eventually take them. Prisoners of the past, propelled by hatred only, can never be expected to deliver a bright future. As soon as the dismissed judges were restored, they dug out their demolished "work in progress" sign boards and spent all energy in dealing with the old enemy while those who brought them back to their court rooms with promises of an unprecedented rosy future look on in disbelief. Was it worth all the effort? Has the common man or the present generation benefitted in any way? Was someone who entered into or was dragged into litigation as a teenager and is still involved in court battles as a pensioner in any sight of relief in this life?

On present evidence, none amongst those unsure of life the next morning seem to think that anything whatsoever has changed in their fortunes through restoration of judges of superior courts. Even though some commendable incidences of judicial interventions that have blocked high profile corruption cases or attempts before damage could have been done are on record, the investment of valuable resource on high profile cases has been enormously disproportionate and the neglect of the most needy and deserving has been almost clean sweeping. The pattern of wrong priorities and excluding the common citizen from the affairs of the state has been amongst the few consistent patterns of governance.

High flying "Tableeghi" activists

This concept of *Tableegh* [*missionary preaching*] raises more questions than it answers. Is money spent on expensive missions abroad a better utilisation of resource than spending it directly on people in need of basic necessities of life at home? During one of my official trips from Dubai to a destination in Africa, while travelling in the expensive business class as officially entitled, the partition curtain ahead to cordon off First Class passengers was pulled apart as is the normal procedure at various flight stages. Every passenger in business class section of travel was astonished to discover that the entire First Class was inhabited by the typical *Tableeghi* characters on some mission. Passengers from Western countries could infer that a religious group of some description was affluent enough to afford as comfortable and expensive an air journey as modern aviation could offer in present times. So who was paying for that adventure? If paid from personal pockets, then as a professional tax man, the first instinctive question is, are these people really in as high income brackets in tax records as their travel style suggested? If the bill was footed by some charity, do people contribute to reputed registered charities so their selected beneficiaries or any level of staff should travel in such luxury in the name of religious preaching?

But why travel to preach others from a place that is shrouded in allegations of corruption, not by outsiders but by every citizen who is offered a media mike from studio rooms to busy streets? Why travel across the ocean to preach right from wrong when the entire local neighbourhood needs preaching first? What answer could this group possibly give if asked whether everything at home was lawful and prosperous? Most tax administrators have a fairly good idea of the actual financial position of known taxpayers. Sometimes informal knowledge is not enough to make a defendable assessment or in other cases even if evidence is available, the taxpayer is in a position to exert enough influence to get away with it but the fact remains, his activities and reputation are often well known.

It is quite common for many such dodgy characters to be part of *Tableeghi* missions. The motives can vary from wearing a simple deceitful persona of noble causes to using such trips for promotion of business interests through social networking. If such activities are funded by incomes from fully lawful means, there can be some justification but where incomes from well documented unlawful activities are involved, it is a manifestation of everything that is wrong in society's package of double standards; not practicing what is loudly preached. Sixty years of such investment may have created many more look alike preachers and followers, which meets the requirements of a structural society but there is no evidence of any functional improvement, no evidence that a better and socially more responsible body of human beings has come into existence who can lead to better times in the future. From a purely psychological perspective, it is an expensive moral cleansing exercise for the performer that in his way of thinking neutralises his indulgences in violations of various laws of the land by pursuing a seemingly holy cause. The holiness of any cause or action must lie in its outcome to the society, especially in helping the most disadvantaged members of society. There seems no relevance on the ground to support that this criteria is even on the agenda.

Private television "chaat masala" shows

For decades the national media was controlled in every possible manner on current affairs programmes and news bulletins. On the other hand, in comparison to that state control, entertainment programmes enjoyed a good deal of freedom in context and visual presentation. Then the media suddenly found unexpected freedom during the period of rule of a military dictator, Gen. Pervaiz Musharaf. But the media having been used to strict controls was not ready and mature enough to handle almost complete freedom. This is not a personal opinion but the aggregate impression one gets from polls conducted on the subject by media itself and the increasing number of complaints from viewers. Someone once asked if it was progress if cannibals used knives and forks? Our media situation is nowhere as bad as that but the point remains valid nevertheless. Technological developments, intellectual development and cultural maturity must go hand in hand in order to produce balanced and coherent products. In some of the political discussion forums, supremacy of the loudest or rudest prevails and he walks away with a feeling of pride. There is hardly any substance or relevance to current issues that could leave viewers wiser or better informed.

Like society in general, the media despite pretending to be a superior breed than the rest unfortunately suffer from the same problem of not being in tune with the order of priorities. When the country was under flood waters, 20 million reported as dislocated by the same media, 8 million rendered homeless; all media discussions were about constitutional amendments that the dead or floating as well as those not affected couldn't care less about. It felt strange watching in amazement as Sky and BBC networks carried live reports from their ground staff in Pakistan, the top indigenous channels organised shouting and counter shouting bouts between guests, some of the learned ones with fake academic degrees. That kind of behaviour seems to work well within the confines of the national boundaries but unfortunately no media anchor or television channel can shut down the rest of the world with high volume nonsense.

It would be most unfair to finish without acknowledging the positive contributions, bold investigations and balanced reporting of events and issues with grace and dignity by a small minority of media persons. Even more so, efforts to bring to public knowledge major stories of financial misappropriation, unacceptable excesses of political actors or state functionaries and other heinous crimes in society that would otherwise go unnoticed and unpunished but for the media's role in bring those to public knowledge and in doing so, offering opportunities for justice to many victims and affected individuals and groups. This is the area in which the media has to play an increasingly effective role. It will get the respect of viewers and society without having to chase viewing numbers and in the process help build a better society and country.

Decisions made in states of strong negative emotions

When a person is angry, his mind is usually not free. A large part of it is preoccupied with thoughts about the target of his anger. In doing so, it is split in many ways. The whole self is no longer available to the angry person. His mental resources are stretched and thinking capacity diminished in proportion to the intensity of the emotion. In that state of mind, it is difficult to think rationally.

Decisions taken in anger are therefore rarely the best ones. People generally end up regretting many decisions and we often say I wish I had not said or done whatever was said or done in haste. It is always best to postpone a decision, if possible, until equanimity is restored to some extent. When anger turns to hatred, the stakes are raised a few notches and the intensity of reaction can sometimes become totally overbearing. The tongue runs faster than the mind, sometimes completely disconnected from the mind, until anger subsides. That is why most people regret things said in a fit of rage because those invariable cause offense to the recipient and embarrassment to the culprit later on. But regret or admission of wrong doing sets in only after some semblance of mental normalcy is restored. As long as it does not happen, regret or realisation of mistakes is an unlikely reaction.

Collectively too, societies and nations engulfed in long term anger and hatred for any reason are unlikely to respond in positive behavioural patterns. Let us look at a few examples of how thought processes involving anger or emotions of retaliation have affected decision making, which under normal circumstances or common logic should or could have been different.

A colossal let off:

There were several aspects of the separation of East Pakistan leading to the creation of Bangladesh that were debated in the media and drawing rooms with great intensity, tempers and regrets. One aspect that was never discussed was the name *Bangladesh* adopted by the newly independent state. The then East Pakistan was the majority province in undivided Pakistan. When declaring their separation and independence, if the Bengalis had taken the position that as the majority population, they would retain the name of "Pakistan" and told the remaining minority to get lost and find a new name, their case would have been stronger than that of the minority population. Even the new name for the former province of North West Frontier is still embroiled in controversy. It was a colossal let off for us and a good example of how hatred driven minds struggle to reach rational and reasoned decisions in their own best interests. At the time, the Bengalis were so incensed and bitter after the way they felt they had been treated, that they did not want to have anything to do with Pakistan.

The merit of their grievances is not relevant to the point. What is relevant is that fortunately for us, their thinking at the time was controlled by anger and hatred, not by what could have been in their best long term interests. It would have been an enduring revenge for them had they thought along the lines of retaining the name Pakistan and a killer headache for us; one that we might still have been struggling to deal with.

Scrapping Asian games hosting rights:

Sports activities are a great source of positive outlet of mental energy and achievement of natural potential. Not only do they inspire the performer, sporting events excite the crowd and bring people together in a unifying bond; identifying with a national team or a professional sports club; the latter cuts across national boundaries in unification experiences. This unfortunately has been another essential that has never been a priority. State sponsored sports facilities are virtually non-existent and the limited contributions are not run along professional lines. While he was in power, Z. A. Bhutto's government won the bidding for the right to host the Asian games in Islamabad in 1978. A huge and impressive purpose built stadium including infrastructure for non-athletic events was constructed in Islamabad. Before the games were due to commence, he was removed from power and the commitment to host the games was immediately withdrawn; the hugely impressive and expensive stadium was buried along with Bhutto. There were taunts from anti-Bhutto lobby about ostentation in the very idea of hosting Asian Games in the country. None seemed educated enough to understand the economic benefits from hosting such a prestigious and mega sports event. We are now in a state where we cannot even host a single international cricket match in the country. The decision was based on hatred for an individual; national interest and international commitment were sacrificed in the most unimaginably irresponsible manner of statesmanship. Many youngsters who could have then been investing their positive energies in rewarding and prestigious pursuits in sporting disciplines for themselves and the country may now be rotting away in militant camps.

Discarding an economic blueprint:

In much the same way as the bid to host the Asian Games in Islamabad was abandoned, a Dubai like vision was set in motion in the form of a prototype casino structure in Karachi well ahead of the onset of economic boom in the United Arab Emirates. The fate of that economic blueprint too was sealed with Bhutto's execution.

Another expensive infrastructure was wasted as a symbolic gesture of undoing everything done in Bhutto's time, negative or positive. Merit and national interest were not a consideration at all. The brand new and unused premises were sealed and described at the time as a reminder of Bhutto's evil mind envisaging a gambling den in the sacred land and with time the haunted structure became the most expensive pigeons' nest in the world! They were for many years to follow the only occupants of a condemned and demonised structure of brick and mortar. Yet another hate based decision that has had only negative implications for the country, in substance and in spirit.

Let us forget for a second that it was Bhutto who was the driving mind and force behind both initiatives and ask ourselves whether those types of visionary moves would still have been abandoned had they been started by someone else? If we could somehow go back in time, would we still take the same negative decisions? If the answer is still in the affirmative, then there is no case for crying about the present state of affairs. The present conditions are the effect or outcome of negative set of choices made at the time. There are occasionally isolated voices reminding their local audiences that Dubai took their economic master plan from us and that personnel from PIA helped set up Emirate Airlines during its teething period. It would be understandable if such reminders were based on regret at lost opportunities, but most of the times it is a case of individuals playing mind games; feeding the mind with empty rationalising reassurances in the face of massive underachievement and frustration. If we feel we should be where many other well-off economies are at present in the Middle East, then that could only have been possible by adopting the full package of implementation. That would have to be built around an attitude of inclusion of outsiders not their exclusion from our hallowed land, extending a friendly welcome, providing security and offering a reasonable degree of freedom to live their way of life away from home. There can be no rewards without the requisite offerings. Our leadership at the time took the opposite stance, not because they believed in it but because that was the basis on which an elected government as overthrown by brute military force; sanitising an allegedly profane set up through a process of visible holiness. Hypocrisy prevailed over common sense and rational thinking in an atmosphere of deliberate poisoning. The adopted direction was unquestionably intentional; the degree to which the pendulum has swung may now be a source of discomfort for the architects of that insane plan but public confessions of poor judgement are most unlikely.

The desired change can still be attempted but that requires a complete washout of the current psychological database dominated more by viruses than any meaningful data. If that is still not an option or none in our leadership has the vision and courage to change track, then those with even a shred of honesty and political vision know which way we are heading.

9

Degeneration of national intellect

Excellence needs no pleading

Temporary success may occasionally land on undeserving shoulders but sustained success can never be achieved in the absence of true quality and excellence. The famous sports slogan, form is temporary but class is permanent illustrates the point. This applies to all walks of life whether manufactured goods, electronics, web services, sports, performing arts, etc. A customer does not have to go seeking reassurances in leading brands such as Mercedes cars or Sony TVs or top brands of mobile phones etc. before buying one, if one can otherwise afford it. Global recognition of quality, however, does not come overnight. It is the cumulative reward for decades of sweat, toil and desire for excellence. The common denominator in all success stories is vision, honest hard work and comprehensive planning.

The desire for success based on true merit and excellence cannot flourish if the spirit of competition, freedom of expression and creative enterprise are taken out of the plot. At the same time, getting rid of comfort or support zones is equally important. Let us take the case of performing arts or literature. We often hear artists from Pakistan self-certify their enormous talent and imply that they do not get their due share of credit or recognition in the region and consequently globally. The implication is usually one of unfair treatment or bias. That kind of attitude is self-defeating and self-demeaning because it betrays an element of begging for support or appreciation rather than creating a product of such quality that naturally triggers a spontaneous "*Ah ha*" response. If quality shines through, admirers and clients will be attracted without explicit pleas for recognition. Acting, singing, dancing, composing instruments have no religion, nationhood, race or colour. The nightingale is a migratory species found in Asia and Europe. It is called so because it frequently sings at night in addition to during the day. Long ago, it was believed that the female sang when in fact the real artist is the male. Without any media service to support it, the nightingale found its way in the lyrics of popular songs and poetry in general. Quality created its own market amongst untold numbers of human admirers. Using race or religious bias as an alibi for lack of recognition or success is a negative attitude. Without dwelling too much on this point, one should look at the examples of the hugely talented *Rahat Fateh Ali* and his predecessor and mentor, the late *Nusrat Fateh Ali*. Even at the height of tensions between Pakistan and India following the senseless killings in Bombay, *Rahat* continued to perform before large, admiring and welcoming audiences in India. In my untrained understanding of music, *Rahat* is already ahead of where *Nusrat* was at that stage in his career but *Nusrat* will always remain as a trend setting legend when historians compile their account of history of music in the sub-continent. No barrier stood in the way of their hard work and professionalism.

Post partition, we inherited true legends in music and singing, *Khawaja Khursheed Anwar*, *Noor Jehan* and *Mehdi Hassan* being examples of either category. The country never produced anyone even close in talent and achievement in later years. To a large extent, that was because of the crisis of identity that corrupts thought processes and value packages, uncertainty over what we can or should own or disown. For years, music was derided as alien to the Islamic religion. Then modern communication technology pulled down many artificial barriers with live reality shows and competitions in both fields registering unprecedented global viewings on international TV entertainment networks and in the process, re-wrote some of the moral codes for music and performing arts to some extent. That commercial generosity offered mouth-watering possibilities that also played a part in silencing large numbers. Suddenly interest in music and dance has been revived.

Pakistan Television in the 1970s

It was the same set of circumstances and thinking processes in other fields. In entertainment, foreign films, especially Indian films remained banned for many years in the name of patriotism, protection of local entertainment industry or any other form of emotional exploitation that worked. At a mental level, it allowed the inertia that held local artists back in comfort zones through absence of competition. As a result, the film industry, if there is one, is an embarrassment today. Compare that to the country's early national television. Through sweat and toil of its founding fathers, their foresight, desire for excellence via international exposure of young producers and artists at prestigious training institutes in developed countries, television productions became an addiction in household viewings. Families would adjust their social commitments for the evenings in order not to miss scheduled popular drama serials in the 1970s.

Then the shadow of Zia-ul-Haq cast its spell on Pakistan. Everything started to go downhill and has not moved in upward direction since then. Indian movies remained popular amongst the masses even when officially banned. Pakistani television drama serials and stage shows were in popular demand on the other side of the border. In fact, on my first visit to Mauritius in 1990, driving from the airport to the hotel, the car radio played wonderful Indian melodies of those times. In the hotel, I was pleasantly surprised that a Pakistani drama serial was listed. Our hosts informed later that Pakistani television programmes were fairly popular with the local population even though they were viewed with subtitles. So where was the national bias then? There wasn't any. For pure quality, there is only a pro-bias within and beyond borders. Quality creates its own market and loyal support base. So is the present oft repeated grievance based on the assumption that our products do not get their due share of market and recognition despite top quality true or simply a combination of the siege mentality and absence of a spirit of competition? If we accept lack of quality and effort in our products, there is no case to argue on grounds of bias. Time will be better served by accepting shortcomings and concentrating on development of skills than complaining all the time about unfair treatment.

Professionalism in TV

Compared to Pakistani movies, in the founding years of Pakistan Television, producers were sent abroad for training at reputed international training institutes under a planned career and professionalism progression path. The benefits of that long term vision of the founding team were reflected in quality of programmes offered to viewers. No one went around pleading for a better treatment from the public for television compared to films. Both got what they deserved! Plays and drama serials in particular became popular in several countries. The first chief of Pakistan's state television, the legendary *Aslam Azhar*, whom I never had the pleasure of meeting or coming across, was known to lead by example of knowledge, professionalism, hard work and dedication. Success and admiration did not come as a surprise. Domestic movie makers are mostly people with no professionalism, education, no appetite for creativity and nothing by way of formal training or international exposure. The outcome and present plight should not surprise anyone.

People from the film industry continually moan about widespread bias against their film industry. Let us try to analyse who is biased against whom, for what reasons and what exactly is that bias? What exactly does bias itself mean? Generally and in dictionary meanings, it is a preference or an inclination that impedes impartial judgment or evaluation; that in a nutshell amounts to irrational behaviour delinked from real facts.

Do ground realities support this hypothesis? How many people with time and opportunity do not play Indian songs and replicate dances from Bollywood movies at private family weddings in Karachi, Lahore or even in very small towns? How many prefer to play local industry songs instead? Whatever people do in this context is mainly a matter of free will and personal preference; a case again of quality creating its own market. By way of example, a local production titled "*Khuda ke liye*" [*For God's sake*] made the rounds a few years ago. I happened to see that movie a few years later on repeated recommendations from family and friends with a taste for good movies and it turned out to be a class above the pretty rotten run of the mill stuff. Quality generated its own whisper advertisement. It won recognition beyond the national boundaries and bias died a natural death, if indeed it was ever alive except in imagination.

People take to entertainment as a recreation or relaxation for the mind, to wean away from real life stresses and allow stressed minds time enough to regroup and re-energise. Depending on the source, there are some very interesting and some embarrassingly stupid interpretations of dreams, in addition to those interpretations that are based on more logical psychological theories. However, what most people are not aware of is that dreams perform a very important pathological function; they preserve sleep. If a person was not to experience a particular dream at a particular time during his sleep, then the continuity of that sleep period would have been broken. When someone has a pleasant dream and subsequently wakes up, he may sometimes wish he were still asleep, even try to fake sleep in the hope of reconnecting to the dream period. Unfortunately, it does not happen but the desire itself reflects the craving of the human mind to prolong its pleasant experiences. If on the other hand, a person has a nightmare instead that heightens stress and anxiety and may even lead him into jumping out of his bed and the nightmare, he feels grateful that his sleep was broken to allow him to escape the unpleasant experience.

Movies are in that sense like dreams. People watch them like men asleep watching real life emotions, aspirations, wishes and desires. If people cannot connect to the content of what is on offer, the experience serves none of the described purposes. A good percentage of movie goers stay away from horror movies. To them these are like nightmares that defeat the mind's pursuit of relaxation and stress release. Some others find as much thrill, if not more in such movies too. The reasons can be varied from pure admiration of art and presentation to less mentally stable individuals who might derive some form of sadistic or masochistic pleasure from the experience. The causes are irrelevant for present purposes but the focal point remains the natural inclination of the mind to drift into pleasant experiences whenever possible.

If, however, the experience is not relatable to the viewer in any way, it does no service to the mind. Unfortunately, the film industry with a few exceptions is ill-equipped and ill-resourced in every way to operate successfully in current times and with the requisite technological knowhow. The average viewer cannot relate to what has now been thrown at them for decades. None of the relaxing experiences or catharsis that the mind craves for by way of passive role playing, living out fantasies or associating with are on offer. Who would go to sleep at night with a last wish for a Punjabi movie like dream? I ask this question being a Punjabi myself so there can be no nationality bias here either. Where exactly do the bias theories come from? Unfortunately these come from the same defeatist attitude that is commonly seen in other aspects of life, an easy escape path to "cognitive consonance".

Ignoring national boundaries – "Sa Re Ga Ma"

The impact of Indian music competitions on a number of Indian television networks has lent a wonderful helping hand in the promotion of cross border cultural activities and in knocking down many irrational emotional barriers. The deceptive persona of religious morality, customised to demonise all forms of art and cultures as evil pursuits created over the years, a sense of guilt for any public appreciation of music, dance and performing arts has been considerably diluted in recent years. People may pretend to dissociate with such pursuits in public but switch on their TV sets behind closed doors to watch everything publicly condemned. In public perception, it peaked during Zia's time. In private, it was a different story. Civil servants stationed as Commercial Counsellors at various diplomatic establishments were tasked with sending to Zia's residence the latest models of the then relatively new and popular product called VCR. The length of their postings at prize stations depended in part on the kind and quality of the services they provided. In one instance, the then Secretary Commerce responsible for the posting and transfers of these counsellors transferred an incumbent without prior clearance from his holiness. The permanent secretary was promptly summoned and ordered to cancel the transfer order. No rewards for guessing that it was promptly done. Names can be provided, if the story is challenged. But real characters are irrelevant; they were just there at the time. Others would have done the same once ordered by that military dictator.

The socio-cultural values of the common citizen were modified under duress to accommodate separate sets for public and private practices. He had come to power in the darkness of the night overthrowing an elected left leaning government by orchestrating a fake agitation through a proxy group of religious parties to justify his act of treason. His public faking of holiness was a compulsion to sustain his position in power. The damage he did to society, education, morals, art and culture is beyond measure and perhaps more tragically, seems irreversible in the foreseeable future.

Recognition surge of Indian Muslims

The single most convincing case in support of the deterioration of our national IQs and creative instincts during a period of at 3 or 4 decades and my contention that it is the direct result of the shift in our socio-political drift from a reasonably moderate previous position to extreme right wing politics is a comparative scrutiny of development and achievements of Muslims in Pakistan and India, especially in the field of education and performing art. Race and genetics are common denominators. Since development of the human mind and personality is the outcome of interactions between heredity and environment and in this case, heredity is common, the subject of analysis can only be environmental variables. We can follow two strategies of analysis. A longitudinal approach, one which looks at changes in our own context over a period of time, and secondly, a cross-sectional approach that compares the environmental differences of two religious and cultural groups at the same point in time.

A lot has already been expressed by way of analysis about the changes in our society over a period of four decades under various topics and subtopics. One can therefore rest that case for now, on the basis of evidence and analysis already offered. That leaves us with the cross-sectional analysis or comparison of the present mind-sets and professional performance of Muslims groups in Pakistan and India. It would be a huge task to take the aggregate population for analysis. We can pick a particular sector for comparison. The one sector that lends itself to perfect comparison is that of performing arts. It is perfect in the sense that the scope of its coverage and outreach extends to a bigger segment of population than any other sector that comes to mind readily.

Some of the more conservative segments of population in our society often contend that the field of performing arts is un-Islamic in many ways without ever producing evidence in support of such drivel. There are even isolated noises that the art of music and singing is forbidden in Islam. That does not, however, deter them from watching popular singing and dancing acts in the privacy of their homes as long as others do not catch them red handed. It also has not stopped many amongst the clergy from singing "*naats*" [*songs of praise for the holy prophet*] through the loudspeakers of mosques that are set on the background score of popular film songs in the sub-continent. In doing so, they have held back so much of potential amongst the youth through a combination of inculcating feelings of guilt and social reprimand for involvement in so called evil pursuits. The divided self plays an important accommodating role in aiding reconciliation between the acts of condemning these kinds of activities but watching them in private. The watcher and his family members retain their holiness by not being involved in these activities themselves.

The average Muslim in India is definitely intellectually ahead of his counterpart in Pakistan in present times. Whether one refuses to accept the reality from motives of jealousy or plain denial of verifiable facts is irrelevant. This should come as no surprise to any balanced and realistic mind. Two factors are considered in psychology to be the shapers of intellectual and personality types. When in a comparative study, one factor [heredity] is common and the second [environment] is decidedly more favourable for one study group, the causal outcome of the product based on the foundation causes should not make a difficult analysis. If more supporting evidence is needed, we need not look further than the qualitative distinction within the Muslim population as a whole. Those Muslims who are more conservative and abrasive in their social attitudes and behaviour lag behind their own Muslim fraternity within India. If some people still cannot see the difference between the role of freedom of thought and purposeful education on the one hand, and voluntary social isolation in combination with a refusal to move on with the time on the other hand, then there is no point in wasting time in communicating with that kind of species.

Maulana Bhashani

Maulana Abdul Hamid Khan Bhashani was a popular political leader in Pakistan and Bangladesh and a *maulana* with a somewhat different mission. He was rural based and within that context, a rare self-educated person. In January 1968, he organized the Cooperative for the Cultivators of East Pakistan. When the nation was in search of a credible candidate to contest elections against Ayub Khan, many turned to Ms. Fatima Jinnah, sister of Mohammad Ali Jinnah to play that role. She was initially reported to have been unimpressed with the idea of being the opposition's nominee. However, Bhashani intervened personally to persuade her to agree to be the joint opposition candidate. That was a progressive Maulana Bhashani in 1968. Since then the world has moved forward towards liberation, equality of rights, rejection of older values of class and gender discrimination, etc. Four decades later, in our present society, the *maulanas* of today have moved in the opposite direction. Far from following the Bhashani template that included persuading a female leader into taking on an important political role in national interest, they sung in unison "*a women cannot rule in an Islamic society*" song every time Benazir stood as a candidate in any constituency. The thought of including the downtrodden and expendable cultivators in any welfare cause in their respective brand of religious politics will never even have crossed their minds.

This brief description of Bhashani points out to clear differences between his personal circumstances or political direction and the religious mercenaries of today. Firstly, that Bhashani had a desire for knowledge and education, and those two attributes made him a rare progressive political actor in a religious mould. Secondly, because of that progressive streak, he had the vision for thinking about the masses ahead of party finances. While that example is a source of satisfaction and role playing for every reader, it symbolises the warning bells that start to ring in the minds of those who exploit the name of religion in pursuit of political power. Therefore having uneducated and indoctrinated followers with physical attributes normally associated with the local clergy is a far safer course than having potentially troublesome Bhashanis amongst their lower ranks. The theme of perpetuation of ignorance and indoctrination is recurrent in so many aspects of our political structures.

Changing times

آج ہم دار پر کھینچے گئے جن باتوں پر
کیا عجب کل وہ زمانے کو نصابوں میں ملیں

Aaj hum daar par khinche gaye jin batoon par
Kya ajab kal wo zamaney ko kitaboon mein milain
Faraz

[Principles for which we might be taken to the gallows today
Who knows may tomorrow become part of academic syllabi]

There was a time when it was a crime to be an anti-slavery activist, to talk of the rights of workers, peasants and women, freedom of speech, majority rule and so on. Many spent lives in jails; some even went to the gallows refusing to give up their convictions and struggles. Today, most of these subjects are essential elements of modern academic syllabi from schools to universities. A wise Chinese proverb states that "*a journey of a thousand miles beings with a single step*". Another wise saying states that one who asks a question may be a fool for a day, but someone who asks no question will remain a fool for life. Given the present sorry state of the common man in society and the terminal dangers that loom overhead, should anyone still hesitate to take that first step in a long overdue journey in support of a change in thinking patterns and decadent values? If the house can be put in order, if divisive tendencies can be identified and marginalised and if the foundations for respecting the will of the people can be established, external threats and pressures can be handled more effectively.

10

Manifestations of structuralism in behaviour

The world is a sort of theatre; full of endless plots and roles. Every human being is a role player in an infinite story. But like theatres in real life, some stage reality shows or art films deal with real life issues, others with pure fantasy.

Visibility over substance

Motorway vs Hub Power Project

Since in societies where structuralism dominates values and practice, and attention is concentrated on form over substance, most activities undertaken by individuals, groups but above all by national leaders tilt invariably towards activities or projects that are more visible and can be clearly exhibited to the public instead of more productive pursuits that will not catch the public eye. Two mega projects in which I represented the Federal Board of Revenue come readily to mind. The Hub Power Project undertaken by the Benazir government was at the time, the biggest private sector power project in the world. How many people were aware of this fact? I suspect, very few indeed. Even though I was involved throughout the duration of lengthy negotiations on tax matters only, I never actually visited the project site in the far flung Hub area. The second mega project was the Islamabad- Lahore motorway during the Nawaz Sharif government. That always remained in public and media focus because the end product was expected to be there for everyone to see and physically use. Without going into the details of the often unprofessional style and contents of negotiations and decision making, the factual reality is painfully evident now is that many power projects like HUBCO should have been undertaken in preference to the still under-utilised motorways. Let us not get distracted by the allegations of wrong doings in setting power tariffs because that is more a question of implementation, not the theoretical necessity for greater power generation. That does not justify altering priorities and requirements. Unfortunately, due to our collective inability to make objective analysis, we often confuse the issue of faulty implementation with wrong decision or choice of activity.

The discrepancies between theory and practice, between policy and administration, between law and implementation of it have never really been clearly understood. The logic goes like, if taxes are not being collected, surely the laws must be inappropriate. That is normally taken to mean it is time for another tax reforms effort which is visible activity for governments to show and for the populace to see but strict application of tax laws, any law for that matter, is more difficult to showcase and is a function of tough political decisions, administrative integrity and visionary planning. That is the kind of manhandling we have been doing with our national constitution. Instead of having the political and social will to ensure strict adherence to constitutional provisions, which is a matter of following the spirit of the documents by all state institutions, we have resorted to the easier and wishful solution of constitutional amendments; something that those in governance can be seen to be doing. Following the letter and spirit of law can hardly be held up for demonstration of achievement by political leaders, even more by military dictators at public gatherings or television performances.

The extent to which structuralism laden, form dominated frame of mind can go to in terms of self-deception at times defies belief. My grandfather graduated as a *Ravian* in 1889 and retired later as a session judge. My father also graduated as a *Ravian* in 1929 and died while still in service in the public sector. He was a law graduate and also a Hafiz of the Quran. Both were therefore equipped with academic and religious knowledge in equal measure. Both were very religious individuals but being well educated never let any form of fundamentalism or radicalism influences their views. Most of the other family elders had religious leanings and knowledge in varying degrees. All through their lives they referred to God as "*Khuda*". Punjabi speaking people including ourselves would refer to God as "*Rab*" in the Punjabi language. Neither ever caused any problem, neither was ever put to any question or controversy; not until we came to the era of radicalisation and divisiveness. Conflicting religious sects and sub-sects were encouraged. Each had to carve out its own sphere of influence and sub-brand of interpretations to stay in business. It suddenly dawned on one of them that Muslims had been addressing God by the wrong name by referring to Him as "*Khuda*". The God that Muslims needed to believe in and worship should be "*Allah*" and Him alone! The underlying thinking that this change of name would transform the fortunes of the Muslims, rectify all wrong doings in society – real or imaginary because all past sins would be forgiven. There must have been several other arguments extended that are not to my knowledge but the gist must be that the change would lead to better times.

So the old traditions followed by our ancestors for centuries with utmost respect and convention were set aside as misled and misguided! I have no problem with referring to God as "*Allah*" or "*Khuda*" but the rationale or the underlying assumptions for the change are unconvincing, if not deliberately deceptive. Respect for and obedience to God will not change for individuals simply because they start addressing Him by a different name. Many Muslims refer to God by any one of the 99 attributes listed for Him in the Quran such as "*Raheem*" or "*Kareem*". It is the spirit that matters in societies that fall into the "functional" classification. It was the form which became the basis of the shift in our society or in some other Muslim societies too where the rule of thumb is form over essence; a misguided but genuine make belief in many cases, a fake belief with the schemers that a change in name would please God more and therefore lead to more favours. In the process, many preachers and so called religious scholars carved out for themselves their own sphere of influence and support following, commonly known as "*fiqahs*". That the Quran does not sanction or justify divisiveness in its believers is conveniently ignored in practical life. This in itself is another example how discrepancies in theory and practice can be both misleading and hugely problematic. That is how and why differences in religious interpretations and minor deviations in practical rituals such as the structure of rows at funeral prayers feed the attention seeking egos and the financial needs of those who lead the chants. Those who follow are not essentially part of the scheming but play a part nevertheless by blindly following whatever is conveyed to them in the name of fictional religious authority.

Like in other matters, the vital question remains the same. Has our lot improved since the new trend of addressing God as "*Allah*" instead of "*Khuda*" was adopted by thousands of converts? It has not and will not because it is irrelevant to our problems nor will it pull a blanket over wrong doings. But the change has generated more controversy and introduced a new topic for division amongst Muslims; even between Muslims and others. Some have even gone a step further in demanding that none other than Muslims alone can refer to God as "*Allah*". The dispute has been taken up in litigation by a tiny minority to the level of superior courts in at least one Muslim country. It also brings us back to the issue of accountability and divine control at all times. If the case for divine control at all times was taken to be true and so too the fact that God should always have been addressed as Allah by all Muslims, how could such a huge proportion of mankind have been acting incorrectly despite divine control? The obvious conclusion is that right or wrong choices could only be made if there is freedom of decision making for human beings. All these wrong approaches have contributed immensely to why instant accountability under human laws has always taken a battering in our society and why so many criminals and law breakers have gotten away using deliberately distorted interpretations of religion.

A massive change in approach to understanding of issues, practices and priorities is the immediate need; a shift of focus from form and structure to the more productive approach of dealing with issues in the light of the spirit and objectives sought to be achieved will produce much better and quicker results. Even if no dramatic improvement comes about, things cannot get any worse than what they have become by doing what we have always done.

Travel prayer before air travel

Anyone who has travelled on Pakistan's international airline will know that during the take-off phase of every journey, a short pre-travel prayer in Arabic language is recited through the cabin's public address system. Very few passengers are aware of the translation of the contents of the Arabic text and even though few will have shown interest in learning about the meaning, all Muslim passengers show complete respect for the duration of the prayer. At some point, the Urdu translation of the prayer was also introduced but after a few months that was discontinued in response to passenger feedback. Part of the prayer states that this could be my last journey. That distressed some passengers, especially those with an inherent fear of flying.

The Arabic version of the prayer still continues till today and devotees of the Muslim faith continue to show the respect and discipline normally associated with all prayers. This, however, is a tailor made example of behavioural patterns in societies that are classified as structural societies in social psychology. The physical manifestation of the ritual gets all the time and respect that can be expressed; interest in the meaning of or spirit behind the ritual remains secondary, in this case there is even a conscious attempt by some to deliberately exclude knowledge of the very message towards which respect is on public display. If translation of every aspect of religious dictates and duties had been mandatory, some of those who violate fundamental moral values of honesty, justice and fair play, etc. without ever feeling guilty in the least might feel some inner embarrassment while practicing the opposite of what they preach. It is essential that ONLY translations are made, NOT interpretations by different sects and sub-sects. That would be suicidal given the politico-religious predators in waiting on every issue on which any controversy can be generated. We need to turn to the basics in all possible aspects of life. This strategy will gradually nudge behavioural tendencies in society towards functionalism which entails giving more importance to why a moral value or a ritual is followed or performed, not how it is normally acted out. That will serve society better than the opposite approach that has failed to serve to any desirable extent.

Exterior looks and concealed realities

Role playing and customary rituals have always been and will remain an integral part of socio-cultural life of human beings. The more advanced a society becomes, the number of significant social role playing and rituals deceases. Conversely, the more backward a society is, the quantum of social and cultural roles and rituals multiplies disproportionately. We therefore see that tribal societies are so top heavy with all kinds of rituals that can range from very few benevolent ones to scores of rituals that have no place in the 21st century such as the frequent sacrifice of a black goat for imaginary threats or beating the devil out of someone who suffers from nothing more than symptoms of mild hysteria.

Sometimes these rituals serve a purpose even though those who believe and follow many silly practices do not understand the dynamics of mental processes involved. Let us take the case of someone manifesting physical symptoms of an attack of hysteria. Quite often, fits of hysteria and epilepsy may look strikingly similar. In their dynamics, they are miles apart. A fit of hysteria is usually driven by unconscious motives of attention seeking while an epileptic fit has pathological causes, mainly through neuronal activity in the brain. For the uninformed observer, it is difficult to make out the difference. A fit of hysteria is basically loss of self-control triggered by an overpowering fear resident in the unconscious part of the individual's mind and can be the cumulative effect of a series of events in the past involving severe mental conflict. When the emotion gets out of control from time to time, the individual goes into what is commonly called a "fit of hysteria" that invariably attracts attention from everyone around and the patient is helped out of his severe state of tension. It is an unconscious attention seeking reaction of the mind and body, a desperate cry for help to overcome the situation. Even though it is controlled by the unconscious mind, the instinct of self-preservation is not completely lost on the mind. It is therefore most unlikely that someone suffering from symptoms of hysteria will go into a fit at the top of a stair case but may suddenly do so when on the last step or having reached the relative safety of floor level. Avoiding long term harm is appended to the agenda. The person does not set out to deliberately deceive in this manner but his unconscious mind usually takes care of that. A problem that he cannot handle on his own is temporarily overcome with the help of outside assistance. On the other hand, an epileptic fit has no such control mechanisms of the mind. That fit can take place anywhere without relating to consequential harm because the basis is physical, unlike hysteria.

One final point in this is that what is seen externally is the physical symptom of psychological problems that reside in the deepest recesses of the unconscious mind. Each individual can display symptoms in a different way, from limited involvement of body parts such as twisted arms or hands to engulfing the whole body in seizure. After a fit, the symptom may be gone for that moment but the deep rooted real problem does not go away with it.

This may seem an unnecessary digression but it is important to clarify this before reverting to the traditional subject of primitive rituals of "*driving the devil out of those under such evil spells*". Primitive rituals for curing physical manifestations of hysteria and epilepsy focus mainly on forms of torture and beatings in various degrees to drive out the target evil captivating the body. Since an attack of hysteria is attention seeking, torture or methodical beating have the opposite effect. The individual's unconscious mind withdraws external symptoms temporarily to avoid further infliction. For the faith healer and those who go to him, that amounts to curing and the business of healing imposter continues to not only flourish, he uses his claims of supernatural powers to maximise his influence and earnings from a fake profession. In reality, the temporary retreat of symptoms by the unconscious mind of the patient only helps to avoid temporary threats of unwanted discomfort instead of added attention. The symptoms either reappear or appear in a different form later because the problem remains unattended. In the meantime the faith healer will have pocketed a healthy sum of money from ignorant and unsuspecting family members. Unfortunately, for someone suffering from epilepsy, there is no respite because it is a completely different problem. He suffers more at the hands of phony faith healers and most often it is too late before proper medical help is sought.

Two very important lessons to be learnt are; firstly, that visually observable forms of behaviour do not necessarily mean or represent what they appear to seemingly convey. Until the real causes, spirit or intent of physically observable behavioural actions are analysed and understood, the outcomes will usually be unproductive at best to totally futile or even destructive in worst cases. Secondly, the single most significant difference between achieving right results and solutions to problems is being equipped with scientific knowledge which is the foundation for reason and logic in the thinking processes. Since our social emphasis is so heavily tilted towards external forms and appearances, while at the same time levels of knowledge and purposeful education are embarrassingly low, as a socio-cultural group we are easy to mislead and be driven into futile pursuits while those who so drive us carry on with their selfish and greedy agendas of loot and plunder.

Decades of deprivation from education in numbers for a start and development of higher skills cannot be reversed in a short space of time. Many unhealthy acquisitions need to be unlearnt and off-loaded before a start can be made in the right direction. At present awareness of the current precarious situation is in very short supply; the time at our disposal to deal with it effectively even shorter.

11

Hypocrisy; a parallel religion

Hypocrisy is the most difficult and nerve-racking vice that any man can pursue; it needs an unceasing vigilance and a rare detachment of spirit. It cannot, like adultery or gluttony, be practiced at spare moments; it is a whole-time job.
W. Somerset Maugham

If one speaks the truth most of the time, if not always, life becomes far easier. One does not have to remember what was said to whom. When a person generally likes most people around him and is able to get along with them, the mind feels less stressed because getting along with others, joining them in their joys and sorrows or cooperating with them in common objectives requires no special skills and is largely stress free. But having made five misstatements to different people during the day, the mind is less at peace when night comes because it is burdened with the additional assignment of remembering what was said to whom or in framing excuses for not joining someone different from himself in that other person's moment of joy or ritual.

How many of us actually put down keeping it simple as a priority in life? Unfortunately, the percentage of such people compared to 30 years ago has fallen dramatically. The reasons for fragmentation in society have been discussed under various sub-topics. Whatever the reason, each fragmentation comes with its cost and collateral damage. Each fragmented mind works overtime to stay tuned to its separatist brand of beliefs, values and practices. More damagingly, it invests a large amount of inherently positive energy into negative pursuits such as finding flaws in other camps that justify its solo flight and maintain its own consonance. That approach is doomed to failure especially when most individuals or other camps are struck by the same collective obsession. Arguments and counter arguments continue to occupy the minds of the subjects to the exclusion of positive attitude building and productive role playing. Continual friction with fellow beings leads to the familiar pattern of anger, anxiety, hatred, negative attitudes and eventually to individual or collective violence.

Hypocrisy, almost a second religion

We choose our joys and sorrows long before we experience them.
Kahlil Gibran

Zia died in an air crash. Air crashes are normally called disasters. Eleven years of his treacherous misrule has left the country scared, traumatised, fragmented, top heavy with hatred and intolerance. Had he lived on for another 5 years, a lot of us may now have been writing about history, not an existing state. Ironically that air disaster was the only disaster during his period that was not made by himself. The countless unexploded bombs and booby traps of conflict and hatred that he scattered around the length and breadth of Pakistan continue to explode with unscheduled regularity causing death and destruction on innocent individuals, families, communities, and races and setting off "*to whom it may concern*" tragedies. His plane crash may have prevented him from driving the proverbial last nail in the nation's coffin, but a coffin produced and directed by him and his equally evil comrades might still come back to haunt us if we keep moving in the direction on which he set the country.

Domestic axis of evil

"**It is the times plague when mad men lead the blind**" said Shakespeare once. In the circles of power, even today, the history of accountability starts from the year of the Lord when Gen. Musharaf usurped power. How ironical that Zia, the architect of religious mass floggings and assignations, who only could think of the use of human dynamite as "investment in human resource" or "development of strategic assets" to prolong his grip on power himself became the first big casualty of that evil scheme. **"That we but teach bloody instructions, and which being taught, return to plague the inventor"**. Usual prophetic and time tested words from Shakespeare again; uttered through Macbeth while contemplating the plot to kill his trusting king while being his host and eventually meeting a worse fate than his victim.

Emperors and dictators

When oppressive and suffocating dictatorships are at their ruthless and nastiest peak, harassed and mentally scarred minds vent their hatred and despair in indirect ways. Individual minds select their own best suited defence mechanisms to deal with the stress and insecurity. Insulting jokes that portray dominant evil traits of dictators are one way of safer catharsis; self-preservation being the top priority. Many unprompted and low profile social groups pop up and jokes about dictators in power in the assured safety of their living rooms become a nervous tension releasing social activity.

Very effective whisper campaigns can be run through the seemingly casual and benign medium of innocent jokes. Each human mind finds its customised psychic defence mechanisms to deal with stress. If that safety regulator were to be taken away from over bearing stress and anxiety, insanity would be far more common under repressive regimes than is the case in reality, even though as it is the incidence is still pretty high.

The appallingly cold-blooded donkey ride

For people with short memories and those who were too young to remember Zia's dictatorial witchcraft, the extent of viciousness and heartlessness in Zia's nature when it came to protecting his stranglehold on power, by hook or by crook, largely by crook only, is symbolised by an act in the name of justice that would have embarrassed Dracula, but which his holiness would have highlighted with pride in a biography if he had lived on to write one. A retired bureaucrat or local judge of good repute was playing a game of cards at a local club in the town of Sahiwal. During a social conversation, he narrated a dream to his game partners, one in which Zia goes into extinction. That narration was conveyed to Zia's wandering intelligence prowlers at the time. The judge owned a hotel that was raided in retaliation at the audacity of an ordinary mortal wishing the end of Zia, even if in an unsolicited dream. The hotel was charged with being the wicked den for every punishable evil deed, real or imaginary. The elderly well respected senior citizen was mounted on a donkey with his face painted black, paraded through streets by way of exemplary punishment and not surprisingly, died a few months later from the shock and humiliation of that treatment! It was claimed at the time that this was the Islamic way of punishment. Whether it is or not, is beside the point. The reality is that there was no such punishment under any operative law in the country at the time to executive that kind of punishment in the name of justice or religion.

In many rural and remote areas of India, this type of traditional punishment was intended to humiliate those guilty of petty crimes, non-conformity or socio-cultural offences. Such punishments were generally handed out by village elders commonly referred to as the local "*panchayat*" or a system of primitive justice delivered by village elders. The guilty person's head was usually shaved and a garland of discarded footwear hung around his neck before being paraded through and around the village or town on a donkey to be mocked and ridiculed by ignorant and mostly subjugated onlookers. That is how backwards Zia's mind-set was logged in and he dragged a fairly balanced society right back to his primitive age in terms of values and practices.

Eid-ul-Azha & the spirit of sacrifice

آ گیء فصل سکوں چاک گریباں والو
سل گئے ہونٹ کوئ زخم سلے یا نا سلے
دوستو بزم سجاؤ کے بہار آئ ہے
کھل گئے زخم کوئ پھول کھلے یا نا کھلے

Aa gaee fasal-e-sukoon, chaak gireban waloo
Sil gaye hoont, koi zakhm sile ya na sile
Doosto bazm sajao ke bahaar aayi hai
Khil gae zakm, koi phool khiley ya na khiley
Faiz

Urdu channels in London recently showed people in Karachi enjoying Bar-e-Q parties following Eid sacrifice [*qurbani*] at home. Though no one should grudge the right of exhausted souls of average citizens improvising ways to voluntarily regress in the service of their stressed existences, but is that the envisaged spirit of "*qurbani*" for Eid-ul-Azha? Slaughter animals and enjoy the meat ourselves? It is interesting to observe the tactics for receiving and sending meat from friends and family in most households, predominantly on the basis of reciprocity. At the end of the day, almost every family retains almost a full animal even though quite literally in bits and pieces. This year saw the worst floods in the country's history with hundreds of thousands, if not millions dead and homeless. While leaders were making passionate appeals to humanity at large to come to the aid of the victims of that natural calamity, it would have made perfect sense to follow the spirit of "*qurbani*" instead of the ritual and donating in cash or kind directly to those living in tents or even under open skies. Even the money spent on slaughter of animals during the Haj pilgrimage in Saudi Arabia could and should have been donated directly to those in instant need and mortal danger. The great humanitarian warrior, *Abdul Sattar Edhi* has been begging people to do exactly that for decades now. It requires a generic cynic to doubt Edhi's intentions and awareness of real needs of the most deprived members of the population, but form and public showing of actions so dominates psyches that even the most educated will prefer the social display over any out of sight donation. Even those who may have considered the option will eventually either succumb to the unconscious fear that not performing the public ritual might come back to haunt them later in life or simply feel undermined socially for not showcasing their religious ritual. In reality, helping those in greatest need of help without retaining the donor's share of *qurbani* would be the real sacrifice.

There is an element of latent selfishness too, spending money, even that earned from unlawful and immoral livelihoods to try to secure their personal comfort and reward in Heaven ahead of contributing to any effort to deal with the miseries of others. If we analyse this specific mind game, it is the exact opposite of the spirit of sacrifice; putting self-interest before that of anyone else, especially those who would currently be the deserving recipients of acts of generosity.

Ironically, even as late as December 2010, a private television channel carried a news report from a correspondent covering the

A ritual meant to be a spirit of sacrifice degraded into a social display farce

plight of flood victims, including women and infants still confined to living in fabric tents, without adequate warm clothing and cover at the height of cold weather. If anyone argues that their need for survival, not comfortable living, was any less than the need to sacrifice animals for meat distribution to those already well housed and adequately provided, I am afraid that logic or view point is difficult to understand, if at all it can be called a view point; at best it is callous neglect of those suffering right under the eyes of ones making a sacrifice; just the opposite of the spirit of sacrifice that the "*qurbani*" is supposed to represent.

The scourge of money making in the name of religion

The past three decades have witnessed an increasing trend in money making in the garb of religious activities. There was always an accepted level of routine religious roles that entailed some financial package. Young children were taught how to read the Quran in almost every home by a visiting priest from a local mosque. The mutually agreed fees for that particular service was usually affordable and offered a respectable livelihood to the teacher, instead of him remaining wholly dependent on voluntary contributions. When any private individual performs his religious obligations, there is no element of money making. On the contrary, there are expenses involved such as payment of Zakat, performance of Haj or the sacrificial ritual at Eid-ul-Azha. Where a religious role involves income or donations, the dynamics change completely. Where minor sums are involved such as the teaching of Quran or Arabic at homes, there are hardly any problems. As the level of receipts start to rise, so do social complications. In recent times, the sums involved in religious activities have at times being huge and so too the troubles that are generated when stakes begin to rise.

Political parties that wear the religious persona to promote their agenda have been regularly accused of money making when in power and political blackmail when out of it. It is not just a coincidence that those who perform religious duties in private cause no concern to or friction in society. On the other hand, those who use religion for money making are at the forefront of most conflicts, sectarian troubles, socially divisive trends and even involvement in violence abroad that has severely dented national and international image and reputation. That in turn adversely affects the country's international relationship and loss of support or sympathy for even just causes. The recent frequently expressed reservations by foreign governments and other donor sources in helping victims of flood is in large measure the outcome of troublesome involvement abroad. Though corruption was also cited as a concern, with a more positive international profile, guarantees of fair distribution of aid for flood devastation would definitely have been easier to sell.

The nation needs to analyse the ever increasing role of money in religious activities and the ill effects it has had on our domestic and international situations. What has been going on in recent years has hardly had a single positive outcome. It is time to revisit this methodology and to collectively think whether one can afford to carry on with current practices. If society carries on as it is, it will continue to get what it has been getting in return and with the passage of time with decidedly increasing intensity.

Social satire on religious matters

In Pakistan's political culture, it has always been traditional for a head of state to have his address to the nation preceded with either a brief recitation from the holy Quran or the national anthem or both. Following completion of the address, the occasion was almost invariably followed by a repeat of the national anthem. Zia being the generic hypocrite that he was may have felt that his deceit and richly wrapped packet of lies were too difficult to sell unless a holy recitation was included before the start and after he finished his speeches. That became the norm for him. Did it work? Yes, it did for a while, especially with those who were his target audience, too innocent to concede that a fraud of the magnitude of Zia's production could be perpetrated in the name of religion. Very few of his followers are now around willing to put up their hands in his support, but at the time many were carried away by the persona of holiness that he wore in public. Behind the scenes, he probably dined with the devil on a daily basis.

But as is the case with all such profane set ups, collateral damage was being inflicted continually even though it went largely unnoticed at the time. While serving as an income tax officer in Lahore during Zia's period, a reasonably senior retired army officer then dealing in the business of import of goods was a regular visitor to one of my deceased colleagues as a family friend. My colleague and I had nothing but contempt for Zia and expressed our views with calculated risk at appropriate times but still discovered later through another colleague that I was a subject of investigation for that reason. This retired army man turned businessman would try to defend Zia in very apologetic language because he was aware of the futility of his attempts in the given company. After a few months he developed some confidence in the relationship and started to be more honest in sharing his views. He then suddenly volunteered to tell a tale that showed how damaging Zia's influence was. He said that he had recently been hospitalised with a heart ailment. During his recovery period, he was once driving back from his army hospital when he felt slight discomfort in his chest. Given his heart condition he thought it wise to take a short break before resuming his home run. He settled on a roadside bench in the front lawns of the Fortress Stadium in Lahore. A few typically *Lahori* citizens well equipped with street humour were having a good time. Not realising that they had been joined by an ex-soldier not in uniform they carried on with their session. The specific anecdote the retired soldier cum businessman narrated in utmost confidence was that one of the characters in the group made a confession to his friends. He said that in the past, when someone asked him to "*swear by God*" in confirmation of anything, a false swear used to be loaded with guilt if it became unavoidable. But then referring to Zia's practice of recitation from the holy book before and after all his speeches, he said that now with "a recitation before and after blatant lies", that inhibition had been overcome! This is one more example of the enduring damage Zia has done to society by his blatant misuse of religion.

Multiple mosques grouped together

In the early days of Islam, in the absence of electricity at the time, the *Azaan* [*call to prayer*] was delivered from a minaret top and pitched to a level that maximised the outreach of the call. In present times that outreach is immensely extended courtesy of present day technology and by analogy the distance between the physical locations of mosques can be considerably longer. The justification for multiple mosques in the same locality, even during planning phase in new settlements can be none other than segregated followers attending only mosques that claim to be representing their sects.

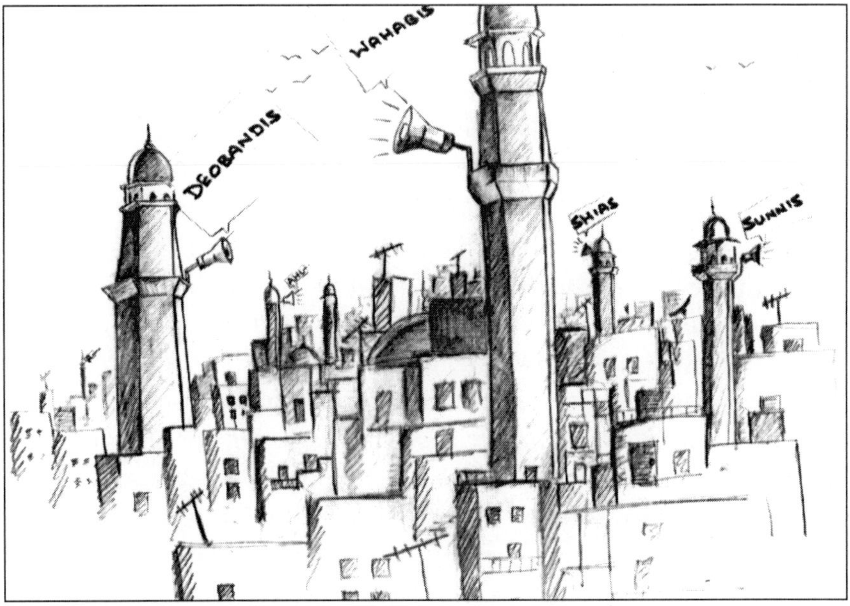

"Haram e paak bhi, Allah bhi Quran bhi ek
Kuchh bari baat thi hote jo musalman bhi ek?"
Allama Iqbal

The management of each mosque far from making any effort to encourage other sects to join in their prayers actually ensure that no one external to their school of adopted belief enters their mosque. That from the clergy's perspective could set a very dangerous trend for Muslims of all sects getting closer in common prayer. I was informed of an incident in a London mosque where the imam of one mosque having found out that someone from an opposing sect had offered his prayers uninvited, actually had that spot washed thoroughly to restore its holiness. It is irrelevant whether the parties involved were Shias, Sunnis, Wahhabis or others. The narrow minded in each such sub-group are of the same divisive and confrontational material. A softer approach would certainly run contrary to their long term interests of solo sectarian flights. Society alone can defeat this strategy by encouraging common worship. After all, people of all sects join together at one off funeral prayers and during Haj rituals. So why break up in daily prayers?

Drug carrying Haajis

Of the five pillars of the Islamic faith, the one held in highest regard is Haj, perhaps mainly for the reason that not all Muslims get an opportunity or sometimes despite opportunity do not have the financial means to perform Haj in their life time. There is therefore a certain degree of pomp and social exhibition by those who make it, partly out of satisfaction or thankfulness and at times even an egotistic satisfaction of being a privileged Muslim although the latter is based on cultural values only, not religious dictates. So how can someone who goes for Haj with the package of religious obligations and in the knowledge that he represents a privileged tiny minority of the population then be caught on arrival for smuggling while in possession of goods and materials that are expressly forbidden under Saudi law? That takes us back to the dominant mental processes of structural and functional societies. Those driven by structural mind sets see the performance of the ritual as the means as well as the end and will generally be the ones who demand that a large entourage of friends and relatives receive them on return from Haj. The act of carrying drugs or gold is part of practical life, Haj is part of religious obligation in divided selves and both need to be kept apart. The real spirit and rationale of the occasion is less significant, if at all. Someone more motivated towards the spirit of Haj would be less inclined to showcase his religious obligation and definitely not get involved in activities that are expressly forbidden.

Minister for Religious Affairs and corruption

Haj for Haajis; Eid for ministry officials!!!!

This year's Haj operations administered by the Ministry of Religious Affairs headed by a minister being a representative of one of the major religious parties in the country degenerated into an embarrassing scandal of corruption and massive monetary bungling. Such was the scale of resentment and protest that the minister, regularly clad in as many religiously holy symbols that can be loaded on one person had to be dismissed. Dismissal of ministers on charges of corruption is a very rare occurrence in our set up since almost every politician, military men included, has skeletons in his cabinet. So this must have been an indefensibly dare devil performance to merit this rare distinction, though it must be added that the charges have not yet been proven in any court proceedings. It does reinforce the point that religious parties and religion's self-appointed ground personnel should never be equated with religion itself.

Social stratification of Haajis

That there was large scale corruption in the organisation of Haj affairs should not come as a surprise to anyone. It is not because of the occasion itself but because those involved come from the same representative breed of limitless greed that cannot see right from wrong. While state functionaries plan their take of financial benefits from arrangements that are so easy to exploit and like all matters, immune from any accountability, affluent private citizens set their stalls for competitive display of resources in the performance of Haj. There are package travels, just as with tourism that offer high luxury comfort in travel, accommodation and other facilities. These include stay in top class hotels and air conditioned tents in Saudi Arabia as well as post Haj excursions in the Kingdom. The quoted prices range from Rs1.5 to Rs3 million per person. That is about more than six times the cost of a state supported official Haj! Some families come back to boost about a very comfortable Haj and *a great family picnic* because many take these package offers for entire families. Does that not generate competition in society to spend more money as a symbol of financial status, irrespective of whether the earning are through legal activity or unlawful, if not through immoral pursuits? Is the concept of Haj not based on equality of all believers of the Islamic faith? When the religious obligation can be offered at a reasonable cost, despite the margin of corrupt practices, is it morally justifiable to spend huge sums instead especially when there are millions of fellow citizens in need of help as they spend life under fabric roofs and exposed to elements of nature?

Implications of contradictory Hadiths

One of the rare universal consensuses amongst Muslims is the belief that the Quran is for them a completely undisputed holy book and one which has remained a totally unedited message from God to His followers since it came into existence. However, the current reality is that Muslims are deeply divided into camps, sects and sub-sects that are not just willing but methodically programmed to resort to violence for the supremacy of their particular brand of religion. So how can the followers of an originally undisputed divine message and by universal admission one that still remains untouched by editorial intervention in the slightest be so rigidly divided on countless important matters from birth to death? A web site that can be logged on at *http://www.quranic.org/quran_article/7/contradictory_hadiths.htm* while confirming that God says that the Quran is protected and free from all contradictions, then goes on to explain the role of hadiths in the development of splinter groups of Muslims. The web site explains that God brings testimony to His statement by the fact that the Quran is His own word. By analogy, the authors deduce that hadiths cannot constitute a source for religion as many clash not only with each other; some are even inconsistent with the Quran. The following illustrative discrepancies are cited as proofs of their contention. The site contains a long list of examples. We can take only the following two as authoritative examples in support of that particular point of view on the issue.

Drawing blood during fast

The first illustrative hadith says; "*Drawing blood violates a fast*". The sources quoted are Tirmizi, Abu Daud, Bukhari. The contradictory hadith states; "*Drawing blood was administered to the Prophet while observing the fast*". Sources quoted include Abu Daud, Tirmizi, Bukhari.

Without taking sides with either hadith, it goes without saying that had drawing blood violated his fast, the Prophet would not have let his blood be taken. This clearly highlights that not only the two hadiths exclude each other but the first also contradicts the Quran. This quotation is taken from three books considered the most reliable sources of hadiths, is evidence of the incorporation of opposing hadiths into books.

Drinking water

The first hadith hypothesises that "*Drinking water while standing was prohibited by the Prophet*". The authority referred to is Abu Daud. The second hadith that contradicts the first one states; "*I saw the Prophet drinking water standing like you and me*". The quoted authority is once again Abu Daud.

The first cited hadith received greater approval among the public but nevertheless clashed with the second one. We often watch especially at sports events followers of practices drinking water in the sitting position and in three gulps, assuming thereby to have performed a pious act.

Whichever is true or more reliable is completely irrelevant for our present discussion. Let us make sure that the argument is not hijacked into contesting the reliability or superiority of different versions. The ground reality is that the followers of any **hadith** remain quite inflexible in their adopted beliefs and those sorts of belligerent stances are often the fuel on which arguments, strong disagreements and confrontations are fed. So why look for corroborative or circumstantial evidence instead of relying totally on the undisputed source? Those who use hadiths to create their own spheres of influence and followings certainly do no service to anyone by taking groups of people from the main body of believers and creating sub-groups that feed their parochial agendas. Surely the way forward in reducing disagreements is in accepting only what is clearly stated in the Holy Book, not individual narrations or apperceptions.

That, however, is easier said than done because those who have built their sub-empires and dominions of influence and control will not suddenly have a change of heart, even less likely let individual or group egos become subservient to the collective welfare of the entire Muslim race. That will require an enormous effort and investment of resource, aided by common sense and tolerance. The theoretical opportunity for reducing one major source of confrontation and friction is clearly available. Getting the message and acceptability across, and creating the awareness is the real challenge.

Glorification of invasions

"You don't have a peaceful revolution. You don't have a turn-the-other-cheek revolution. There's no such thing as a nonviolent

revolution. Revolution is bloody. Revolution is hostile. Revolution knows no compromise. Revolution overturns and destroys everything that gets in its way".
Malcolm X

Like revolutions, invasions are inherently bloody and violently demolish every obstacle in their way. No matter which side sheds blood, it will always be red and fall into the known five categories of blood types, without exception; period. Historians and intellectuals can gift wrap their cases in noble causes for justification, if not glamorisation, the hard realities will not change and pains inflicted on innocent millions cannot be eliminated posthumously. By way of current examples, the pain and tragedy of those Iraqis who died without having anything to do with Saddam or that of the innocent thousands who have died in Pakistan, and according to one report more have died in Pakistan than Afghanistan in the holy war waged by the Taliban in the name of Islam. Some historians will write their version of distorted history in times to come to glorify the misdeeds of Al-Qaeda and Taliban, just as some still glorify the atrocities of Emperor Aurengzeb. What such narrations that romanticise aggression in any name and any religion do is that they instigate vulnerable and susceptible minds into glorification of misunderstood or misconceived causes. That is what has happened to the hundreds of young boys and girls turned suicide bombers, inspired by glorified and romanticised accounts of Muslim invasions at various times in history.

Once indoctrinated the victims believe it is their destiny to enshrine their names in history in the same manner in which they have been taught to believe their ancestors did so in their times. Add to that the promise of a wonderful life of comfort in the company of "*hoors*" in Heaven for all times to come as an instant reward that awaits them, the destruction package is well and truly ready to pass down the assembly line, irreversibly programmed for delivery. The death, destruction and sorrow their misguided actions leave behind for the survivors or families of victims are none of their concern. None of them have ever bothered to insist that their spiritual and political leaders should lead the way on a suicide bombing mission to litmus test real intents. It is therefore important that educational curriculum be drafted in a more responsible way; one in which the negative consequences of wars and invasions are also highlighted no matter how noble or unavoidable each might have been. This potent tool in the hands of the producers of mental software packages for suicide bombings needs to be disabled if any meaningful and long term results are to be achieved. The inherently flawed but unchallenged assumptions injected in young minds also need to be highlighted. For instance, when a Shia suicide bomber blows up worshipers in a Sunni mosque or vice versa, do they go into different Heavens? Both having carried out a religious duty in opposite directions cannot logically be rewarded the same way. Without taking any sides as usual, since both cannot be right, the wrong one will have wasted his life and in that case, which one? The same basics apply to other parallels such as Christian crusades, their equivalent of "*fatuhats*" except that Muslims were on receiving end. In present times one of the most horrible examples is the Israeli occupation – Zionist equivalent of religious wars in pursuit of promised lands.

Jazya

Under Islamic law, **jizya** or **jizyah** a per capita tax was levied on a section of an Islamic state's non-Muslim citizens, who met certain criteria. For instance the said tax was levied on able bodied adult males of military age and other applicable conditions. This was meant to compliment the levy of Zakat on the Muslim population. While Zakat still continues to be discussed and applied, in some cases by use of unreasonable systems, no one seems to remember *Jazya*. This is not a case for advocating its reintroduction but the fact that it is no longer part of present day society is proof that adjustments need to be made and have been made, in some cases pretty much unnoticed to relate to life as it exists today. It is perhaps a good example of why and how, some of the ritualistic practices that were very relevant at the time can and should be redesigned to meet the requirements of today's ground realities. There is a positive message of flexibility in its non-use in present times.

The curious case for Islamic Banking – but for whom?

The concept of "usury" has a long historical life, most of which refers to *the practice of charging financial interest in excess of the principal amount of a loan*, although in some instances and more especially in more recent times, it has been interpreted as *interest above the legal or socially acceptable rate.* Based on this broad definition, the practice of usury can be traced back approximately 4000 years. Criticism has come mainly from the religious institutions of Hinduism, Buddhism, Judaism, Islam and Christianity.

The oldest references to usury are found in ancient Indian religious manuscripts. The earliest such record is from the *Vedic* texts of Ancient India (2,000-1,400 BC), the "usurer" (*kusidin*) mentioned repeatedly as any lender charging interest. Detailed references to interest payments are also found in the later Sutra texts (700-100 BC), as well as the Buddhist *Jatakas* (600-400 BC). Ancient Western philosophers who condemned usury include Plato, Aristotle, Seneca and Plutarch. Criticism of usury in Judaism has roots in several Biblical passages in which the taking of interest is either forbidden, discouraged or scorned. The Hebrew word for interest is *neshekh*, which literally means "*a bite*" and is believed to refer to the exaction of interest from the point of view of the debtor.

The criticism of usury in Islam was well established during Prophet Mohammed's life, the original word used for usury in this context was *riba* which literally means "*excess or addition*".

In a nutshell the charging of interest has been the subject of criticism in all religions at various points in time. There is no known sustained period, especially in modern history during which interest free banking or lending remained in practice or as a burning social issue. My objections to the heavily disproportionate investment of human and financial resource on an issue that impacts directly on not more than 1% of the population at the most is an example of how we have strolled down wrong lanes, ignoring fundamental priorities or the welfare of the majority of the population. Islamic banking is part of the larger Shariat system slogan, which in itself is a politically deceptive and make-belief escape from reality, namely that the introduction or adoption of unclear religious concepts will in itself lead to some miraculous solution to nation's self-created mess.

What the Taliban preach is in their opinion the only pure form of Islamic society. There were many silent sympathisers of their claims without any knowledge of how those claims would turn out in reality. As the forces of extremism started to encroach beyond their previous tribal confines and almost knocked at Islamabad's main entrance, there were sudden calls for swift action to nip the approaching menace in their original strong holds. The dynamics of interest free banking are quite similar in that the overwhelming majority of potential sympathisers have absolutely no clue of the working details. But the single biggest objection one can have to the diversion of resource and focus is that issue of interest free banking has no relationship what so ever to the burning issues that threaten the existence today.

The present limited movement for Islamic banking or interest free lending dates back to the catalogue of fraudulent movements triggered by Zia in the name of religion. For the first time then all conventional savings accounts in banks were renamed under a Presidential Ordinance as "*profit & loss accounts*". In reality and practice, nothing changed on the ground. Just like interest, so called bank profits continued to be declared as percentages of deposits. Surprise, surprise, most banks declared more or less the same percentage by way of profit as they did for interest! But the deceptive change allowed Zia to tick another box in his list of time gaining measures in power in the name of religion. He must have had several laughs in the privacy of his existence about how effortlessly his plans seemed to sink in. Just as everything he did has since then turned to dust, nothing meaningful and productive will come out of this device too for the common man. This propensity of the average citizen to fall so easily for calculated deception is a product of an education system in which attendants think they are being educated, come out of institutions with only years of attendance to count and a certificate or degree at the end. The real success of the feudal stranglehold has been the percentage of population that has been kept away from purposeful education. It is a point already made but worthy of a repeat.

Advocates for Islamic banking base their case on moral and ethical grounds only; a system that they claim is in accordance with Islamic beliefs. Apart from other concerns about the real motives, the more important question is why should a system based solely on religious grounds limit itself to one or two religious principles only? What about higher levels of honesty in financial matters, or following the Islamic calendar instead of the Christian one? After all for purposes of fasting, we follow the month of Ramzan in the Islamic lunar calendar, alter the working hours for business, education and the affairs of the state too. Haj too is performed according to the Islamic calendar, not the solar calendar. All institutions that base themselves in the name of Shariah, whether banks or courts must as a logical corollary adopt the whole religious package, Islamic banking or courts run in conjunction with all other Islamic principles. That by the way, will also mean paying out shares and profit more frequently given that the lunar calendar is shorter than the solar one; which will make it a more even-handed, equitable and generous form of business. That could also imply for instance people reaching the retirement age of 60 years based on the lunar calendar two years earlier than on the basis of the solar year. It would enable the followers of such strict religious interpretations to perform all collateral Islamic duties in the bargain.

What about taxation? A business with claims to higher moral values for conducting its affairs must be more accountable on all its legal obligations. Apart from state taxation in the source country, would it not be better and consistent with their own concept if Islamic banks also paid Zakat on their total income on a voluntary basis? Is there any justification for not doing so? There could of course be a perfectly rational reason for not doing so but it would make better sense for everyone to understand their viewpoint better.

This part of the proposed package will not go down very well with our friends. For the sake of argument, if the lunar calendar was to be made the basis of career management in Shariat courts at all levels, a lot of individuals might opt out of careers in that branch of judiciary for fear of early retirement. Those with rigidly firm beliefs may still opt to pursue their convictions but the majority jumping on the proverbial bandwagon from structural attitudes are more likely to abandon the ship in a rush. If anyone does opt to stay the course out of genuine belief, then fair play to him. People should certainly have far more respect for him than for someone only making selective choices of religious beliefs and practices based on pragmatic convenience or simply to put up a deceitful persona of religious holiness for society's consumption.

This approach whereby activities are seemingly based on religious practices and rituals rather than the underlying spirit and original purpose is further confirmation of the behaviour that reflects features of predominantly structural societies. Their output is also comparatively less than functional societies would normally achieve in similar situations. When purpose and functionality become subservient to form or the visible structure, societies will always progress less and remain continually distracted from priorities, realities and hardships of common citizens. This inefficient employment of resources tantamount to a negligent wastage, especially when resources are scarce and times are difficult.

Amongst several sources of information on the subject is a very different but valid set of reservations on the subject. *Asharq Al-Awsat- Syria's Mufti, Dr. Ahmed Hassoun* decreed to rename Islamic banking as "*partnership*" which reportedly caused uproar in the world of Islamic finance and its followers. Dr Hassoun justified his call for renaming them as "partnerships" by the fact that he was afraid of hearing in the future of "Jewish banks" or "Christian banks," because now there are those who call for establishing "Hindu banks." Dr Hassoun added, "*Faith descended from God to serve man, and not to exploit him; let faith facilitate the life of man, and not to shackle his life.*" This in itself is worthy of serious consideration. The world is already divided into too many confrontational camps to create a new set of financial instruments of division and unnecessary friction.

Similar disproportionate attention and allocation of resource compared to real life issues faced by the common man is in evidence in other areas too. The judiciary's allocation of 17 judges to hear lengthy constitutional petitions is a symbolic example of how the lives and welfare of the common citizen simply do not fit into the current systems of governance.

On 13 Jan 2011, a private television channel by the name of Geo telecast a report based on a visit by one of its field correspondents about a locality in Karachi. It was reported to be just a handshaking distance from the most affluent "*Defence*" residential sectors of Karachi. The video made very painful viewing. If there was ever a juxtaposition of economic contrasts, this was it. Almost everyone in the locality was on drugs. While the cost of living is skyrocketing elsewhere, the correspondent reported that the cost of a small packet of heroin had dropped from Rs50 to Rs5! Every individual captured on camera, including women and children either held a syringe in their hands or drug sniffing paper rolls; pain and desperation etched on every face. They were reported as selling their belongings to buy drugs, belongings that included daily essentials, even doors and windows pulled out of their shattered homes to fetch anything in return. When nothing was left, some tore down their walls to pluck out the steel bars used in construction to sell to willing vultures so they could buy more dr ugs for a few more days.

Drug addicts sitting under open skies with exposed cuts, wounds, ulcers from drug use and decay did not portray a picture that should have a place in the 21st century. Even if this was to happen in some remote corner of the country it would still be a horrible tragedy but for this heartbreak to be played out right under the noses of affluence and seat of provincial governance is an unbelievable moral crime. It brings back graphic flashes of a part of another great poem by ***Faiz***:

انگنت صدیوں کے تاریک و بہیما تلسم
ریشم و اتلس و کمخواب میں بنوائے ہوئے
جا بجا کوچا و بازار میین بکتے ہوے جسم
خاق میں لتھڑے ہوئے خون میں نہلائے ہوئے
جسم امراض کے تپتے ہوے تانوروں سے
پیپ بہتی ہوئ گلتے ہوئے ناسوروں سے
لوٹ جاتی ہے اُدھر کو بھی نظر کیا کیجے
اب بھی دلکش تیرا حسن مگر کیا کیجے

Un ginnat sadiyon ke tareeq-o-bahimana talism
Resham-o-atlas-o-kamkhab mein bunwaye huay
Ja baja kucha-o-bazaar mein biktey huay jism
Khaak mein litharey huay, khoon mein nehlae huey
Jism amraz ke taptey huay tanuroon sey
Peep behti hui, galtey huay nasuroon sey
Laut jati hai udhar ko bhi nazar kya kijey
Ab bhi dilkhas hai tera husn magar kya kijey

Given the insensitivity that prevails in society at present, it is quite likely that some may have changed the TV channel instead of watching this "*boring*" documentary if they accidentally switched to it. At the same time, it is a huge compliment to the young female correspondent covering that report in intensely intimidating surroundings and in her own words, attacked by women on drugs and protected by other women also on drugs. It is the presence of this tiny minority of committed citizens, especially the comparatively enlightened younger generation that lends some faint hope for the future and has so far prevented the total disintegration of society.

Is interest-free banking of any relevance or use to such people living in sub-human conditions? Is there any chance their past, present or future paths will ever cross through banks of any kind? That never was nor will be the concern of the masters of deception. The real plot is that having conceded that some indigenous bankers cannot reach levels of competitive banking efficiency in the international market, this disguise takes them away from a competitive level playing field by creating a sub-market that seeks to attract customers by exploitation of their religious sentiments in place of open competition. Lack of knowledge amongst customers about the true dynamics and role of interest in today's banking operations makes that job far easier than it would otherwise be.

Before we wind up this sub-topic, here is a fact that should raise many eye brows. The system of Profit and Loss Savings Accounts [*PLS Account*] was introduced by Zia in the late 1970s. That dates back about four decades. Having spoken to a number of bankers in Pakistan, there is not a single reported case in public knowledge where a bank has formally declared a loss as far as its deposit holders are concerned while the bank was still in business. Not only that, the so called profit is declared as a percentage of the deposit and that percentage has remained at the same levels as for the rate of interest on deposits in the previous periods. That means the pre-PLS accounting systems have also remained unchanged. The reason is simple. If a bank were to inform its account holders, used to getting fixed rates of interest on deposits for generations, that far from getting interest payments on investment, their deposits have been reduced to the extent of losses suffered by that bank, then belief or no belief, every account holder would make a run on the bank. In today's economic realities, is a fixed interest based monthly return on investment a more assured and preferred option for investment for old age pensioners and other senior citizens with no other income options or the alternate option of having at least a theoretical possibility of no income at all on savings if a loss in incurred, even though in reality none has ever been declared?

So let us move on from our very own WMDs, *weapons of massive deceptions* and attend to the real bread and butter issues of income earners. That will require wholesale review towards policies that address the problems of masses for a change instead of the economic gurus. In the planning phase of this book, I informally consulted around 20 of my former colleagues to list what each considered the top ten problems or concerns that needed to be tackled immediately. In the 200 hundred problems listed in aggregate, not one mentioned interest charged under current banking system as a problem. This was a representative group of people in reasonably good economic conditions who had regular dealings with banks. Those millions who will never have seen the interior look of a bank would probably not even include this in their top 100 problems!

Tolerance – a religious virtue or not?

The Holy Prophet Muhammad (PBUH) is quoted to have said, **"A strong person is not the person who throws his adversaries to the ground. A strong person is the person who contains himself when he**

is angry." He is also quoted to have said, **"When one of you becomes angry while standing he should sit down. If the anger leaves him, well and good; otherwise he should lie down."**

It is highly unlikely that we would hear such quotes from any of the Muslim priests. If any Muslim was to be asked whether the holy prophet himself was an intolerant man or not, the answer invariably would be that he was most tolerant indeed. So how does religious intolerance relate to his teachings then? It does not, just like most other practices on the ground. How can one claim to be a true Muslim by doing the exact opposite of tolerance? The current anger often referred to in conversations is not religious. It is more out of social and economic injustices, and inequalities in wealth and incomes, redirected mischievously towards misconceived religious causes by those who make rewarding careers out of it. What is worth more serious consideration is what will the reaction be when and if a realization sets in that a whole generation has been used and misguided for unholy agendas? How will that affect people's attitude towards religion in future? Will that add up to a service or a disservice to religion in the long run by its self-appointed custodians? As usual very few of us seem to think of the long term consequences of current myopic misdeeds. That will not alter the causal course of history in the times to come. It is something that those at the forefront of such conservative thinking need to consider themselves. The disastrous consequences of their actions now will be visited upon their own future generations.

Doctrine of necessity

Political compromises are decisions to martyr one right, advantage or principle in the hope of acquiring a somewhat lesser advantage or principle in the long run. Experience shows that it is hardly ever worth the effort in the long run and most of the time, both possibilities are lost. Starting with the controversial first application by Pakistan's then *Chief Justice Muhammad Munir* in 1954 through a judgment validating the extra-constitutional use of emergency powers by then *Governor General, Ghulam Mohammad*, it has been used more frequently than the regular intake of painkillers by a patient in great pain. It has become a joke, but it certainly has never been funny. What is necessity? Does a starving man stealing a loaf of bread to keep body and soul together constitute necessity in the eyes of law? For him there could be no bigger necessity. But would a judge who has ruled generously in favour of the law of political necessity make a similar allowance to a hungry thief? That is why it is a cruel joke and still not funny! No one should be above law but by the same token or principle no one should be below it too simply because he is too insignificant in social ratings. Linking law and principles to the socio-economic status or indeed any other criteria is a stab in the heart of the legal system. The patient may survive but will never lead a normal life. That is what the highest judiciary has done to the country. It is part of the feudal mind set again; the rustic pragmatism of not offending the village or tribal chief, in this case the martial law administrator or governor general. It is another example of how governance has been engineered to look after the welfare of the carefully chosen ones only. Judiciary's historically generous use may have saved the jobs of a few Lordships from time to time but each use has weakened the body with additional stabs while it was still recovering from previous grievous bodily harms.

Another recent example of a compromise was the when the government agreed to allow the introduction of Shariat laws in some parts of Swat valley, presumably on the understanding that the local Taliban's would limit themselves to the agreed areas. How strange was that? Laws that are not acceptable for application in Islamabad, were agreed for imposition on behalf of an excluded from consultation population, leaving them to be the sacrificial lambs at the expenses of the saved majority. No sooner had the compromise been made, videos of national image shattering public lashings of male and female victims filled the screens of local and international news media the world over and the Talibans came knocking at the outskirts of the capital. That prompted the military operation which still continues till today. Compromises made on principles that leave both parties satisfied make sense. Those made to shun responsibility or escape more difficult but effective solutions will always back fire in the long run. Our history is littered with examples of wrongs choices, decisions or compromises that have left us worse off every time.

On a lighter note, it seems our forefathers too were in the habit of making wrong choices for centuries. *Mohammad bin Qasim* was the first Muslim General from the Middle East who, at the age of 17, began the conquest of the provinces of Sindh and Punjab regions in the early 8th century. According to historians, his interest in the region arose from the ambition to control the trade route down the Indus River valley to the seaports of Sindh. Little would he have known then that the land he walked on all his life and eventually away from was floating on oil which was to become today's most sought after natural resource and the land that seemed so attractive to him from afar would at the same stage in history hardly have a natural resource worth economic appeal but plenty of poverty and social disorder! The land where our original forefathers came from is now out of bounds for us and can only be visited after meeting tough visa requirements. It now remains territory where thousands in our workforce earn their livelihoods to ensure a better future for themselves and their future generations while the land captured by Mohammad bin Qasim remains nothing beyond a vast desert. How ironic is it now that Muslims in the sub-continent crave for moving back in that direction to earn decent livings, sometimes away from families for years. While many Muslim immigrants have succeeded in getting visas for permanent residence all over Europe and the United States, they are completely barred from that same possibility in the lands from where their first ancestors came!

The Prophet's personal credibility

Several years ago, there was a very insightful comment in social conversation by someone who was not of a religious bent of mind. He said even if he accepted that the Quran was dictated by God, it was the credibility of the source who said so that was most important. Had those who were told that the contents were coming directly from above not had complete and unflinching faith in the honesty, integrity and reliability of Prophet Mohammad, there may not have been a Quran with such global following today if the intermediary between God and man did not have such unquestionable acceptance of reliability. Such is the importance of who says what over whatever is being said.

The near absence of that reality is precisely the tragedy in today's set up. No one believes a word of what the current breed of religious sermonisers and political leaders have to say. They cannot be aggrieved about that reputation because they themselves often do not believe in, even less practice what they preach. Most of them are fully aware of their lack of credibility but in order to stay in the positions of power and financial affluence, they simply cannot afford to be bogged down by morals.

The Bhutto phenomenon

Today's Muslim Leagues, whether A, N, Q or Z are essentially marriages of mutual convenience by various Bhutto hatred groups. If the Bhutto phenomena and his legacy of PPP were to mysteriously disappear from current affairs, would these Muslim Leagues stand to gain or strengthen themselves? They would explode into ten new splinter groups, each suspicious of the other, each gunning for power by front, back or side doors, with no political philosophy except power at all costs. This is an extension of the same mind set in which hatred or fear of real or imaginary enemies is the only unifying bond.

Bhutto was portrayed as a socialist being who sought to destroy the Islamic ideology that we have been brought up to believe is the only definition of Pakistan and the perpetuation of the feudal mind-set has ensured we have never bothered to understand what it means or how the population has been held back by a tiny minority from understanding what the nation's best interests are. People were brought up to mistrust Russia or the Soviet Union as a communist block that can only be an enemy of Islam but at the same time, consider another Communist power, the Peoples Republic of China to be the nation's most trusted ally. In very much the same way, while the country continues to have an enduring love affair with communist friends in China, people find them more trustworthy than their own fellow citizens with leftist leanings. This is not meant to take sides here, but to highlight the massive contradictions that most are comfortable with because the analytical thinking process that develops with awareness and purposeful education has never been part of the development agenda.

Floor crossing

Mirza Ghalib who lived during the 19th century was one of the most respected and popular poets the sub-continent has known, almost equally popular amongst Muslims and Hindus in the region. In one of his numerous well known pieces of poetry he state;

وفاداری بشرط استواری اصل ایماں ہے
مرے بت خانے میں تو کعبے میں گاڑھو براھمن کو

Wafadari, bashart-e-ustawari asl imaan hai
Marey but khaney mein to Kahbey mein garho Brahman ko

Loyalty based on true steadfastness is the real faith;
A loyal Brahman who dies in a temple deserves burial in the Ka`aba

A lifelong supporter of the Labour Party lying on his death bed suddenly decided to join the Tory party. His puzzled friend asked, *"But why? You're Labour through and through. Why change now?"* The man leaned forward and explained, " *Well, I'd rather it was one of them that died and not one of us!*"

We have come a long way since the days of Ghalib. Loyalty is a political liability in today's politics. Legislators are very sensitive about their privileges and have an insatiable appetite for bringing up privilege motions on the proverbial drop of the hat. But self-demeaning acts that keep them on the right side of power are not a problem. Floor crossing, switching political loyalties half way through elected terms were relatively rare concepts not so long ago. In our current political madhouse, not switching sides or loyalties has become a symbol of lack of political acumen.

While in theory everyone agrees that loyalty is a great virtue, when it comes to performing in real life situations, the thought process suddenly becomes subservient to political prejudices. A young political activist, especially during the life time of Bhutto senior, who displayed party loyalty and commitment with intensity, was called a ***Jiyala***. It is difficult to figure out as to why opponents came to treat a *Jiyala* in derogatory terms. Where a political culture is plagued by disloyalty and floor crossing, such a character should be worth his weight in gold. One could completely disagree with his views or conduct but to condemn him for extreme loyalty reflects a mind where all wirings are crossed. The only other political activist with some degree of commitment and consistency was the grass root worker of the *Jamaat-e-Islami*. I can hardly agree with anything said or pursued by the *Jamaat* but for that reason alone one cannot take away a positive trait in addition to the fact that it is not confined to ancestral leadership, rare traits in our society. Muslim Leagues in the country do not have workers. They have leaders and stake holders like wholesalers and retail traders. The committed worker is not part of their culture since there is no ideological centre of gravity. Each of recent Muslim league groups leans on the symbolic respect that Jinnah enjoyed amongst the masses as leader of the original Muslim League. Declaration of association with Jinnah's name sort of compensates the intellectual and ideological void in the current claimants.

"When I point my finger at someone, three fingers point back at me"
Chinese proverb

Whenever the national cricket team has performed poorly in recent years, a committee of the national assembly or senate springs into action, demanding judicial inquiries and issuing summons to cricketers, managers, officials of the cricket board, etc. to appear before them to answer questions. Apart from the fact that some do not understand the fundamentals of the game as reflected in many public statements, the real irony is that they themselves are charged with a long list of offences and malpractices, ranging from financial misappropriations, violations of their own rules of business, floor crossing to fake academic degrees. All seems to slip their minds and conscience in that sudden surge of "structural" patriotism and questions are put by them in a manner that would suggest their own lives are personifications of *"the truth and nothing but the whole truth"*.

The origins of religious sects

Were there any sub-groups of Muslims in the life time of the holy Prophet? We all know the answer. So can a departure from a single brand of Islam be made by anyone after his death? Those who have done so are the ones who insists that the only Islamic way of life and thinking must be based on "*Sunnat-e-Rasul*", the teachings and practices of the holy Prophet himself and that his way of life should be viewed as a model for Muslims. Therefore in the light of their own logic, practicing something that was non-existent in the Prophet's time would constitute a violation of "*Sunnat-e-Rasul*". If it is not so, then other variations in practices adopted by Muslims such as not keeping a beard cannot be condemned for the same reasons for which Muslims can be sub-divided today but were only a unified single group in his lifetime. Not only are there so many religious sects today, each claims to be the only true representative of Islam and is willing to go to war against each other. All that simply does not add up in reasoning except that it is deliberate and richly rewarding hypocrisy.

Video of female lashing in Swat

"I can stand brute force, but brute reason is quite unbearable. There is something unfair about its use. It is hitting below the intellect."
Oscar Wilde

About a year ago, a video of public lashing of a female victim in Swat was suddenly telecast by some private television channels in the country. Religious party representatives called it a conspiracy against religion; a perfect example of equating themselves and their actions with religion itself. Not one had the honesty to clarify their real position on the issue. If in their view such punishment is in according with Islamic principles, then why feel apologetic about it? Why deny the occurrence of an event which in their wisdom is the right punishment for specific crimes? The honest approach would have been to say, yes this is the Islamic way of punishment and we offer no apologies for that. If they believe lashing is not prescribed for the particular charge the victim was said to be guilty of, the only decent position to be taken would have been to roundly condemn that act as un-Islamic and to recommend exemplary punishment for those who took law in their own hands to bring religion into disrepute. Does it make any logical sense to deny being in agreement with public lashing and still call it a conspiracy against religion?

Girl whipping in public in Sudan for wearing trousers

In a news report on Sky News in the United Kingdom on 14 December 2010, a young girl in Sudan was shown in a privately recorded video to be whipped in public, apparently on a public road by two able bodied bullies swinging their whip ruthlessly and randomly until the girl is also struck on the face. All through the whipping the victim is heard screaming in pain. The telecast created an international outcry at the sheer savageness of the treatment. In response, an unrepentant apology was offered by the government of Sudan, not for the inhuman law but for the manner in which it was carried out. The act caused no shame; that it was privately recorded and exposed the brutality of the regime was the only point of inconvenience. The real tragedy in the whole farcical episode is the hypocrisy and double standards in social equations. The victim charged with the heinous crime of wearing trousers in public is lashed mercilessly. The president of the country in which such perverted justice was meted out is listed in international media for war crimes and alleged to have swindled billions of dollars into bank accounts in European countries!

While those are issues for relevant competent authorities to pursue, the misuse of religion for rationalising governance excesses is graphically highlighted. If the manner in which the punishment was implemented was based on religious conviction, then all that the country's authorities needed to say to the rest of the world was that this was based on their religious beliefs, that it was in accordance with their interpretation of Islamic jurisprudence and that the rest of the world can take a running jump. Why carry out a mode of punishment that a country is ashamed to admit or own publicly? Why offer apologies for any act that is based on religious ethics or conviction? May be it has nothing to do with religion after all and the guilty parties are fully aware of their attempted deceit with the sole objective of hanging on to power and promotion of self-interests.

Lack of credibility of preachers

The main reason that the common man no longer has faith in those who preach in the name of religion is because their practical lives contradict their preaching almost every step of the way. So many *Tablighis* [*religious preachers*] talk about leading a simple life and to convey that message by travelling in the most expensive and luxurious manner available simply do not add up. One needs to demonstrate before preaching in order to create even a minor impression, let alone any lasting impact. If any evidence is needed in support of this contention, one needs to look no further than the almost mythical *Abdul Sattar Edhi*, the silent executioner of his social welfare beliefs. His silence has earned him more admirers than all the loud speakers and auditorium mikes used by formal preachers of the country put together. He is a shining little island of honesty, dedication and practical work surrounded by an ocean of dishonest and deceitful sermonizing.

Is it a coincidence that Nawaz Sharif indirectly patronises *Tablighi* activities around his imperial palace in Raiwind made out of unaccountable income sources? Not at all because he derives great satisfaction from an annual gathering under his wings, a gathering that despite being fully aware of his route to affluence will never utter a word against him. It is his show of strength to powers abroad that he has religious following in addition to that of the business community and the feudal lords. Therefore he is the one political figure that the developed world needs to deal with in Pakistan. No wonder anyone who has dealt with him officially or diplomatically at home or abroad in the past, is unwilling to trust him anymore, with the possible exception of Saudi Arabia. Some of the "Wikileaks" documents recently circulated on the internet on this specific subject make this point repeatedly and consistently. Let us as a society try to set our records and reputations in order of some respectability before some of us can set out to preach others.

Enforcement of Ramzan

As part of the Islamisation measures introduced by Zia, a raid was once carried out during lunch time on a restaurant led by a magistrate near the famous Punjab University premises in Lahore for lunch eating Muslims in the fasting month of Ramzan. Amongst the sinners was a senior civil servant, who narrated the story the following day. So what happened to you then was my obvious question? He smiled and added, "*Well all law breakers were hauled up by the police and taken away*". Then he and the invading magistrate had a good exclusive lunch in the chartered restaurant! Everyone knew the political fraudulence in that ban on eating during fasting hours. Most of those arrested from that restaurant that day will have been released after payment of a "*Tasfiyah*" [*compromise*] amount to the police. When we were growing up and right till the time Zia came into power, the concept of "*Ehtaram-e,Ramzan*" [*enforcement of fasting*] was never brought up in social conversation. Those who were fasting never bothered or felt offended if someone else not fasting for any reason had a bite in their presence. It was a popular option in those times for families to proceed to hill stations during the peak of summer heat in the plains of Punjab. During the Zia period, our family took a trip to the now famous for negative reasons valley of Swat for a few days. The month of Ramzan started while we were still out there a couple of days earlier than anticipated in the province of Punjab so we left for Lahore two days later. My elder son was three years of age at the time. The journey from Swat to Lahore was a very long one, especially in the oppressive heat. A couple of hours later, the child felt thirsty. We stopped at a road side kiosk to ask for an ice-cream for the child. The owner refused on the ground that he was strictly forbidden from doing so. We tried to explain to him that the request was for only one piece of ice cream for a three year old child, who even under the terms of religion was not old enough to fast. The pleadings fell on deaf ears. We must have stopped half a dozen times after that and got the same rote memory answer. Eventually a private road side well was spotted when just about a couple of hours short of Lahore. We managed to pull up some water through the suspended bucket and that was given to the child immediately. It was a huge relief for the family but for those that we dealt with on the way, common sense and even the prescribed age for fasting never entered the thinking process. It had less to do with religion itself but more because of the fear and intimidation of military rule using religion as its basis for justification that could have caused a severe case of dehydration in a minor child.

Ignoring long term consequences

The post-Salman Taseer scenario is more alarming than appears on the surface at present. Taseer was a politician with strong views on many issues and expressed them without too much editing that most politicians normally do. History has many instances where strong opinionated leaders have fallen to the bullets of intolerant fanatics. Even if for the sake of argument it is accepted that the fault was entirely with Taseer, if individuals and in particular those entrusted with the task of guarding someone decide that any individual can not only pass judgement but also become the executioner, then where does this stop? He was accused of committing blasphemy by his assassin. If so, there is a law called the Blasphemy Act and Taseer should have been tried under that act in accordance with the very law which he had allegedly violated. The same sentiment can trickle down to lowers levels of governance and religion too, even into private businesses. Given the intense rivalries between various religious groups, if a single follower of one group feels that the leader of an opposing group or his boss in office has deeply insulted the leader of his religious sect and also decides to take decisive action when opportunity presents itself, it could become common practice. There is an old sitting room fairy tale from the city of Lucknow in India. The story goes that a *Nawab* [*local ruler*] disgusted with the antics of an opponent summoned a local scoundrel [*badmash*] and gave him a decent sum of money to slap his opponent in public. The scoundrel took the money and assured compliance but before leaving, paused for a while. The Nawab asked him if he was having second thoughts. The man denied any chance of having second thoughts but said that he was just wondering that in his life, such activities were a routine if not a full time profession. He said that the only thought that crossed his mind was that if the to be roughed up opponent offered him more money in return to slap the nawab on his behalf, what would he do then? As the story goes, the *Nawab* took back his money and thanked the *badmash* for showing him the stupidity of his plans.

There are numerous incidents of political murders in history involving such figures as Lincoln, John and Robert Kennedy, Martin Luther King, Gandhi, Rajiv Gandhi, Liaqat Ali Khan, Benazir Bhutto and others. In each case, a fanatic individual or group has been involved. One can go through details and follow events in each of these eliminations but not find a single example where following the assassinations there was ever widespread support on the streets portraying the assassin as some kind of a hero. There were smaller groups of less vocal sympathisers of Bin Laden following 9/11 but never on a scale seen this time. It is time for society to think again whether this and similar actions should be supported or treated as unacceptable? If there is any consolation, it is that even the largest crowd of protestors has been estimated by organisers to be around the one hundred thousand mark. In terms of the total population, it is still a tiny fraction but it is the trend that needs to be watched carefully.

A dream of a divorce

During the period *Ayub Khan* was president of the country, the then leading religious political party in the country, the *Jamaat-e-Islami* was headed by the fairly respected and learned *Maulana Maududi*. An anonymous citizen had a dream, or so he claimed, in which he uttered the word "*talaak*" [*divorce*] three times to his wife. That in real waking life, under one particular school of thought completes the mandatory knock out count for divorcing a troublesome or an un-resourceful wife. So he approached an intermediate level leader of the *Jamaat* to query whether that word delivered thrice in a dream amounted to completion of the virtual extermination order. To his delight he was told that deliverance had been well and truly done and dusted. That the wife was not part of that dream was irrelevant because even if awake, she had no mechanism at her disposal to reverse the outcome if the magic word had been delivered thrice in full consciousness. It was time for her to pack up and leave!

A group of young progressive students with different views approached Maulana Maududi to seek clarification in a face to face dialogue. Maududi was held in reasonably good esteem by even those who disagreed with what he represented and to his credit he would receive such visitors in the knowledge that a question answer session was to follow. That is another throwback to the far more tolerant society we once had. The students referred to the religious decree by one of his lieutenants and asked whether it made sense? To their delight and relief they were told the interpretation was misconstrued. One of the students therefore requested Maududi to issue a clarification in the press to offer relief to the unsuspecting divorcee. That request was declined on the grounds that it would create unnecessary dissention in party ranks and society. What about the wrong done? What about defending the rights of someone wronged in a reported dream scenario? That matter was trivial and subservient to higher causes and in Jamaat parlance, "*ends justified means*". Therefore if in pursuit of their vision of an Islamic society, some people in the wrong place at the wrong time had to be sacrificed as insignificant pawns; they were destined to be so treated and evidence in support of that was recorded in the palm of their hands.

12

Corruption – Is society a victim or catalyst?

"Sometimes I lie awake at night, and I ask, 'Where have I gone wrong?' Then a voice says to me, 'This is going to take more than one night!"
Charlie Brown

To concede or not to concede; one of many questions

Not a single media report seems complete these days without outcries of unbridled corruption, callous and cold blooded practices in governance and society in general. But when the same sentiment is echoed from a foreign country by a frustrated expatriate individual or any international watchdog organisation, it raises immediate protests of prejudice or deliberate disinformation, etc. If society's own view of its domestic situation is one of uncontrolled and unbearable corruption, it should be seeking all possible help home and abroad to identify and expose it. Just as everyone seeks a constructive role by the national media in highlighting corrupt, unjust governance and socio-cultural practices, so should external evaluations by internationally recognised bodies such as the United Nations or the Commonwealth, etc. be deemed helpful intervention in support of the struggle against injustices at home. If our own perception was one to suggest that a noticeable improvement in national morality was in evidence, there would be some basis for feeling aggrieved but when the general view is one of continual deterioration, why should anyone have issues with those saying the same thing from abroad?

The ground reality is that the present level of choking corruption has a narrow base and is the monopoly of not more than 10 per cent of the population. The remaining 90 per cent may or may not have exemplary morals but are essentially the victims of greed of the exploitative 10 per cent. Why should they, the non-guilty happily shoulder the blame for the misdeeds of a small minority who are as much a demon to them as they are a national sigma internationally? Could the answer again be found in our traditional crises of identity? Can anyone ever deal with a problem without first conceding that he has one?

Serial bluffing

No vested interest gives up its selfish pursuit unless that interest is forced away from it. That is natural and instinctive in human nature and simply complaining about it is like a child's complaint about another child snatching away his toy, though that will happen through an innocent childish desire to be in possession of something. The real bluff does not have a shred of innocence about it and it is certainly not child's play. If there is any innocence, it is in the victims of corruption; being fooled once the shame might be on the manipulator but to be deceived time and time again, the honour must be conferred squarely on the serially bluffed one. By definition, every vested interest has to be a minority, though the percentage of that minority to the total population will vary. Conversely, the majority can never be a vested interest. It will always be the victim for some minority vested interest but any pursuit that is for the good of any majority will most likely be for a good cause or for noble intentions. A large group can be misled into becoming a tool of short term exploitation but that will never be a sustainable position for ever. Weapons of mass destruction at the global level and Zia's Islamisation mask on an evil face at the domestic level are examples of how a majority can be sucked into seemingly sacred causes. With time, however, the process is invariably corrected and there is hardly a surviving vocal supporter of the Iraqi WMDs or Zia's Islamisation.

There is too much emphasis on crisis management in our case but too little, if any, on crisis prevention. Those who have stood to benefit and thrive from the use of traditional weapons of control and subjugation will continue to weave their webs in the name of emotional vulnerabilities especially religion because that is exactly what such moves are; use of religion in a manner that pre-empts opposition. It will take time to change hardened positions set in for generations but a change in perspective is the only answer to bringing about a change in our fortunes. The attempt will definitely counter aggressive resistance but some people can be fooled for some time, everyone cannot be fooled forever.

Expenditure estimate on CATA conference

Spending public funds in a responsible manner is an essential part of good governance. There has always been a psychological disconnection between what is seen as governments and those who are governed in many developing countries. One can go a step further and see even those in positions of power and authority see public funds as the ownership of an organisation that they too are not really part of. That is the extension of historical relationships between colonial rulers and hostile local populations. The fact that the old pattern lingers on till today is symptomatic of the static medieval mental state that has failed to move on with time because the real ground realities and opportunities for a post-independence better life have not changed too much. The deep seated public image of successive Governments since independence has been one of a body of rulers that is not part of them and therefore it can be to be disobeyed and fleeced whenever possible.

Pakistan hosted a prestigious international Commonwealth conference in 1993. As chairman of the organising committee, my first task was preparing an estimate of expenditure on all arrangements which was then sent to the ministry of finance for approval. To my surprise, it was sent back with the query whether it was possible to host the conference in the amount of money requested? That planted some seeds of doubt in my mind too and a revised estimate with a slight increase was re-sent. The approval was received after about a fortnight. When the conference ended with a very high rating by all delegates, we were still left with a small amount of unused fund which was returned to the ministry.

Now comes the interesting part. A number of us involved were surprised that the finance ministry had chosen to seek an upward revision in expenditure that was contrary to the conventional role of seeking reductions. Credit must go where it is due; the original estimate sent by me could have been insufficient to offer all the hospitality, organisational detail and quality of conference halls that were eventually put in place. To that extent it was a good gesture of national spirit in support of an international event. It later emerged that when our original summary was sent, a simultaneous request had been received from another ministry seeking funds for a conference on foreign investment. The amount sought in that summary was roughly 20 times that sought on behalf of the Board of Revenue! Approval of tax conference summary before the huge amount would have had implications of comparison ahead of approval. Once the request for a smaller amount had been referred back, the other request was cleared immediately. The Commonwealth conference was a great success. It leaves one wondering as to what else could have been done for our tax conference in addition to what was actually done that could need twenty times more money? Without implying corruption or foul play, it highlights how public money is spent with a completely different set of financial morals compared to personal funds. The answer lies in the fact that most governments have never shown any interest in the welfare of the majority, who in turn have never seen it as part of them. The only time there was a relationship between the government and the population was in Z.A. Bhutto's government and interestingly most developments that took place then have stood the test of time, starting with the constitution of 1973.

There is obviously no external influence in shaping these types of attitudes. Three factors that can bring about any positive change are effective accountability at all levels, starting with the very top; involvement of the population in decision making through regularly repeated fair elections and purposeful education that creates awareness of rights and responsibilities. Is there any chance that some other nation may suddenly have an uncontrollable surge of sympathy for our current situation and offer to provide these services instead of the country's leaders themselves taking matters in their own hands? If not, can anyone justify or explain the inaction on the part of civil society, except that the obvious to everyone solutions are not in the interest of a privileged group or vested interest within the country.

As low as it gets!

Some might think this is a fairy tale. It is embarrassing to even narrate this but it should give the reader an accurate picture of "*as low as it gets*". One might even wish it was not so but it is "*the truth and nothing but the whole truth*"! If matters have improved now, it would be a miracle but when all other socio-cultural indicators are in inverted perpendicular position, it is hard to image that this type of social greed would have taken a solo U-turn. It is common for parents in our society to browse other families through friends and relatives in search of the right partner for their children, especially for girls of marriageable age. There is nothing wrong with this traditionally accepted practice, as long as it does not force young children into matrimonial contracts under pressure or threats. Some of my colleagues will confirm parents of marriageable girls occasionally used to browse corridors of the Board of Revenue looking to verify from their personal contacts the earning potential of young revenue services officers; satisfying themselves about the "*underground resourcefulness*" of potential sons-in-law! Honest young officers living off salaries alone were seen by this low life breed as "unbranded" and financially unattractive investment. The likes of them then have the audacity to complain about corruption in society when their own incomes and businesses are selected for tax audits. If one were to struggle to reconcile with this most embarrassingly hypocritical conduct, it could only be that this is a very tiny minority. If their kids decide for any reason to marry of their own choice, that will be an affront to their honour and enough provocation to go bloodthirsty at their own young ones, but spreading a bait themselves to net the most corrupt specimen as their own future generation; well what is so fussy about that?

Organs trade

The existence of organised rackets for stealing human parts from ignorant, exploited and helpless persons is often reported in the media. Such set ups have to involve surgeons, anaesthetists, cold storage stockists, kidnappers, carriers of the expensive stolen merchandise, etc. Not one of them falls in an economic distress category that can claim involvement in such greedy and inhuman pursuits as a desperate act of survival. They know what they are doing, that it is immoral and criminal but as long as it lasts and generates silly money, or unless someone involved discovers that his son or daughter was kidnapped and has returned home one kidney less, they will not stop on moral grounds alone. In one incident in Islamabad several years ago, a six year old girl was reported to have been kidnapped from the private drive of her residence. She remained missing for six days and was suddenly seen back home apparently in good health. The parents took a closer look and found a scar in the abdominal area. Medical check-up confirmed that she had come back with one kidney less than when she was kidnapped! The kidnappers, however, did have some morals after all. Before dropping her back home, they decorated one of her wrists with a gold bangle. It was an act of clearing their conscience in cash or kind and for them it was calling it quits. When their misdeeds "*counter*" will have reached a certain level of reading, some might have decided it was time for a Haj or an Umra to seek forgiveness and start all over again with a clean slate. A perfect example of a structural society in which performance of a scared religious duty is deemed enough to wash away misdeeds committed up to that point in time. At the risk of repetition, until the approach to life shifts from rituals and visible role playing in society to placing value on the purpose or spirit of religious duties, current levels of social, moral and financial accountability will not change for the better. Can it get worse? It certainly can and will except that there is not much room now further down that route.

Politicians' safety lockers

Hundreds of millions, if not billions have been taken abroad; not in trouser pockets nor suit cases but through more formal channels; banks or informal set ups that are illegal for a labourer sending his meagre hard earnings to family members back home but the astronomical sums swindled in corrupt practices have never seriously been investigated, sometimes simply for fear of the "*investigator becoming the investigated*" later. Michael Moore once described Congressional inquiries on corrupt practices as usually ending in certificates of clean health. His take was that when congressmen clear fellow colleagues it is not saying they did nothing wrong but simply saying that they did not do anything we would not do or may not have done in the past. Basically a template for mafia scratching each other's back. There is some consolation in there that at least we still remain part of some dodgy international practices and fraternities. It may not be too lonely out there after all for swindlers international!

Interests abroad; politics at home

It will not violate any national official secret information act by stating that the national interests of top politicians, military personnel, judiciary and civil servants are maintained at a minimal essential inside Pakistan, just enough to lead a relaxing and enjoyable life at home. Most of their movable and immovable assets, cash, second and additional homes, education of children, medical treatments, holiday homes and holiday trip locations are overseas, mainly in exotic settings rather than in some troubled societies. So what are their interests at home? Very few indeed, except those that satisfy inflated egos and social personas through privileged treatment, VIP protocol and fast track channels for most activities in daily life. It is the most rudimentary manifestation of a lack of confidence in the effectiveness and durability of national systems and institutions. How do they expect others to come and invest when the indigenous dons feel insecure keeping their mainly illegally and untaxed earnings at home for reinvestment?

The scourge of social status

To put the world right in order, we must first put the nation in order; to put the nation in order, we must first put the family in order; to put the family in order, we must first cultivate our personal life; we must first set our hearts right.
Confucius

One is occasionally led to wonder why senior officers are rarely invited to any family event amongst the lower grades of office staff. In line with our structural society syndromes, existence is slashed into so many artificial segments that individual personalities struggle to cope with the stresses and strains of each such split. Ethnic divides that cannot be corrected by human cosmetic surgeries, religious segregations that expressly unwelcome "*others*", caste competitions that have never allowed merit as the sole or even prime criteria for judgement, civil and military service groups that cannot associate based on self-certified superiority claims and so on. But perhaps the most damaging and sinful of all is the economic stratification of society. It puts the burden of living up to frivolous intra-group expectations, to perform the same insane and punishing rituals of daily life and special occasions to minimum expected standards, to remain part of their respective social set ups or to avoid relegation to a lower league, to put in football terms. Each of these groupings has inherently loaded flaws that outweigh positives, if any. Each such divide is worse than the other and that in a nation or society where Iqbal's famous line is quoted ad nauseous, "*Eik hi suf mein kharey ho gaye Mahmood o Ayaaz*" *[King and slave praying side by side].*

That is mere lip service as with most other aspects of life because in practice, most seek promotion to the highest and seemingly most prestigious socio-economic group, while at the same time looking down on those who fly at lower altitudes. Seeking progression and betterment are natural desires but there is a world of difference between a positive desire and a sick obsession.

Because of such social pressures and expectations, lower income groups often feel hesitant, even embarrassed to involve those they consider very well off in society in order not to expose their lack of economic clout. If someone does endeavour to invite a higher class icon, that invitee will most likely feel equally uneasy at associating with the underprivileged. Not any aspect of the entire description has a single point of merit in this horrible package of flawed values. Such is the intensity of this affliction that there are unfortunate incidences of domestic cooks, not themselves in flattering company, refusing to drink water from the same glass that was offered to the domestic house cleaner from a different religion! Could this person have been born with that prejudice imbedded in his mind at birth? Obviously not, for every infant is born with a clean slate; the concept of "*Tabula Rasa*" dating back to the time of Aristotle which stipulates that the mind of the new born is like a "*white paper*" on which experiences are gradually filled in. Immediately after birth, most conservative societies immediately put up their "*work in progress*" sign boards and transform that *Tabula Rasa* into such a divided and reclusive unit that he is unable to associate with most others in different ways. Most societies do that in varying degrees, but our conservative masters must rank amongst the finest artisans of social disintegration and this in large measure is an attribute of structural societies.

We need to set our hearts and priorities straight, put our families in order before society as a whole can improve. Charity must start at home, so too must reform and correction.

13

Leaders and unsung heroes

The continent of Africa is full of fascination and unique experiences. The one that is relevant to the current issue is the way in which wild life operates in many parts of Africa. In 1992, I had the experience of an overnight stay in a tent in the midst of wild life in the famous *Masai Mara National Reserve,* a large game reserve in Kenya.

It is famous for its exceptional population of Big Five and the large cat family. Every year from July to October, most animals undertake a migration to the north into Tanzania, a gathering so massive that it is called the Great Migration. Wild life video recorded documentaries showing the event make a fascinating viewing. It is probably one of the most impressive natural events in the world. Several estimates claim that around 1,300,000 wildebeest, 500,000 gazelles, 95,000 antelopes and over 200,000 zebras amongst other smaller groups are involved in the mass exodus. They are followed all along their known annual circular routes by the usual predators such as lions and hyenas making sure they do not relax while proceeding on holiday!

Despite this unbelievable organisation and regulated annual timing, there is one important element that is non-existent and that is leadership; no intellect, civil society or vision for the future otherwise they would not migrate to new pastures each year in the company of their traditional predators. That attribute is reserved for the human species; that is one of the few important characteristics that sets the two groups of species apart. Unfortunately, that attribute is often also the cause of misery and downfall of many races, nations and societies of human beings because unlike animals, human leaders have the ability to redirect people in their desired directions. Leaders are in that sense the helmsmen or the curse of the human race depending on who emerges or ends up where and when. Good leaders, especially those who contribute to shaping history, therefore need to have special attributes that ordinary mortals are not blessed with.

Prisoners of history

Nelson Mandela is perhaps one of the most towering leadership personalities to have walked on planet earth during the past century. I had the privilege of visiting the former prison on *Robben Island* in South Africa where he along with his close associates spent substantial parts of their lives in subhuman conditions. Mandela was the longest resident prisoner for 27 years; so easily said but an eternity in a real life time. So how could anyone so persecuted, mentally and physically abused for so long react with a "*reconciliation commission*" that covered even those who treated him so instead of plotting instant revenge, once the tables were overturned completely?

When Mandela was on his first official visit to the United States after assuming power in South Africa during the presidency of Bill Clinton, his reception in Washington was an event that was telecast live by many international channels. Clinton as his host and a gifted orator made an excellent speech. During that he shared his interaction with Mandela with the audience. He said he asked Mandela as to how did he feel towards those who had kept him behind bars in deliberate humiliation for almost 3 decades? Whether he felt anger or hatred or an urge to take revenge? According to Clinton in that live telecast speech, the reply was that Mandela felt that he had been a prisoner for so long, he just wanted to be a free man. Had he opted for a campaign of vendetta and revenge, he would have remained their prisoner all his life and never really a free man in his own mind. The capacity to exclude unpleasant past experiences from affecting current thinking or future planning is a great asset for any healthy mind. For visionary leadership, it is an absolute must.

Learning from past experiences is great, getting trapped in the past is a great tragedy and nothing positive has ever come out of such static attitudes throughout history.

Visions – dreams of realism

A vision is a hypothetical dream, well thought out, seen with eyes wide open, based on realistic possibilities, set into a definite and consistent direction, with steps allocated into time frames. Within all this apparent rigidity or inflexibility is the vital ingredient of flexibility for change and adaptation based not on avoiding temporary inconvenience or the stress of taking honest and difficult decisions but on the visionary prognosis of changing circumstances dictating appropriate adjustments. Reverting to Jinnah, the two quotes from him about the future direction of nationhood clearly demonstrate that there was no ambiguity in his mind as to what were clearly acceptable guidelines or not, as core values of governance and policy direction.

But what options do we have at present? A leader cannot lead without having a clear vision, based on knowledge and formal education of his clearly defined goals and directions. He naturally cannot lead if he does not himself know which way he is headed.

Sunday Market Revolutions

Those who make peaceful revolution impossible, make violent revolution inevitable
John F. Kennedy

There are often unmistakeably discernable economic types amongst voters that align with particular political parties. When the Pakistan Peoples Party was created, a new political terminology of "*roti, kapra aur makaan*" [*bread, clothing and housing*] was launched. It captured the imagination of the masses because for the first time a politician made an economic slogan the basis of his election manifesto. Prior to that, party differences were usually in terms of variations in the same ideological positions and slogans, with the exception of one secular party in the north-west province of Khyber Pukhtoonkhwa. If the masses felt neglected by political leaders in the past, all evidence today suggests that the feeling has now aggravated into one of severe seething antagonism.

In comparison with the urban working class and rural peasants, urban shop keepers of most descriptions, middle level businesses particularly those affected by the nationalisation policies of Bhutto aligned on the opposite side. They still continue to do so till today. The overwhelming majority of wholesale and retail shopkeepers support Nawaz Sharif. *Bread, clothing and housing* were never their issues in life; they were and still are driven by greedy motives of preserving ill-gotten wealth and their social privileges over their working class. Now this is the interesting bit. The overwhelming majority of down trodden, illiterate urban based workers, rural farmers and tillers of agricultural land associated strongly with Bhutto, himself educated in top institutions in the west, knowledgeable, articulate and used to a visibly modern style of living. The comparatively literate, though not necessarily knowledgeable shop keepers and small businesses identify with a far less educated and hardly articulate Nawaz Sharif and other factions of Muslim Leagues. There appears to be no role for religious ideology in this divide! The divisions are essentially based on economic perspectives and priorities. One top international politician was once quoted to have remarked that Bhutto was too educated a leader for a developing country but is it not strange that within the country those at least on paper who had some claim to education failed to associate with him, while those totally deprived of literacy identified with his policies and most of those still do so till today? Is there something fundamentally wrong with the education system? Another interesting noticeable trend in our society is that while in most countries in the world, students tend to be progressive compared to conservative influences elsewhere, in most of Pakistan's colleges and universities, student unions are dominated by the student wings of major religion based political parties. The education system simply does not impart knowledge or education that is directly relatable to improving the quality and understanding of life. Most of those who come out of their schools, colleges and universities have nothing more to count on except the numbers of years spent there. Those with religious bent of mind, however, do manage to infiltrate important state institutions as part of the political strategy and that influence has been visible in the trends, performance and priorities throughout our history. A fundamental change in the social psyche is required if the trend is to be reversed and there is no sign on the horizon of that happening under existing set ups.

Consequently there is recurrent talk of a pending or approaching revolution in many circles and in the media. Talk from those who probably have never read a word about famous revolutions in history or any other book of knowledge for that matter, even from those who should logically be the natural targets of a peoples' revolution. It is almost like fashion talk at present. When feudal landlords and business tycoons talk about leading a revolution of the exploited population, it amounts to saying that the head of a top political party plying its trade in the name of religion will lead a fight for a Communist revolution in the country. It betrays either a hypnotising performance in hypocrisy worthy of an Oscar award or an appalling ignorance of history or understanding of the current domestic situation. Neither is helpful or of relevance to the current state of affairs. Any organised revolution cannot logically be cooked from existing ingredients but if the ruling class continues to remain totally insensitive to the ever increasing misery of the common man, violent anarchy is the more likely outcome in the absence of any revolutionary leadership. Those making light of developments and thinking of hijacking a potential violent upheaval will be the first ones to board flights into safe havens abroad where their riches have always been waiting in residence for decades. Every stake holder who talks of revolution seems to do so with a childish fantasy in which those who they dislike or are inconvenienced by and seem immovable at present will be washed away, opening the way for their turn to assume the throne and recommencing their unfinished business of plundering the nation's wealth. Thinking beyond that is a step too far.

Imran – A Shakespearean Tragedy

In our dark and depressing recent three decades, if there were two flickering lights of hope for any revitalization, those were firstly, Imran Khan's potential as a leader with integrity, respect and achievement on the ground; the second was progressive stewardship under a revitalised judiciary which has already been discussed. Post retirement, when Imran launched his cancer hospital project with high sounding ambitions, many had reservations about the likelihood of success in what seemed an over ambitious and somewhat larger than life project. But he pursued and persevered with single minded dedication. My reservations too were proved to be without foundation and a gross underestimation of his strong character. Misjudgement of his determination was a defeat well worth the suspicion at the time. But more needs to be said on him and his later political role. When the last election schedule was announced, I made a conscious effort talking to anyone I bumped into who spoke about corruption in Pakistan to vote for someone who was not corrupt instead of making the "*always do*" choice and ending with the "*always get*" result in return.

If there was to be another election in the foreseeable future, would I again position myself for the same line of argument? To be honest, I am not too sure now. Is his integrity no longer worthy of trust? For financial integrity, the answer would still be yes he can be trusted on that account, unless I am completely ignorant of facts to the contrary. What about intellectual integrity? Well one would still probably trust his moral integrity though not without a few reservations. However, for moral integrity to be collectively productive, it needs to be a function of vision and a sound sense of judgement. On both counts, unfortunately and regrettably the position now is very indeterminate indeed. No one seems sure now what Imran really stands for? Is he a liberal, of left leaning political inclinations, a progressive leader, clear in his vision and direction for the future, a good student of history, owner of a mature and balanced analytical mind that does not lend itself easily to hearsay, prejudices and personal revulsions or just a clean shaven cleric? On each of these counts, the confidence of many of his earlier supporters is left in despair, hope so dampened that one could easily and repeated tear one's limited crop of hair apart several times over. As emphasized earlier, a leader cannot lead if he does not know which way his destination or direction is. All other qualities fall by the way side if the ability to analyse issues dispassionately and in a mode totally detached from futile traditions and unproductive sentimental pursuits cannot be ensured. Above all, if a leader cannot live in his contemporary time and link those conditions to the collective future, then failure and frustration, if not disaster is almost guaranteed. Having dug himself so deep in is opinionated trenches, he seems most unlikely to suddenly dust himself out of those bearings and take off in purposeful and productive new directions. Let us hope he has the ability to prove us all wrong again but his present political billboards do not inspire any confidence whatsoever.

The once adored youth icon who as the nation's beloved son, only political entrant with large acceptance of integrity, educated in premier educational institutions, home and abroad, he should have been shielding and guiding the youth's crisis of identity, not driving a bigger wedge in profusely open and bleeding wounds. Such is the force of uncontrolled and irrational hatred that it provides the shortest and fastest route to self-annihilation without any guiding assist from a satellite navigation system. In a very recent interview in a local network, Imran passionately argued for mid-term polls. Not letting an elected government complete its term has been the biggest argument and "get out" clause to cover for failure. Even without that argument, building systems should always be a higher pursuit than changing it to deal with any undesirable individual or a party. His main argument in support of mid-term polls was excessive corruption. That may be absolutely true but that precisely was the main argument that was used to disrupt many previous elected governments. What about the precedence setting by him? Shakespeare famous words in Macbeth "*that we but teach bloody instructions and which being taught, return to plague the inventor*" might come back to haunt him some day, if his latest wish was to be granted. Supposing mid-term elections are forced on the nation and

Imran's party wins the election. A year later all others get together on any pretext and demand mid-term polls again. What will his stance then be? If that thought has ever crossed his mind but he still cannot overcome his anger towards his usual suspects to even discipline himself, it does not paint a promising picture of change for the future under any potential leadership role for him.

The curse of lost opportunities

That leaves us very short of an alternative leadership package that can be trusted and have the ability to analyse the genetics of the current mess and deliver a change that can redirect the nation towards a brighter future. His obsession with support for fundamentalism, or at least his inability to condemn it, hold it guilty of our present abyss may never set his mind free to do what is the need of the hour. This has been one of the major recent tragedies. A colossal loss of opportunity for a seemingly cursed society; consumed in its own prejudices, stewing in its own juices of ignorance and a crippling crisis of identity. The number of times Imran has spoken out in favour of "*deeni madrassahs*" would suggest that his own children will have been allowed nowhere near any other system of education but as far as common knowledge goes, they have been the beneficiaries of formal, modern, and development oriented education. Should anyone grudge that? Not in the least. On the contrary, every student or would have been student who acquires knowledge and education that keeps him away from the killing fields of religious fundamentalism is one less tragic liability on society and the nation. One hopes Imran's children will grow up without the baggage of recent political bitterness that the present generation simply find to tightly appended to their existence to shake off in this life. That is why this is the equivalent of a write-off generation of political actors.

Until people stop making excuses, stop blaming everyone except themselves for the current disarray, take responsibility, make things happen at the level each one can manage, act as drivers of change, current conditions will continue to drift towards more destruction.

What we do today is what will be our history tomorrow. If we do nothing now, there may not even be a history to write about.

It was Imran's good luck and Pakistan's too that the cricket world cup final in Melbourne was played against England. That team was fortunately not led by a Musharaf, Zardari or an American. Had it been so, Imran would have probably lost the plot and we would have lost the trophy. For whatever reasons, real or imaginary, a reference to any of those three "*red flags*" immediately induces a "*red card*" reaction striping him off all ability to think objectively. Walking out on to the pitch that day, he might have dropped his equanimity down the pavilion stairs, told Wasim and company to forget about wickets or winning and probably said instead, "*Come on boys, just bowl beamers at them, till death do them apart*"! As another benchmark, if Jinnah had been alive today, would he have approved of Imran's political leanings or analysis? Jinnah certainly would have gone into a deep depression listening to some of Imran's political and strategic directions, if at all there is any specific direction. To fancy that an independent judiciary would be the be all and end all of our sufferings so deeply rooted in decades of ignorance, exploitation and neglect amounts to saying that global warming could be sorted out by sprinkling pure cold water in the ozone layer.

If there was a choice between alternates for ensuring financial integrity in a national disaster relief project, I would still tilt towards Imran far more than all other candidates, but trusting his judgement in leading the nation towards a bright and progressive future seems a bridge too far for him. That to me is one more national tragedy in a painfully long list. If Imran had been around when Shakespeare was weaving his literary magic, he might have been tempted to add a fifth tragedy to his "famous four", *Hamlet, Othello, King Lear* and *Macbeth*!

Judicial extermination of a political icon

There are turning points in the history of all nations; some for turning positive corners, others setting them into tragic directions. In our case, that tragic turn undoubtedly has to be the execution of Bhutto and the arrival of Zia. Apart from the judicial witchcraft stage managed by Zia and his selection of poodle judges who volunteered to be happy signatories to a judgement drafted before the trial began, it was the permanent political divide along lines of mutual hatred right through the middle of the nation followed by Zia's gleeful jump into the holy jihad against the Soviet army in Afghanistan. The consequences of both those decisions are at the very foundation of our current potentially disastrous mayhem.

For the current young generation who were fortunate enough to arrive after Zia died, the following brief narration of events recorded by *Tariq Aqil* on December 7, 2004 in a Special Supplement on the eve of 25th Death Anniversary of Z.A. Bhutto in 2004, captioned "*Judicial Murder of a Prime Minister*" is a good reproduction of the fateful night that put a permanent spell of curse on the nation. "*2:00 AM, 4th April 1979, Central Jail Rawalpindi. Zulfiqar Ali Bhutto first elected Prime Minister, former President and former foreign minister of Pakistan was informed by his jailers "Its time". He was removed from the death cell and taken to the gallows or "Phansi Ghar" [execution chamber] for execution. The word had leaked out among the inmates of the jail and the melancholy quiet of the night was now punctuated with recitations from the holy Quran. Head held high, in proud defiance, Bhutto walked the short distance to his place of execution, his tryst with destiny, and the final act in his turbulent chaotic and historical career. Tara Masih the official executioner and hangman tightened the noose around Bhutto's neck and now in the eerie silence of that macabre scene those present heard Bhutto's final words "Finish it, Finish it".*

Whether someone likes it or not, no one can change the real facts of and events in any history. Even if we wanted to forget it all, we are reminded everyday of our current lives of the outcome of such acts of vendetta because of the obsession of the ruling class to deny and defy the rights and political will of the majority of the population. An attempt was made by Zia to wish away Bhutto's period in power by deleting that period of history from the subject of "Current Affairs" in the academic syllabi of text books for school children for a number of years under a Presidential directive. Obviously that did not work as several subsequent election results showed; they never have throughout history.

Now here is the fundamental question. If the accused had been any other political leader at the time, firstly would the outcome of the trial have been the same? Secondly, would those who supported the outcome at the time and distributed sweets to celebrate an execution still feel proud of their support for that phony trial and their personal misjudgement? If the answer is still "yes", then should any such person have any justification for complaining about the lack of rule of law in the country today? That support could only have come from either a poor understanding of socio-political dynamics or through the thought process of a mind captivated by irrational hatred that blocks off all avenues of rational thinking. Neither can be a compliment and none is intended, nor deserved.

Zardari

This might initially shock some readers but in a strange way, Zardari looks like a very straightforward man! It is difficult to recall a single occasion where he has come out to even try to explicitly defend himself against charges of corruption. There is a common saying amongst information technology experts, "*what you see is what you get*". That is basically what his body language seems to suggest; very few pretentions of piousness, exemplary morals and so on. That leaves little room for high expectations. He has changed the very fundamentals of Bhutto's Peoples Party. One cannot cut away from the traditional core support of a political party, carry on the business and expect the traditional support as usual. He has put the party to a major political by-pass surgery, transplanting a Bhutto family heart with a Zardari family one. The real damage will become clearer once he is out of power. For the moment, there will be plenty of support from those whose only political philosophy is "*to Hell with morality and principles*" as long as life is comfortable "*here and now*"; shades of existentialism in that approach but sadly for the worst possible reasons.

By ending up in the presidency, Zardari has played a kind of master stroke for his political longevity, because he has placed himself in control of the epicentre for premature dismissal of all previous elected governments within a democratic set up. The establishment, with its blurred definition is struggling to find an alternate method of dismissal of an elected government with their traditionally effective firing trenches occupied by those who were always fired upon. As a result both sides are continually involved in a never ending wrestling match while the country and its population watch in "*shock and awe*", afraid to take sides openly for fear of betting on the wrong horse. Not much can be said about *Zardari* at the moment because there is nothing substantive to report on.

Nawaz – package of everything wrong with society

Nawaz represents everything that is morally and intellectually wrong with society. He does not shape events; events and developments shape him. By way of illustration, he thought he had a vote winner in suggesting that the nuclear scientist *Dr. Qadeer Khan* would be his candidate for the office of presidency but Khan in turn painted a most uncomplimentary picture of Nawaz in a subsequent television interview. There are dozens of other similar instances. Like his political mentor, he can deny anything that most cannot or would be too embarrassed to do so; or even claim credit for situations in which he was either never involved or held the opposite view at the time. There is a video still accessible on the popular "*YouTube*" web site that is a great illustration of the point. It shows Nawaz addressing the local press after he was out of danger and under some kind of protective assurance from the Saudis in which he is seen boasting about his heroics of defiance despite mortal threats from Musharaf before leaving for Saudi Arabia in the company of *"all the king's horses and all the king's men"*. His claim was [**Quote**] "*But I took this stand the very day Musharaf came and there was an atmosphere of deep fright in the country at the time, but I said you can kill me if you want, or do anything else you want but I will not stamp my signature on this paper. My conscience does not allow me to do it, my spirit of patriotism does not allow me either, my love for Pakistan does not allow me to sign it.* [**Unquote**] While that declaration of self-certified chivalry is visible in the background, an inset figure of Hariri who was credited with brokering the escape agreement between Nawaz and Musharaf, confirms his role in the palace intrigues [**Quote**] "*When Mr Sharif was in prison in Pakistan, I was the person who came back and forth and made the agreement for the release of Mr Sharif out of Pakistan*" [**Unquote**]**.** The reason why Nawaz represents everything wrong with our society is because the foregoing brief can be a perfect fit under most chapters such as "*hypocrisy*", "*double standards*", "*fall in intellectual standards*", *"corruption"*, etc.

His biggest shortcoming is his abrasive ego run on below average intelligence fuel. When Benazir first came to power, it was against all odds. She had a very thin majority of 3 or 4 seats in the National Assembly, faced with a very hostile president in Ishaq Khan, the then army chiefs, media, judiciary and at least two provincial chief ministers. Despite those odds she managed to hang around in power for 18 months.

In the elections that followed, Nawaz's party was helped into power with extra seats through rigging [subsequently publicly confirmed by an ex-chief of Inter-Services Intelligence in a different context]. Nawaz started with almost a two-thirds majority of elected seats, a very supportive president, army, media, judiciary and friendly governments in all four provinces. He lasted two years! In that short period, he managed to offend his benefactor president [*Ishaq*], the army to the extent that the well-respected army chief at the time suddenly died in somewhat controversial circumstances and there were suggestions in some quarters of foul play by Nawaz though nothing was ever proved. His supporters also scaled the boundary walls and stormed the building of the Supreme Court because the then chief justice had differences with him. Many in the press and electronic media who flirted with him during his route to power held different views about him by the time he was shown the door in the traditional way. It requires special ability to offend so many friends in such a short space of time and Nawaz is well equipped with those attributes.

It is not worth devoting more time and space on the subject. The more inquisitive can check out the details for themselves on http://www.youtube.com/watch?v=44dRR-Wf-yg

Political vision and "jacket-potato" politicians

Apart from these options, there is precious little by way of alternates. A few heads of parties that ply their trade in the name of religion and have brought the country to where it is today hardly constitute an alternate option. The image and reputation of politicians, including army men turned politicians amongst the public is in tatters. A lot of engineered or cloned parliamentarians are on show now. For want of a better description, the representative appearance is like a human version of the jacket potato. A jacket of sorts of relatively recent origin, open at the front with over fed bellies bulging out like the fillings in the fast food version of jackets potatoes. In all probability, in many cases the internal content is not too dissimilar; fattening and with little nutritional value. The belt used with trousers is a good monitor of the waistline of the user. An increase or decrease is noticeable to the user straight away. The fabric chord used to do the belt's job on the "*shalwar*" [*local traditional dress*] is unlimited in its generosity. The user would hardly notice a difference of even 12-inches in extended waistline. Metaphorically it can provide service to two users simultaneously though that is purely a hypothetical illustration to emphasize that for those lacking in weight or health consciousness, its use is not recommended.

The reason that particular dress has become more common in recent years is that with political reputations as they are, a fall back to a visible dress form that is meant to encompass a more patriotic look is a useful cognitive digression for the user and in his wishful opinion, limits the damage to his image to some extent. The extent to which the deceptive dress code card is played by some politicians can be seen in the following incident. During Nawaz Sharif's period in power, an agreement for the avoidance of double taxation was negotiated and concluded with a Muslim country in the Middle East. The signing ceremony was scheduled to be held in the Prime Minister's House Islamabad in the evening. As the principal negotiator of the agreement on behalf of Pakistan, I was directed to be present on the occasion. At the scheduled time, I reached the venue in a normal suit and tie. As I entered the ceremony hall, security and protocol staff reacted with a strange sense of annoyance and discomfort, asking me why I had not come dressed in a *Sherwani*? I explained that firstly, there was no instruction for a specific dress code and secondly, I did not have a *Sherwani* to wear anyway. But they insisted that I go back immediately and return with the change in dress. Alternately, the advice was that when the Prime Minister arrives for the ceremony, I should hide behind a specific pillar to remain out of his sight because as they put it, he was very stern about the dress code and would be very upset to see that a government functionary had dressed differently. My response was that if my presence was not essential at the signing ceremony, there was no point in hiding behind pillars and that I would prefer to leave instead. Even though it did not go down well with Nawaz's loyal servants, I left the premises to let someone else in a *sherwani* do the job instead even if he did not understand a single word in a rather technical document.

What signing the bilateral agreement and the ceremony represented was not important for the ones in-charge of proceedings on the day nor did they have the faintest idea what a very technical agreement on complicated tax clauses meant. Wearing a *Sherwani* was the be all and end all for them. Incidentally earlier today Nawaz was shown on local TV channels making a political statement. He was dressed in a formal suit with a bright red tie! So what was the fuss about compulsory *Sherwanis* while he was in office? Was he more patriotic when in office covered in *Sherwani* or dressed in a western suit on another day when accusing his opponents of being the carriers of all conceivable evils? The fact of the matter is that most of our leaders have wasted valuable time on such issues which are irrelevant in themselves and which these leaders themselves adopt only as political gimmicks.

Unless a new breed of young, educated and liberated leadership emerges outside of the feudal stranglehold, continuing to rely on the present lot is bound to end in more tears.

Unsung heroes

It is a sad fact of the our political life that not a single top leader from any national or provincial political party stood out openly in support of Bhutto during the period of his mock trial and subsequent judicial murder. The unorganised struggle against Zia was defiantly led by two female leaders, his wife *Begum Nusrat Bhutto* and daughter *Benazir Bhutto*. It is an insulting reflection on all those conservative political leaders who scoff at the idea of a woman leading a political party, let alone the nation. There was, however, a third figure of open defiance and steadfastness in ***Yahya Bakhtiar***, an Attorney General in Bhutto's cabinet who took up the challenge of defending Bhutto in the Supreme Court in the face of intense intimidation outside the court room and deliberate contempt and ridicule by those judges on the bench who were dancing to the military tunes played from the presidential palace. He must go down as one of the most unsung and underrated heroes in the nation's history.

On the same note, it would be unjust not to pay premier tributes to those judges on the bench who withstood great pressure and intimidation but passed judgement based on their independent judgement. Just before the trial, Zia replaced the non-compliant chief justice at the time [*Justice Yaqub Ali Khan*] with his stooge *Justice Anwar ul Haq*, who the common man in the street at the time referred to as the Chief Injustice of Pakistan. A full bench of 9 judges started the hearing. During the trial period, that number was reduced to seven. ***Justice Qaiser Khan*** retired from service and ***Justice Wahid ud Din*** suffered a stroke. Both were men of independent thinking. ***Justice Dorab Patel, Justice Haleem Sidiqui,*** and ***Justice Safdar Shah*** were the three surviving judges who adjudicated as they deemed right. They were truly worthy of the title of an independent judiciary. About the four judges who signed the death sentence judgement drafted in Zia's presidency, the less said the better. They, and even more so, *Justice Maulvi Mushtaq* the despicable chief justice of the Lahore High Court who passed the initial death sentence, will forever remain repulsive scars on the country's judicial history.

There were many others; intellectuals, lawyers, student leaders, leaders of working class, even some from performing arts who offered resistance in varying degrees with consequences ranging from physical extermination to imprisonment sentences on unproven charges. All of them should qualify as unsung heroes in the nation's darkest hour of history.

14

Israel – Masters of deception & digression

While most religious extremism in the Muslim world is home grown, there is one global external factor that outmuscles all other indigenous competitor causes. So credit then where it is due! No other single factor has so pig-headedly frustrated strategies for curbing religious extremism in the Muslim world than the attitude and behaviour of the state of Israel and the "*advance permanent pre-arrest bail status*" it has enjoyed in international affairs for nearly half a century now.

The Israeli leadership is either completely deluded in its assessment of ground realities or is living in imaginary castles in the air which they somehow see as so well insulated from earthly threats and so impregnable in their defence capabilities that events on the ground never have nor ever will pose to them a threat of any kind.

The strategy and thinking process are totally flawed. If the strategic assumption is that excessive force will eventually tame the other side into a timid submission, evidence to-date suggests the opposite. Have the militant wings in the forefront of struggle for liberation of territories occupied by Israel weakened or become stronger as time has gone by? Will the trend reverse in the future or the quantum of arms of combat become larger and qualitatively more destructive in times to come? There is only one answer to both questions and the whole world knows that. Those who have been without a homeland or shelter for decades will not suddenly break down and call it a day. It has not happened till now and will not ever happen in the future. The strategy has nevertheless lent itself as a cause for not only genuine anger and disgust for millions, it has also allowed those with destructive minds and agendas the perfect "*justification clause*" needed to propel any call for arms in the name of aggression, exploitation or simply sacred religious duty.

The persecuted executioner

First things first! Before the rapid fire anti-Semitism shots can be fired, let us get this out of the way. The state of Israel is one matter, the entire Jewish race a completely different matter, just as criticism of Muslim religious extremism and its unholy alliance with the feudal grip on Pakistan's political fate is not criticism of religion itself or the entire national population. Despite this unequivocal clarification, if anyone tries a different spin, it can only come from either motives of deliberate dishonesty or simply poor comprehension. Both are not worthy of undue attention.

While sticking with the honest conviction that most problems currently faced by Muslims including extremism are largely of our own making, there is one external factor that provides fuel for exploitation and incitement of domestic frustrations and angers into a seemingly just cause. There is no way anyone can defend rationally the role that the state of Israel has played since its occupation of Arab lands in the war in 1967 and that it still continues to play by its incremental encroachment and annexation of disputed territories by unlawful settlement constructions. Far from feeling under any pressure or embarrassment at its conduct and lack of respect for international opinion, it almost sticks out a dare devil virtual finger in an obscene gesture to the international community. It seems to feel so securely insulated from any threat or retaliation for its arrogant conduct that it walks in and out of negotiations with the Palestinians under a planned time gaining strategy that suits its settlements construction schedules.

When many of us try to discuss emotively sensitive issues with our friends and fellow citizens, there is no way we can defend allegations of favouritism, high handedness, duplicity in policies and practices, and in the frequent disproportionate use of force on civilians by Israel that is meant to be less a response to specific incidents and more a symbolic demonstration of muscle for general intimidation. The single biggest factor outside the activities of the Muslim race itself that has aided the enlistment of sympathisers of religious extremism as a supposedly pious cause is the provocative, insensitive and taunting attitude of defiance and disregard for international opinion by Israel.

A painful and damaging love affair

In the post-Vietnam war era, the United States has repeatedly tangled itself in many situations in its international dealings and operations that have given rise to hostility towards it in many parts of the globe, culminating in the insane and greedy invasion of Iraq. The regime change drama later on was as big a deception as that of WMDs itself. But that too is irrelevant to the case in point. During the intervening period it can also take some credit for its intervention in stopping the massacre in Bosnia. The general global adverse reaction and reputation is above all due to one particular role that the United States continues to play by way of total insensitivity towards the feelings and perception of the international community of its unconditional love affair with Israel. Israel occupied massive chunks of Arab land in the 1967 war, which is quite common in wars. However, what is unparalleled in modern history is the brazenness with which occupied territory has been retained, steps taken to perpetuate that occupation and the blatant deceptions put in motion to digress from accusations that the occupation is totally illegal and needs to be reversed. Four years after the 1967 Middle East war, a deadly conflict broke out between Pakistan and India commonly referred to as the December 1971 war. That dismembered Pakistan leading to the creation of Bangladesh. During that conflict, India managed to occupy over 1000 square miles of territory along the borders of what is now the state of Pakistan and had in its custody over 90,000 prisoners of war following the demise of the then East Pakistan. Within a period of a few months, a summit meeting diplomatically promoted and supported by the international fraternity took place between prime ministers *Zulfiqar Ali Bhutto* and *Indira Ghandi* in New Delhi. The outcome is known as the *Simla Agreement*. All occupied territory was returned to Pakistan; all POWS returned to Pakistan. Argentina occupied the Falkland Islands. Did that occupation last long? Iraq invaded Kuwait under some misconceived notion or a false sense of security. Did that occupation last long?

So the question that every common man in the streets of developing countries asks or is opportunely led into asking by domestic religious forces is what is so different about Israel's occupation of Arab lands that normal international laws, laws of common decency and human rights do not apply. Not only that, but even bringing up the issue of Israeli occupation results in the objector being made to feel guilty for the audacity of bringing up such vulgar conversation in decent company. If some aspect of the issue somehow made it to the files of the Security Council, a veto by the United States was a foregone conclusion. There have been several UN and Security Council resolutions against PLO [now PLA], Iraq and others, perhaps a few with justification too. They are all part of the CVs or charge sheets of each such declared guilty party. But if we catalogue the number of resolutions that would have been part of Israel's CV had these not been torpedoed by the use of Veto by the United States in each case, that non-existent list would be distant winner by a long margin compared to any other accused party charge sheet in the region.

Creating new calamities the perfect way

I have deliberately not based this perception on any research for the simple reason that if someone relatively better informed and generally himself labelled anti-extremism can come to have this perception, should anyone be surprised if this disgust is shared by the relatively conservative common masses throughout the Muslim world?

No peace loving person wants to see groups like *Hamas* and *Hizbollah* strengthen and flourish. Would they even be a topic of discussion today if Israel's illegal occupation had been corrected even within 10 years of the initial occupation? Extremism feeds off issues that may be real, imaginary, contrived or propagated. It is the oxygen that keeps the fire burning consuming without discrimination in its flames those who support or oppose. A just and swift resolution that gives both sides the right to live peacefully is the only way to take the sting out of Muslim extremism, not necessarily as a direct outcome but by neutralising the most important justification tool used in brain washing frustrated and deprived young men and women into acts of violent revenge. The longer it takes, the stronger and more equipped all resistance organisations will get. The world created and supported the Talibans because they were considered a potent tool in fighting Communist advances in Afghanistan. Once created, they felt under no obligation to stay in control. Though there is a major qualitative difference between *Talibans & Al-Qaeda* on the one hand and *Hamas, Hizbollah*, etc. on the other in that the former are not sons of a specific soil and wreak their brand of havoc worldwide and indiscriminately, the actions of the latter groups have so far been confined to the war zones in the Middle East. The latter have not been involved in international acts of terror like 9/11 or 7/7 etc. Israel may be quick to remind the world of the attack on its athletes during the Olympic events in Germany but at the time PLO was not part of the international political community. At the same time, Israel itself has subsequently carried its own acts of terror by raiding relief goods ships in international waters and committing murder in a third state, the U.A.E. to quote just two such recent incidences.

Even if the Palestinian issue is settled but too late, history may repeat itself if armed groups are redirected to other pursuits once they see themselves fully organised and motivated to pursue broader causes. Time is of the essence but there seems no hurry on the part of the United States to get the job done. On the contrary, Israel seems to have been granted a sabbatical from peace negotiations to complete its settlement building process. It is an irrational self-delusion that resistance movements can be made to disappear through brute force, that those living in refugee camps for over four decades will eventually concede they have had enough, go back home into their tents to weep away their sorrows and losses, and Israel will live happily ever after. It will not happen and not learning from history will be a renewed invitation for past and present disasters to revisit the world. The collateral damage to global peace and safe existence is too big and unacceptable a price to pay for keeping the Israeli train of deceit rolling on indefinitely.

Thus far Israel has been like an unscrupulous and brutal minister in the United States cabinet, sanctioned to do as he pleases protected by assurances of no consequences. The United States not only needs to sponsor and support a just and speedy peace deal, it also needs to be seen as the principle driver or engine room for success; justice not only done, but clearly seen to have been done properly. Nothing short of that will ever help it shake off its shattered international credibility. Its role may still not be over if any durable peace is to be ensured. Another *Marshal Plan* for the devastated region may have to be put in place by the developed world to ensure getting young men and women out of their desperately adopted militant roles in the struggle for creation of a homeland for the Palestinians. That would be the minimum price for decades of neglect of the sufferings of displaced populations of Israel's occupation as well as the insensitive and partisan role thus far of the United States in sustaining their misery.

Getting found out by the day

"*Schindiler's List*" is one of the most fascinating and technically captivating movies that I have ever had the pleasure of watching; brilliantly crafted by a brilliant director. Would I like to see another one in the near future on the same theme with the same enthusiasm, even if by the same director? I would be dishonest if I said "yes" today. That is the extent of the self-inflicted negativity the role of the state of Israel has carved out over four decades. The change in this aforementioned attitude is symbolic of changing perception all over the world. It is not a denial of the *Holocaust* as some may rush to suggest, certainly cannot be logically construed after my views on *Schindler's list*. But it certainly leads people to ponder as to how a race that has endured such brutal sufferings and never feels exhausted continually reminding the world about it, can be so totally insensitive to the sufferings of another nation at its own hands? It simply does not add up in any common sense equation unless attributes like greed, senseless hatred, etc. are thrown into the mix. Is this really in the long term interests of the people of Israel? Is it worth the risks and consequences the present approach is sowing today that future generations of Israel may live to face and tragically regret?

More equal than others

Another example of the special "*can't touch this*" status of Israel is the issue of nuclear weapons. Iran's alleged nuclear programme is subject to international debate, suspicion, scrutiny, inspections, threat of consequences, etc. Without offering a value judgement on non-proliferation of nuclear weapons, especially with myself coming from a country with nuclear weapons, this aspect is again irrelevant for this given context. That subject is better left to experts. The moot point is that Israel is alleged to also possess nuclear weapons and while ordinary mortals have no access to verifiable information, in this case the accused party has never unequivocally denied that it does not have the alleged nuclear status.

The following was widely reported on Thursday, 25 February 2010 in the international press through sources in Oslo that [***quote***] *Israeli nuclear whistle blower Mordechai Vanunu has asked the Nobel Peace Prize committee to disregard his nomination for the prestigious award, a Nobel official said Wednesday. In a letter to the Norwegian Nobel Committee, Vanunu wrote that he doesn't want an award previously given to Israeli President Shimon Peres, said Geir Lundestad, the committee's permanent nonvoting secretary. He sees Shimon Peres as the father of the Israeli atomic bomb, and he does not want to be associated with him in any way, Lundestad told The Associated Press. Vanunu, a former low-level technician at an Israeli nuclear plant, served an 18-year prison term in Israel for leaking details of what he alleged was the country's secret nuclear weapons program to the Sunday Times of London in 1986. He was freed in 2004,* *but is not allowed to leave the country or to consort with foreigners for fear he might divulge classified information. Israel neither confirms nor denies having nuclear weapons, but foreign experts concluded from the material Vanunu made public that the country has one of the world's largest nuclear arsenals!* [***Unquote***].

Has the world heard of any UN inspectors in hot pursuit of Israel's nuclear programme with half as much vigour and enthusiasm as with Iran's programme? One can have no sympathy whatsoever with the current regime in Iran or other similar ones anywhere in the world. That adds to the strength of my contention. Israel's decades of assured status quo in its position of occupancy of Arab land through a network of deception has now gone past its "*sell by*" date. If even a persecuted opponent of the fundamentalist regime in Iran still has sympathy for his country's nuclear programme on grounds of blatant international discrimination when it comes to Israel, then surely it cannot serve the long term interests of those in Israel who may have misconceived delusions of survival and prosperity for all times to come despite its "*in your face*" approach towards the international community.

Very intriguing that despite a series of bloody episodes over four and a half decades, Israel does not have a single Security Council resolution registered against its name. It is somewhat like a terrorising antisocial mafia "*Don*" who benefits from the absence of witnesses even when he commits murder in a city centre in broad daylight. It has managed to escape altogether what no other nation could have ever done through a combination of lies, smartly designed deceptions, disinformation, intimidation and use of brutal and disproportionate force at various stages. But all deceptions and distortions have an eventual exposure period and the real Israel is gradually being found out the world over. Some of those states that would not even accept hearing a negative comment about Israel are now joining the demands for controlling what in more recent years has become somewhat like a wild bull in a china shop.

This is no imaginary apportionment of blame; if it can be so construed because by the same logic then, every word I have said about socio-cultural hypocrisy and all else in the name of my own religion is then logically "*Islam phobia*"! Either both contentions are true or neither is. It surely can't be true for one, but not for the other, even if the other is the eternally protected Israel. The overplayed and opportunely played anti-Semitism card is also now an ineffective and tired argument. The state of Israel is not synonymous with all Jews, just as the states of Pakistan and Iran are not synonymous with all Muslims.

Invasions and annexations throughout history have been inherently painful and never without bloodshed of the innocent. Occupying forces and invaded locals can never co-exist peacefully; invasions and annexations are not made in this way. History may record events differently, depending on authors but the ground realities are different or else there would never have been any occupation. No one would allow any intruder to enter his house without resistance. It therefore follows that no peaceful or non-aggressive visitor can occupy property not belonging to him simply for his good looks or pleasant conversation. On the other hand, a robber or dacoit or someone simply intoxicated with power can force his way in and will either not meet any resistance because of his preceding reputation or just bulldoze his way in destroying and brushing aside any resistance in his path. He can later try to justify his actions to others or rationalise his actions for his own mind's consonance. Let us take the case of the Talibans for instance. Their public justification for the senseless bloodshed is that of fighting occupation of Afghanistan by western allies and the general injustices inflicted on Muslims worldwide. For their own mind's consumption, it is a holy war in the name of religion and therefore, ends justify all means used. The real irony of the Talibans is that they were created by the very forces against whom they now fight in the name of God whereas then both fought side by side in their joint hatred for the Soviet Union and Communism; another example of how hatred driven decisions never flourish in the long run. Occupation of alien lands can be called by any name, jihad, crusade, weapons of mass destruction, etc. but all will be equally violent, brutal, never without bloodshed including that of innocent people, especially the more vulnerable men, women and children.

"If someone's deeds lower his position, his pedigree cannot elevate it".
Hazrat Ali

Israel's overuse of the Holocaust argument is also flawed for another reason. Can anyone approach the Home Office in the United Kingdom and seek citizenship on the grounds that his great grandfather was horribly mistreated by a delinquent soldier of the then British colonial army which occupied the sub-continent? Constant reminders of previous injustices may evoke temporary sympathy amongst the neutral. In the long run, they start to irritate the same ears and that is exactly what is happening at present. Seeing Israel's ability to manipulate facts, distort realities and to indulge in open acts of violence has injected suspicions amongst the current generation of other nations. They can understandably be justified in suspecting whether this too might be yet another Israeli ploy of employing exaggerations and excesses in defence of their positions and wrong doings? In doing so, the current and previous Israeli generation have themselves not only done injustice to the victims of *Holocaust*, they have been disloyal and disrespectful to their own ancestors and forefathers. How can they expect others to be more holy than the Pope?

Lots of leaders have urged Israel to understand that they can only get enduring peace by trading occupied land for it. That is a truly innocent proposition. Is it possible that Israelis do not understand this? It is too simple an argument and too basic a logic to miss out. But the persona of deception and disinformation has served Israel so well and for so long that they still feel tempted to try to appear to be part of the peace process but hope that they will eventually manage to get not only peace but retain the land too. The mushroom growth of settlements is one of the principle manifestations of this wishful strategy. It is up to the rest of the world to ensure that they do not suffer any more by being silent spectators in this magnificent disguise.

No one should grudge an Israeli state that could co-exist peacefully with its neighbours in the future provided it is built on a just settlement that is also acceptable to the Palestinians. Those who talk about removing the very existence of Israel, are doing no service to the Palestinians too because in doing so they provide an independent alibi in support of its induced paranoia. Once an acceptable political settlement, containing no element of bullied contents is reached, those with extreme views would be disarmed from holding the single biggest weapon for instigating discontent, frustration and anger in the minds of those whom they target to enlist as supporters. The more extremely frustrated ones or those carefully indoctrinated from childhood from amongst them eventually become the work tools of fundamentalism and suicide missions. Why assist in the growth of that assembly line simply not to offend Israel and its financial governors, wherever they may be based? Whether those who are in a position to influence current events and consequently history remain in their current state of inertia either because taking the opposite view is not financially affordable or because they fall too easily for political fairy tales, neither can be good for the future of this planet.

The cruel game must end soonest. If not, we may see the start of the end-game for modern civilisation if fundamentalism leading to extremism on the one hand, and counter- fundamentalism leading to extreme reactions are allowed to grow and flourish, aided indirectly by inaction. The world does not owe the current generation of Israelis any favours for past events, but Israel itself certainly owes the present generation of mankind immediate reprieve from the ill effects of its territorial greed and its "*now you see it, now you don't*" mind games.

The "*Leaked*" Ash clouds

Recent domestic large scale upheavals and uprisings in several Middle East countries are a huge wake-up call for Israel too, in addition to the countries concerned. Whereas most popular movements are against socio-economic injustices and political exploitation, there is always the risk that religious extremists and rouge elements will jump into power vacuums. We all remember how chaos, destruction and death that took over when a dictatorial regime entrenched for decades suddenly collapsed under an ill-thought and dishonestly conceived international policing action in Iraq. If many of these unrepresentative and oppressive regimes start to fall at the same time, some of the affected countries may fall into the hands of militant bodies. While that will be bad news for the voices of progress and moderation, it will be a catastrophe for the state of Israel; surrounded on all sides by hatred and perils. Retaining fifty square miles of extra usurped territory over a trade-off for potential enduring peace will not make it a superpower but it could be the difference between boiling water at 99 degrees turning to unbearable steam with the rise of one more degree in temperature. It is also time for an immediate final choice for Israel and its unconditional supporters.

In history, the timing of decisions is decisive to the outcomes. Some of the falling regimes are now making desperate offers of major concessions to agitating populations. It will be a case of too little too late at this stage, whereas even lesser concessions made a few years ago would have been acceptable at that stage. Going back to the subject of *Existentialism*, insuring that there is a future in existence in the first place has to take precedence over worrying about what shape any future might have or someone may want it to have. Once the unrepresentative regimes fall in many Arab countries, they will be replaced by representative regimes in varying degrees because most protesting populations are concentrating on demanding modern democratic set ups. Whether they get their wish or not is a different matter. Once that happens, Israel will lose the last card from its pack of deceptive assertions, this being its claim as the only democratic country in the region.

15

Connecting with the world

One of the finest pieces of English literature is a short passage by *John Donne*:

"No man is an island entire of itself; every man is a piece of the continent, a part of the main; if a clod be washed away by the sea, Europe is the less. Every man's death diminishes me, because I am involved in mankind, and therefore never send to know for whom the bell tolls; it tolls for thee".

A major strength of analytical psychology consists of concepts that emphasise common denominators in human traits not only across the globe but also as patterns of thinking processes or behaviour that transcend generations, the collective wisdom of mankind passed on from generation to generation.

Each country interacts with the world in countless ways. Every contact influences both parties in different ways. Some forms of contact are more influential modes which leave lasting impacts or imprints on the minds and memories of others. These are mostly in the form of what people practice not what they preach; how they treat others, especially those who do not matter too much; whether they communicate with respect and clarity; and finally how nations present themselves visibly to the world.

The Commonwealth Games 2010 in India were preceded by immense adverse publicity about management and organisational flaws by the host country. Reputations are not built in a day or by a single incident alone. Once built, they may be hit by temporary setbacks but long established images and perceptions are usually restored with time. As soon as the opening ceremony got underway, the now well branded immense cultural richness of the country showcased at the occasion swept aside whatever had happened in the lead up to the event. India managed to put up a cultural show that left audiences the world over in aesthetic awe and admiration. All was forgiven and forgotten in the space of two hours of cultural excellence and hospitality.

The way nations and races present themselves to the world over long periods of time cannot be destroyed in the short term. Self-destruction takes time and effort of a different nature. Building reputations and perceptions takes even longer but once built, can afford the luxury of a few blips. Negative perceptions have similar dynamics. Even a few acts of benevolence and appreciation cannot completely wash off whatever negative image is developed over a period of time. In today's world, soft power achievements dominate hearts and minds. Unfortunately, not all persons and nations seem to understand that fully. Those who do understand, reap the rewards. Those who do not realise the outreach and financial potential not only deprive themselves of a huge tool of development and progression but also leave themselves vulnerable to negative fall outs. The offerings of Hollywood, Bollywood, Microsoft, Apple, tourism attractions like the Niagara or Victoria Falls, Taj Mahal, Masai Mara, etc. hosting and showcasing art and culture at sports world cups and Olympics of today's world are examples of how much durable goodwill and multiple advantages can be achieved without violence or coercion and without shedding a drop of human blood. The greater the sweat and toil in the efforts, the sweeter are the rewards of these endeavours.

Conservative societies being comparatively more inward looking appear occasionally seemingly eccentric in the way they sometimes react to developments. Lack of interaction creates its own prejudices and psychological distances. As with local neighbourhood relationships the loner of each locality becomes the object of most suspicions and negative developments. Most attitudes attributed to such characters have negative undertones. If a loner suddenly decides for any reason to start building relationships and friendly bridges, a lot is gradually forgiven and forgotten. The choices individuals and societies make in life play a major part in the eventual outcomes.

Scapegoating

Everyone thinks of changing the world, but no one thinks of changing himself.
Leo Tolstoy

It refers to a tendency of the mind to single out a person, group, organisation, nation, and the like for negative comments, blame, condemnation, etc. In psychoanalytic theory defence mechanisms are unconscious psychological strategies to reduce the mind's anxiety. A way of escaping stressful thoughts or situations, by mentally forming new thoughts detached from reality; a self-protection system designed to lessen or repress unpleasant thoughts. Some others have approached similar mental processors with independent theories of their own. A relatively later theory is that of *cognitive dissonance.* It stipulates that the human mind constantly seeks to be at peace or consonance. When that balance of mental equilibrium is disturbed, the mind tries to get back to that consonance by two methods; either changing the objective situation that causes the imbalance or dissonance, or if changing the problem situation is out of reach, then the fall back reaction is to change one's perception of it. Supposing one is informed that someone whom he considers to be an icon of honesty and integrity has been arrested for possession of drugs. The first reaction would be to try to prove innocence somehow, but if that is not possible and the development continues to disturb, the alternation escape reaction could to change one's perception and start believing that either the case is bogus or the accused is a victim of some conspiracy. In taking the latter course, the mind tries to restore calm or consonance through an escape away from reality.

The weaker or anxiety loaded a mind is, the greater is the tendency to scapegoat or take the easier option of perceiving things the way one would want things to be, not how they are in reality. Individual reactions can and do extend to large groups or nations, even an entire religious or ethnic race. As the propensity of this attitude intensifies, it makes that individual or group mentally weaker and more vulnerable. People who tend to blame others rather than take responsibility for their own conduct or actions keep digging themselves deeper into this negative spiral because problems remain unattended and therefore grow further in numbers and intensity. The proportional reaction also continues to perpetuate in intensity and frequency, the outcome is never one to remember or quote by way of example, unless the purpose is to attempt a cure or warn others of consequences of such negative psychological fall back reactions. In matters of statehood and national issues, the first tendency is to blame others for domestic problems. It can take the form of trading insults and allegations, direct confrontation, conspiracies and so on. It is important to differentiate between natural reactions of this sort and a deliberately designed deception that may look similar in pattern.

During the last two or three decades, the tendency of blaming external interference and conspiracy theories for all our woes has continually been on the increase. That in turn has aggravated problems. The aggravated problems then in turn increase mental anxiety or insecurity and the reactions get proportionately more intense, upgrading mere accusations or suspicions into levels of hatred and revenge. The cycle is unending. Part of the perception may be true in reality but it is the imaginary part that is particularly harmful. Real problems can be tackled with real solutions but it is more difficult dealing with problems that do not exist in reality but only in the minds of some people.

All aspects of daily life can be affected in this way, including livelihoods, personal safety and security, even sports. Let us look at the less serious matter of sports first. It is in the inherent nature of sports that at the end of an event, someone must lose. One can either take defeat in sporting events as a fact of life, try to understand the cause of each defeat in an analytical way in order to learn from it or take the easy course and blame someone or other factors through the defence mechanism of scapegoating. The recent incidences implicating players and management of wrong doings and match fixing are examples. A methodical analysis requires a proper understanding of the dynamics of a particular sport, its rules and codes of conducts. For the easier reaction of scapegoating, knowledge of the technicalities plays virtually no part at all. Since success rarely comes without identification of the true dynamics of each sports discipline, more failure leads to more frustration and consequently more scapegoating. It is not surprising that in recent times, the frequency of accusations of wrong doings is continually on the increase with our national cricket team in particular. This is not to suggest that all is well in practice but it is the kneejerk and bandwagon emotional scapegoating reactions that are covered under these mental processes at work.

Logical fallacies

Logical fallacies are essentially flaws in logical thinking or arguments. One of the principal fallacies identified by Aristotle in his *Organon* is referred to as "*ignoratio elenchi*", the English equivalent of this Greek term would be "*irrelevant conclusion*". What it means is that the argument itself may be valid but is being used on an irrelevant issue. Aristotle believed that all fallacies were derivatives of *ignoratio elenchi*. Some of the better known ones in Latin expressions include *argumentum ad hominem* [characteristic or belief], *argumentum ad populum* [appeal to the people], a*rgumentum ad baculum* [threat or force]. To make matters simple, let us expand on just one as an example. The "*populum*" fallacy refers to attempts to prove a contention on the grounds that since all or most people believe in it, so it must be true. Most rumours are spread or supported through this logical fallacy because rumours are mostly based on speculation rather than verifiable facts. For instance, someone might claim that the whole cricket team is involved in corrupt practices but having no evidence of that, most often he will try to assert his point by claiming that everyone is saying that so it must be true. That claim in itself is false because of the use of the term "everyone". How many people constitute "everyone" normally used in arguments? In our political context, a common expression used in media discussions by politicians and anchors alike is "*16 crore awam*" [*160 million people*] as loyal witnesses in support of their adopted positions when no better evidence is available to them.

Fear and anxiety generated by several years of internal unrest, strife, suicide bombings, loss of livelihoods, destroyed businesses and so on have taken their collective toll on the ability of most citizens, including both the educated and the illiterate to think clearly or judge objectively the dynamics of the conflict causing damage to daily life and property. Positions and perceptions change from day to day even on the same incidents as well as the role of various sides in the war on terror. Logical thinking has taken a battering and stressed minds think and express themselves through flawed arguments or logical fallacies.

For instance when some Pakistanis were accused of a role in the 9/11 aircraft bombings in New York, the senseless killing of transport passengers on the roads and underground trains in the United kingdom and the tragedy which unfolded in Mumbai, many people in Pakistan took mental refuge in claiming that the Americans themselves masterminded the New York bombings. Many others took the view that the London bombings too had wrongly been placed on Muslims and that the Indians had no clue who caused the havoc in Mumbai and as usual blamed Pakistan for their internal problems. Let us for the sake of argument accept that all three allegations were correct. But then for every incident at home, someone from outside was deemed responsible by the same lot! Those subscribing to such theories seemed to completely forget how their previous arguments were placed completely on their head once the tragedies were taking place within the country.

Similarly, a lot of people thought that the sole surviving Mumbai terrorist was actually an Indian boy having no links with Pakistan. Once he was found guilty and sentenced, media persons took to the streets of Karachi and each person interviewed stated that the guilty sentence was indeed a travesty of justice against Pakistan, completely forgetting that the accused had earlier been disowned as a fellow citizen when the charges were first made. A lot of such confused persons were victims of their own stressed minds playing games with themselves. Following decades of international accusations and suspicions of involvement of our governments and especially intelligence agencies in militant endeavours, average minds have become too weak and exhausted to keep taking accumulated accusations without some sort of a cognitive breakdown.

These fluctuating reactions of scapegoating and seeking quick consonance are also visible in relation to domestic troubles. In the immediate aftermath of suicide bombings with high casualties in domestic cities or random panic generating firing episodes, the first reaction is one of condemnation. "*Islam does not preach violence*", "*these people are not Muslims*", "*we will not be intimidated by such acts*", "*the government should find them out and eliminate them*" are standard responses in television interviews of ordinary citizens or eye witnesses at targeted sites. As soon as anxiety levels drop in a couple of days, the tone changes to "*this is not our war*", "*the West is in a propaganda war against our country*", "*foreign agents are involved in these acts*", etc. None of this has helped in any way in either levels of mental stress or in developing effective solutions to situations that cause these escape reactions. Of course, political, military and religious agencies often thrive on the state of collective fear and apprehensions in different ways. Some flourish only in conflict and the show goes on, with the string pullers and puppets acting out their traditional and well documented roles.

To friend or not to friend

One popular national poet of humour and satire, *Zameer Jafri* is sometimes not taken serious as a thinker or someone with a vision. That is at times the tragedy with comedy. It is a good moment to introduce the thoughtful aspect of his poetry to our current generation:

جس کو کسی سے پیار نہیں
اس سا کوئ بیمار نہیں
سب سے اچھا ہے وہ گھر
جس کی کوئ دیوار نہیں
بھوکے لوگوں کا کلچر
شہر تو ہے بازار نہیں
انساں بھی اک چیتا ہے
بس یہ دھاری دار نہیں

Jis ko kisi se pyar nahi
Uss sa koi bimaar nahi
[He who loves no one
Is more sick than all others]

Sab se acha hai who ghar
Jis ki koi diwar nahi
[The best of all homes is
One that has no walls]

Bhokey logon ka kalchar
Sheher to hai, bazaar nahi
[The culture of the hungry
May be the city but not its life]

Insaan bhi ik cheeta hai
Bas ye dhari daar nahi
[Man too is a wild "cheeta"
Except that he has no stripes]

During more than two decades of interacting with people across the globe, I found getting on with people was far easier and came more naturally than sustained confrontation or disagreement which requires constant effort, vigil and diverting valuable mental energy into negative pursuits. Why would anyone take that course of action as a conscious choice or as a cause? It is simply not the natural indulgence of every healthy and balanced mind. The Commonwealth represents a massive range of races, cultures, religions and geographical regions. The workplace is a great example of all these diversities at work in harmony and in rare cases a demonstration of the type who simply cannot co-exist whether at home or abroad. The problem is not in the physical environment but in the mind sets of those individuals. The Commonwealth Association of Tax Administrators is the largest inter-governmental tax organisation in the world in terms of membership. In my association spanning nearly two decades almost every decision worth remembering was based on consensus, sometimes achieved after a fair amount of serious debate but all in the best common interests. If there were a few exceptions, they could be counted on finger tips. The important approach in all this was to focus on commonalities or agreements and the put dissensions on the back burners.

A nostalgic memory of top tax officials from the past. The president of CATA, Mr. Michael Waweru [R], Commissioner General from Kenya, the chairman Tan Sri Dato' Zainol Abidin [l], Director General from Malaysia, the vice chairman Mr. Gerry Cook MBE from United Kingdom and the executive director from Pakistan. It is difficult to recall a single point on which consensus was not eventually achieved by this team during its 3 years term

Delegates from most Commonwealth countries that I had the pleasure of interacting with at my very first Commonwealth conference in 1990 remained friends till completion of my assignment in late 2010 and many still continue to remain so till today. The basis of that enduring relationship was mutual respect and straightforward dealings. But a major contributor that secured the enduring bond was the warm welcome and hospitality that we managed to extend to all delegates who attended the conference hosted by Pakistan in Islamabad in 1993. There is no better gesture of sincerity than being good hosts and making the time spent by visitors as comfortable and memorable as possible. As simple as that; no rocket science, no spin, and definitely no personas of false pretences.

With H.E. Prof. John Atta Mills, the former President of Ghana at the inaugural ceremony of the Commonwealth Tax Conference brilliantly hosted and organised by Ghana in 2004. President Mills was an immensely respected Commonwealth personality whom I had the pleasure of first meeting in 1990 in the Commonwealth *conference in Mauritius.*

Similarly, equally important is the manner in which long associations with friends and colleagues are brought to an end. That is facilitated most by leaving at the right time, while still wanted and not after all members break their daily sleep to pray for someone's riddance in the middle of the night. It is said of finance ministers that there are only two types of them. Those who fail; and those who leave in time! Judging the right time to call it a day in any top assignment is the secret to either leaving with one's respect in tact or in tatters. A few appropriately chosen farewell and thank you courtesy calls while leaving always help in building lasting goodwill. It is a kind of indirect message that we were not in it for professional dealings alone and that personal respect and admiration were never missing from working relationships.

Mauritius always had a special place in my heart where my long association with CATA first started. The final farewell call had to be there. Photo taken at the farewell courtesy call on Hon. Pravind Kumar Jugnauth, Vice- Prime Minister & Minister of Finance of Mauritius [L] & Mr M. S. Lal, Director General, Mauritius Revenue Authority and current President of CATA [R]

During long haul flights, passengers meet many strangers, often leading to pleasant conversation and a good handshake at the end with mutual exchanges of best wishes for unknown futures. Both sides might recall with a bit of nostalgia at some later stage having met a Greek, Japanese or Pakistani person during a long journey and enjoying the company while it lasted. On the other hand, once in a while, one can came across the opposite species that specialises in offending most co-passengers, cabin crew and those at check-in counters. Why would anyone ever want to remember such unfriendly creatures except by way of negative examples? One does not need to be at an airport or on board a super airbus to have pleasant conversation. That can be done to equally good effect during a short market visit or waiting for one's turn at a doctor's clinic. The only requirement is a willing mind that does not erect defensive walls to cordon off communication with those around.

London is a multi-cultural city and Londoners generally take pride in that well recognised attribute. All religious, ethnic and racial groups celebrate their respective festivals from time to time. Many invite friends and families from outside their own roots to join in celebration. Some, however, prefer to stay with themselves. Having met a friend after a while and the Muslim festival of Eid had fallen during the intervening period, I enquired from him as to how had he celebrated the occasion? He had been invited to a communal gathering courtesy of a communal Eid party. Instead of enjoying the occasion, he was distressed that the organisers had invited non-Muslims also to an Eid party. On asking him as to why would he want to exclude others from his happy moments, he struggled for a convincing answer but seemed to register without an explicit confession that there was perhaps nothing seriously wrong after all in inviting persons of other religions. Many negative cultural practices remain entrenched in collective thinking simply because they are hardly ever questioned.

The extreme manifestation of divisiveness of more recent origin is the trend of claiming that "Allah" is the God of Muslims only not to be shared with others? I have referred elsewhere to a stance taken by a Malaysian group as reported in detail in the media which is a practical manifestation of the isolationist mind set. What sort of insecurity or crazy suspicion would lead someone to not even share his "exclusive" God with someone else, or claim an exclusive relationship especially if the same Allah continues to produce human beings of other faiths too? Would that not suggest that Allah has interest in all religions and faiths, even in non-believers? This is food for thought in particular for those who firmly believe that every event on earth is subject to complete divine control because they cannot hold that point of view and at the same time then suddenly exclude some developments from their belief package. Uncertainty about whom to befriend or not; whom to own or disown? Those precisely are the kind of scrambled minds, mostly indoctrinated with malicious intents that are at the foundation of current conflicts and fragmentation of mental processes.

To friend or not to friend

Tourism serves several objectives, including income generation and livelihoods, developing infrastructure, creating a hospitable and welcoming environment where those who come once are tempted to come again. This puts all those who are involved in a testing and responsible situation; each person an informal ambassador for his country. How have we fared on these fundamentals?

The daily ***Dawn*** newspaper in Pakistan reported on Sunday, 13 Jun, 2010 that *"The Global Peace Index (GPI) released by the US Department of State termed Pakistan as the world's fifth most unstable country, better only than Iraq, Somalia, Afghanistan and Sudan. Pakistan's ranking according to the GPI is 145 on a list of 149 countries"*. Factors considered in leading to the assessment included (1) internal conflicts, (2) deteriorating law and order situation, (3) bad governance, (4) suicide bombings and (5) large-scale violence in different regions. Mercifully the subject of internal daily cries of corruption is not part of this list. Probably because there are a few countries that compete in this field but are nevertheless more peaceful at home and more welcoming for outsiders.

Forgetting for a minute the source of this assessment, let us look independently at the relevance of each of the 5 listed variables to current state of affairs in the country.

Internal conflicts

Can anyone amongst us disagree that there are presently far too many conflicts at home? Where do we start when worshipers cannot go to the mosques of their choosing unless those places of worship are protected by fully armed security personnel? There could be many a publication on this subject alone. Without going into details on this distraction, given objective realities we have to accept this as a fair basis for assessment of the present country situation.

Deteriorating law and order situation

When parents deem it important to remind on a daily basis from school to university going children of the need to be careful about places to go, to come back home as soon as possible, when market places are deserted for fear of the unexpected, when cars full of family members are checked by security personnel at virtually every street corner, motor cycle riding is restricted to the rider only, many families in the biggest city in the country go into mourning every day at target killings or killings at random and so on, there is no case for defence of the current law and order situation. It does not matter in whose kitchen the poisonous dishes are regularly cooked, because a bullet is a bullet and every fatality is a human tragedy. If names do not get mentioned on TV channels because channel viewing numbers are not inflated by it, it is no less significant. In fact it is a bigger tragedy when a human life is only referred to as part of a fatality count. When a cricket team from a neighbouring country is invited with assurances of security levels equivalent to head of states visits and is attacked as defenceless sitting ducks en-route to the stadium, what does that say about current rule of law, security and hospitality assurances? There are jokes in circulation in social circles on the subject. A minister for law in the Punjab is regularly cited in the media for many incidences of ultra-legal activities. He may not be the only offending minister in the country but he is currently the popular quote. When the Afghan crisis was at its peak during the Soviet invasion, an Afghan refugee was reportedly apprehended trying to cross the border into Pakistan illegally. He warned the apprehending authorities of consequences because he claimed to be an ex-minister in the Afghan cabinet. When asked about his portfolio, he informed that he was the minister in-charge of railways. Security personnel scoffed at the claim and reminded him that there was no railway in Afghanistan so how could there be a minister for railways? Thick skinned politicians don't go down for the count so easily and he is quoted to have returned fire aggressively, "*Don't you have a minister for law*?" Whether this anecdote is true or not, it reflects the general perception about lack of respect for law at all levels. So if we do not score well on this variable too, should it come as a surprise?

Poor governance

Poor governance is quite common in many countries but near absence of governance is not as common. When the international community sees our natural disasters on international electronic media, accepts the scale of the disaster, when those rendered homeless need help without delay but potential donors are reluctant to hand over funds due to lack of confidence about their use, when parliamentarians trusted through votes with the task of framing the laws of the country feel no hesitation in moving about with body guards loaded with totally banned lethal weapons on the main roads of busy towns in full view of capturing cameras, when the judiciary cannot see the injustices in the streets, homes and offices meted out to the common citizen who led the movement for the restoration of ousted judges and is obsessed with settling political scores and in their preoccupation betraying the very people who put them back in place wondering what the fuss was all about, talk of governance naturally seems totally out of place. Our media channels spend countless hours in shouting and counter shouting matches, live and repeated telecasts between uneducated and uncultured political opponents that the common man does not even want to watch, totally unmindful of the fact the viewers did not subscribe to selected channels to have such meaningless horror shows thrust upon them. There is hardly a strong case too in support of good governance in the public and private sector.

Suicide bombings

Without going into details of who is behind such serial killings, it is presently the single biggest fear that every living being in the country carries in his heart and mind in his home, in offices, schools, colleges, market places, places of workshops, trains, planes; the list is endless. It is presently our biggest PR disaster internationally and if truth be told we have no hiding place from this charge. Excuses and explanations for the happenings are drying up very fast if indeed any more are left now. So it seems there is virtually no case for defence or denial of this charge too.

Large-scale violence in different regions

There is a widespread revolt like situation in at least two provinces in the country. A full scale army operation is in place in the famous tribal belt and its neighbouring areas, the loss of valuable life, civilian as well as military, cross border attacks and counter attacks including by unmanned drones on selected targets are a daily routine. That is enough to deter any outsider to even consider visiting those places when even aid workers and engineers of our strongest neighbouring ally are kidnapped and murdered. In fact it is worth considering whether what we insist on calling our areas are even free and safe to visit by ourselves? If not, is it not equivalent to having a part of our territory under foreign occupation? It is understandable if in any armed conflict, armed forces personnel become targets but why should these regions become no go areas for teachers, doctors, engineers, posted civil servants and even aid workers? The strategy defies all common sense and logic, but common sense, logic and compassion do not make an extremist.

It does not matter whatever explanations are offered in defence. As long as the situation does not change, the evaluations of the world about us as a nation will remain unchanged. When things at home are not conducive to inviting others, it becomes more important to earn additional good will abroad. After the events of 9/11 and 7/7 in New York and London and the more recent attempted bombing in New York, that seems a non-starter too. So what is the option? Do we just leave matters as they are or play a more active role in trying to rectify our situation? Time does not wait. In present circumstances it is a case of now or may be never. Waiting for those to lead us who are the root cause of problems will only lead to more deterioration. Each citizen, home and abroad has to play his part and the starting point has to be an honest admission of current woes and to act with common sense devoid of anger and hatred. Unless that happens, our international reputation, even less our seemingly gloomy future will remain cause for even more depression.

Growing influence of "soft power" in image building

"There is no greater sorrow than to recall in misery the time when we were happy".
Dante

Whereas most of our behavioural manifestations at home are heavily tilted towards outward display and maintaining socially approved physical appearances, there is a visible "*couldn't care less*" attitude in interaction with the rest of the world. It is most unlikely from a psychological point of view that two almost opposite sets of behaviour packages can so comfortably co-exist in the same mentally healthy personality type. The sudden display of a completely different attitude is both out of ignorance of current global attitudes and a general contempt for any different value system that is worthy of contempt purely for the reason that it is different. Appreciation of socio-cultural and religious diversity is a product of education and tolerance which unfortunately are in very short supply at present.

In a very recent chat with a Pakistani airline car driver tasked with driving his employer airline's passengers to designated airports in London, the murder of the governor of Punjab popped up in discussion. When asked about his opinion, he said he thought it was totally out of order. He then added that if he had still been in Pakistan instead of having been in London for a decade, his views could have been different. It was only having lived abroad as an ethnic minority that he realised how important it was for every country to treat its minorities well and equally. What happened to *Salman Taseer* cannot be anything other than religious fanaticism. Society at large, the free media but most importantly the educational system should be creating awareness of fundamental human values of freedom of speech and choices, equality of rights of minorities and so on. This lack of contact with what is projected in local media as the largely evil external world has been a major contributor in general intellectual degeneration.

A very important feature of modern life is the role of soft power in image building, constructing bridges of communication and goodwill with others in addition to benefitting from the massive economic benefits of the development and marketing of soft power products. In contrast with the traditional hardware power such as brute military strength, economic dominance through natural resource monopolies like oil reserves, conditional economic assistance, etc. soft power refers to the role of cultural and commercial goods, like movies, music, dance, reality contests like Miss World gatherings, cultural displays at major events such as opening ceremonies for Olympics, sports world cups, firework displays on new year's eve, entertainment hardware and software, provision of IT related services and so on. It is an alternate influence, an ability to showcase talent through possibilities of comfort and attraction, inviting and providing affordable opportunities for holidays away from home, gifts, handicrafts and tourism in respective countries.

It is not a completely new concept though the tools used today are radically different from historical parallels. Past tools included fields like herbal medicine, meditation, etc. The idea of using charm as a form of power base can be traced as far back as the ancient 7th century BC Chinese philosopher *Laozi*. The phrase in its modern context is attributed to *Joseph Nye* of *Harvard University*. It is now widely used in international literature and social conversations.

It is fairly independent of traditional power positions. The former Soviet Union for instance was a mighty power in military terms but its soft power base was virtually non-existent mainly because of its policy or inability to interact in a friendly and welcoming way with the rest of the world that differed from its ideology. While military force can dominate through intimidation or use of brute force, soft power can create friendly domination through the now familiar "*winning hearts and mind*" philosophy.

The term is not completely alien to history of the sub-continent region. The positive role played and influence exercised by the

Muslim *Sufi* saints in the sub-continent in promoting integration of all religions, races and cultures is well documented and equally appreciated by all religions and races in the region. All that goodwill generation without the use of a single tool of coercion and intimidation is a perfect example of how soft power can influence the lives of millions in a constructive way as well as draw collective reverence and admiration. The exact opposite of that today is the Talibanisation of society that is completely alienating as well as intimidating in every comparable way.

Indo-Pak tennis goodwill hunting

During the past couple of years, a rare but most welcome and successful partnership between a tennis player each from Pakistan and India, namely *Aisam ul Haq Qureshi* and *Rohan Bopanna*, respectively has drawn a lot of attention and appreciation in sporting circles and amongst sports lovers. Qualifying for the finals of mixed doubles of US Open in 2010 and in doing so becoming the first Pakistani tennis player ever to reach such a level at any Grand Slam event is a huge achievement in itself. He then partnered the Czech tennis player *Kveta Peschke* in mixed doubles with the same degree of success. But the real success was winning the hearts and minds of millions across the globe. What did not get the attention it probably deserved was the fact that this was achieved by the players for themselves and for their countries in the same city where self-appointed custodians of our religion brought down the mighty twin towers and killed thousands of ordinary citizens, including Muslims. *Aisam* then made a customary short speech of goodwill hunting; one brief speech that had more impact than the mundane effort of entire ministry of foreign affairs for years put together because it was based on real life action. Which of the two feats would we all want to see repeated in the future? If the answer is only a goodwill feat, why do we have people amongst us who still sympathise with what Bin Laden and his criminal gang represent?

Female suicide bomber

A woman in "*burqa*" recently blew herself up and killed 45 innocent people gathered to receive food aid from a UN agency in the northern province of the country on Christmas Day which also happens to be the birthday of Jinnah, the father of the nation. Many of those killed could have been sympathisers of the Talibans. In doing so, she became the first Pakistani female suicide bomber, a sort of dubious distinction shared with *Aisam* but in a terribly different way. Those who support the universal enforcement of "*burqa*" need to think carefully about this unforeseen implication through an act that the suicide bomber will have perpetrator as a holy mission. Did she do a service to the campaign in favour of burqas? The crazy criminal act is a graphic demonstration of why giving utmost importance to outward appearances is a seriously flawed way of thinking. The "burqa" can be used with the best of intentions and probably was when it was first invented for that purpose in times when state policing and social protective laws were totally inadequate, if not non-existent for providing protection to female members of society at the time. The same contraption has now been used for the most evil act that can be inflicted on unsuspecting fellow human beings. This is very much the same way in which religion that is meant to bond people and bring order in the life of its followers is being misused today as a tool to motivate human beings to blow themselves up at carefully chosen vantage points where death and destruction can be optimised. It should not be too difficult to see the distinction, unless someone is determined not to concede fault at any cost.

No my friend, darkness is not everywhere, for here and there I find faces illuminated from within; paper lanterns among the dark trees.
Carole Borges

Now contrast this with our unholy girls out of "burqa", quietly putting in hard work against heavy socio-cultural odds, tucked away from media in carefully concealed surroundings to do the nation proud by winning the gold medal in women's cricket at the

Asian Games in China or the first Pakistani female athlete to win an individual medal at the same games. Which feat would we all want our female members of society to repeat in the future? There is again only one sane answer. These may be only a few seemingly insignificant examples to brag about but it is still better than having none at all; a few paper lanterns among dark trees!

IT leadership & international call centres

Countries that lead the way in information technology innovation and services win admirers directly through their inventive devices and quality of services. In doing so they create for themselves, a great deal of goodwill and positive sentiment. Developing countries, in particular which have made big advances in this field have won considerable business opportunities in IT related fields because of lower costs of services compared to the countries in which these services are actually delivered. In the comparable Asian context, the names of India and Malaysia immediately spring to mind. We did not lose out on such business opportunities because of country bias. We lost because of the policy choices made in the past; the decision to relegate the English language to the status of "*also ran*" in academic priorities. The bias was purely internal and indigenous. There have been very recent reports that the provincial government in Punjab has ordered the closure of post-graduation studies in English literature even in premier colleges like the famous Government College Lahore. If this is true, it should be least surprising given the recent and current ruling groups in the "*Parah Likha Punjab*"! No one could have taken such a retrogressive step except with the ill-informed arrogance of the current Muslim League leadership, or its predecessor fraternity of Muslim League that coined the phrase in the first place. Are their own children also deprived from that option? What a silly question; most have or are still getting education in Europe or the United States, and so will their future generations.

The human mind can think good or evil in any language. Each amongst the whole breed of suicide bombers did not use the logical process of English language to convince himself into his final act.

But if he had not avoided or had not been deprived of access to international languages and sources of knowledge, who knows he might just have opted to pursue a different life. That in itself is reason enough for the control freaks not to risk offering an alternate option that might lead to thinking minds which could threaten to destabilise status quo or evil agendas.

Appealing for world help – "to whom it may concern"

A leading newspaper in the country reported that in a meeting by a top Pakistani politician with Hilary Clinton on 29 October 2010, the United States was urged to ask India to stop interference in Pakistan's internal affairs and also to put pressure on India to negotiate with Pakistan on all subjects including Kashmir. If memory serves correctly, especially for ex-patriots not in daily touch with developments on the ground back home, the Americans have also been reminded repeatedly to get the Hell out of the neighbouring country where their presence is the root cause of our current domestic woes. So far not only have the Americans not paid any attention to repeated warnings, they send unmanned drones deep into our territory to hit selected targets. Our leaders have also repeatedly cautioned the Americans that we have the military capability to stop them any time we want but it is not in our tradition of hospitality in the tribal belt to attack guests. In any case it seems morally improper to attack unmanned American military machines by using other military machines that have also come from the same country.

So when the country's political or military leadership says to the United States or to European partners in the now loosely defined war on terror to get behind us in all matters India, do they think they have gone to their friends with whom they share great traditions of friendship and mutual respect; friends that hold them in higher esteem than other nations do on the basis of common values, interests and objectives? Or do they just go to them in anger to convey that the United States and European nations have caused our nation despite our deeply patriotic leadership enough damage and pain by their unilateral misdemeanours which our leaders never wanted to be part of at any stage? There has to be some rational thinking behind appeals for favourable support or treatment. That can either be on the basis of a very strong and convincing moral high ground or very special friendly relations justifying special favours. The closest our country is involved in such relationship with another sovereign state is in the China-Pakistan relationship. Appealing to China for support makes perfect sense but appealing to those countries which the leadership simultaneously accuses of being against our interests and involved full time in activities for destabilising the state makes very little sense; even lesser sense in expecting a more favoured nation treatment on demand. Support comes through development of common causes, interests and pursuits; even more through mutual trust and respect. If the leadership has the vision and honesty for developing more relationships along the Sino-Pakistan model, support might just come without begging for it. At present there appears no other bilateral equation that could have even twenty five per cent of the ingredients as in the relationship with China.

Like in most domestic matters, our policy makers and political masters seems to have their wires completely crossed in a huge tangle; the only energy that is released from those complex plants is in the form of random short sparks that have no productive value but enough threat to blow up the plant itself at any time. Even without a complete blow up, the units operate at considerably downgraded strengths and the output is both low and erratic. Therefore most of our time and resource is spent in damage control, just as the Supreme Court now seems to be doing at all times.

South Africa – odd one out

More than two decades of association with the Commonwealth and interaction on international tax treaties with dozens of other nations prior to joining the Commonwealth are full of fond memories, professionally satisfying outcomes and richly educating experiences. Given another opportunity in another hypothetical life, one would want to relive all that and revisit friends. However, if I was completely cornered into asking whether there was a negative or forgetful experience, then it will have to be my experience of dealing with most tax officials in South Africa. It is sad that this is a perception despite the exceptionally high esteem in which I hold the legendary Nelson Mandela. Equally sadly, this perception was shared by a number of other Commonwealth colleagues, including those from the African continent.

One would like to believe that the general population is different from the small group of South African officials that I interacted with. However, it also highlights the fact that when someone visits any country as a tourist or on business, every local person he interacts with is an ambassador of sorts for the host country. Similarly, the visiting person is also an ambassador for the country or organisation to which he belongs. A few individuals or a small group can make or mar the long term impression of the visitor or the visited. If a negative image is created, with or without justification, no third party can repair the damage. If our international image has been severely dented in recent times, it places added responsibility on every citizen, home and abroad to try to repair the damage. Good relations and reputations are the bridges on which constructive bilateral and international relationships can be built and developed. Are we doing enough, if anything at all, to repair our badly shattered current standing? It is very important to address this question with calmness and maturity in order to review current attitudes towards the rest of the world.

The "Passive Withdrawal Symptom" Leadership

In 1997, the biennial meeting of the Commonwealth Head of Governments was hosted by the United Kingdom in Edinburgh. It included a number of social events, inaugural lunch and a grand farewell dinner in the exotic Edinburgh Castle. Nawaz Sharif was the Prime Minister at the time and headed the Pakistan delegation, at least on paper.

We frequently read about Kashmiri leaders asking the West to pressurise India into settling the Kashmir dispute. But how many of them ever actually meet their target audience, socialise with them, openly condemn the bombings in New York or London to create goodwill or a rapport? Most simple principles of locality relationships almost equally apply to global relationships too. Friends will always have a soft corner for their friends compared to strangers or those who wilfully maintain a distance until a need arises, not only openly disagree with styles of life different from their own, at home and abroad, but express their contempt for values held by others.

Nobody wins a case in a court sitting at home. People need to associate with other people, share their joys and sorrows before they can communicate effectively. This is no rocket science. In my relatively long international experience, it is not difficult at all if one can just learn to accept and respect the differences in cultures, values and beliefs, just as we enjoy each other's cultural shows, entertainment events and showbiz products. It requires no special effort. In fact creating conflict requires effort and continual devious planning. It is a tragedy that so many opt for the latter course.

At the opening reception hosted by the then Prime Minister of United Kingdom and the closing reception hosted by HM The Queen as Head of the Commonwealth, there were leading political figures from all over the Commonwealth membership. No one from our delegation was in sight at the opening reception. As a Pakistani present at the occasion, I was quizzed by an anchor from an Indian TV network on their whereabouts. For the opening event, I used the alibi of Friday prayers as a possibility. There was no such defence to offer at the closing ceremony. On checking with a colleague from the Pakistan High Commission present there, the explanation was stunning, if true. He said Prime Minister Nawaz Sharif was reluctant to mix up in such informal gatherings. If he was covering up for something else, it sort of confirmed the impression that it was a case of lack of awareness in the leadership about the importance of such opportunities for creating goodwill and new relationships. If it was true, then it reflected poorly on the quality and vision of the country's leadership at the time. It also re-emphasised that our lack of ability to mingle with the rest of humanity has been a major hindrance in not getting our point of view across in a way that could knock down the mental barriers or in creating and maintaining lasting friendships. Should this come as a surprise? If some of us cannot knock down the barriers at home between castes, sects, provinces, classes because of intolerance towards anything different, how can we be expected to be more broadminded towards outsiders? It is a general disease that plagues the entire body and consumes the whole psyche. It is not an incurable condition but it can only be cured in willing patients.

16

Dead end ahead; all change

Changing direction and priorities

What is the use of running when we are on the wrong road?
Bavarian Proverb

Having looked at problems, their origins, major causes and condemned the drivers of deceit and manipulation, it is time to answer the million dollar question. Against the background of the paths followed for almost 65 years, the directions set, the socio-cultural and political set ups that have brought matters to the brink, the false values adopted which have not done any service to the nation or the fake morals which have only deceived society and given plenty of sorrows; is there any sense in carrying on moving along that destructive path or is it high time to change directions and priorities immediately in an attempt to reverse national fortunes and the possibility for a better future?

Despite widespread intense sentiment of contempt and disgust for the overwhelming majority of politicians, especially the current lot, disillusionment with a judiciary that promised much and delivered hardly a fraction of expectations and the general shambolic state of governance and economic management, there is hardly a politician of note or a representative of major state institutions who is heard even talking about, let alone showing genuine concern for issues that are really hurting the common man. These include security of life and property, continually shrinking incomes and livelihoods, punishingly long periods of load shedding, a prohibitive cost of living that is directly leading to higher rates of suicides, complete breakdown of law and order, rampant corruption led by the usual suspects and a population growing out of control in numbers. Why would they? None of that bothers them in any way; it never has for six decades and so many of them might even wonder in the privacy of their living rooms what the public fuss is all about? A complete write off is the only possible solution. Not a single vote at the next opportunity to any of the known lethal political bacteria.

Change does not come about easily or is presented on a platter by those who stand to gain from status quo. The seeds of the problems and tragedies faced today as a nation were sown by some of our past generations and cared for by the current one. What is done today and tomorrow lays the foundations for the rewards or consequences that will visit our future generations in due course. In our given situation, inaction is simply a suicidal option.

A flashback to college research

During my college days under the professorship of the very learned *Dr. Mohammad Ajmal* as head of the Psychology department, at one point all post graduate students were required to undertake a research project. The choice of topic was left to students but needed eventual approval by the great man himself. The reason why this rejigged memory now is that my chosen research project was very relevant to this particular topic. Every individual has notions of himself and those around him; self-evaluations and evaluations of him by others as well as his own judgement of others. Do all these relate to each other? Could there be a reliable relationship between these variables?

Let us make the research synopsis as brief and painless as possible. Supposing there were 50 students available to run the rule on. Each student was provided a questionnaire that included a list of all names. Every student was required to give his ratings for each of his fellow students whose name was on the list against a number of personality traits, including general intelligence, social stimulus value, equanimity, friendliness, helpfulness, honesty, reliability, etc. Every student was required to not only rate others, but also rate himself on each of the listed traits. There was an undertaking that all feedback would remain strictly confidential and nothing would be shared at any stage. That commitment remains in position till today. Nothing short of such assurances can encourage honest comments and evaluations.

The hypothesis was that those who were actually successful and popular in real life were the ones whose self-assessment was closest to assessments made about them by others. If someone considers himself to be some kind of *Lord of the Ring* but others view him as a complete waste of space, it was evidence of a mal-functional mind with a poor sense of judgement. He was likely to be the most unpopular and maladjusted character even though his own evaluations painted a very rosy picture. Those who had a better idea of what others thought about themselves and made realistic evaluations of their own qualities or negative traits were likely to be the best adjusted members of society. Fortunately, the results of data analysis supported the hypothesis. One cannot say the hypothesis was confirmed because the group sample was not large enough to arrive at definite and reliable conclusions in a one-off research but a definite trend was clearly discernable.

Moving quickly on to the real issue in the present context, similar studies about evaluations can be very useful at national and international levels too. Last year during one of many political television chat shows, an anchor known for his aggressive dialogue with invited guests, usually political actors, was having a go at those present in his studio and accusing them of being out of touch with the real issues and worries of those who had voted them to power. The barrage of accusations was relentless and conveyed with real intensity to uncomfortable guests. The point in itself was fair enough but the second part is more interesting. The anchor at the same time contended that the media was doing a great job in bringing up the grievances of the public by being in touch with them. As luck would have it, the web site of the same media house was conducting a survey asking readers to assess whether the public was satisfied with the role of the media or thought it was adding to the problems. A staggering 68 per cent gave a negative feedback about the role of the media at the time. The name of the network is not relevant though the results are preserved in my archives. The important point is whereas public opinion showed a negative image towards politicians and media houses, both held themselves in fairly high self-esteem! That reinforces the research hypothesis that persons or groups that make poor evaluations of their own abilities, output or shortcomings usually fail to deliver and are most unpopular at the same time. That seems to hold true for most of our political and military rulers, past and present.

Something similar is needed in the context of international relations. There are deluded misconceptions in many countries about current domestic situations and their relationships with the rest of the world. It would again make not only very interesting reading but provide useful indication on where someone may think he stands at present, and to find out the opposing responses from external sources; a reliable reality check from time to time that could provide guidance as a basis for correction. This cannot be left to state organs for reasons we all know. There is a quote on this point from one of the professors at the University of Bath during my post-graduation period time spent there. *Prof C. Sanford* wrote in one of his several books, "*Governments use statistics like the drunken man uses the lamp post; for support rather than for illumination*".

It is difficult to understand the justification for a full bench of 17 judges of the Supreme Court hearing political and constitutional cases day after day. Why cannot a smaller bench perform instead? Would it be more difficult or less effective for the court to implement its judgement if passed by a smaller bench? Most probably, the answer lies in the structuralism analysis. A larger bench symbolically represents a more assertive looking judicial presence. What about pending law suits of average citizens during this period? It would make a very interesting study, ascertaining the number of man hours spent on judicial proceedings in political and constitutional cases during the first 12 months of the restored judiciary in comparison to the number of man hours spent in cases of common citizens? It would provide a reasonably reliable analysis of where our priorities have been and are still focused till today.

At least two or three judges of the Supreme Court should be dedicated to social sector related cases and causes; assault cases involving women and children, use of force and blackmail in marital issues, land grabbing, hoarding of essential goods, incidences of extreme police excesses, deaths by negligence in road accidents or children falling to death in uncovered gutters and sewers, blatant violation of dowry exhibition bans and food restrictions at wedding ceremonies, etc. These dedicated judges should not need to hear and pass judgement in every such case. Exemplary punishments dished out to the worst known offenders with extensive media coverage of the outcome will produce a massive demonstration effect on criminals and defaulters operating at lower levels. The electronic media has made some positive contributions by highlighting many ghastly incidents that would otherwise have gone unnoticed. Given the handicap of the low national literacy rate, the electronic media has the capacity and outreach to play a pivotal role through media watchdog programmes. The common man needs an honest demonstration of intent that he is part of the effort to reform society and that finally someone is willing to listen to him. It is a kind of "*taking care of the pennies*" approach, as a stepping stone for pounds to look after themselves. The reason why dedicated judges are most important is that these kind of exemplary hearings need to be on a day to day basis with swift outcomes. Given the social mind-set that has been discussed at length, it is quite possible some judges may feel downgraded dealing with commoners while adjudicating in the highest court of the land. For instance *Justice Chaudhry Ramzan Khan* may feel a higher sense of satisfaction in summoning the prime minister, leader of opposition or the head of FIA to stand before him in his courtroom rather than an insignificant hearing of a personal torture story of a somewhat anonymous *Maskeen Baba* from *Toba Tek Singh*. If society is to be reformed, the first thing that needs change is the mind-set; getting involved with real life issues of ordinary citizens and giving relief to them for a change. That transformation must come from the very highest echelons of the judicial hierarchy in order for it to have a meaningful impact.

In a similar way, the involvement of the higher judiciary in tax investigation matters of biggest tax dodgers is the need of the hour, just like its involvement in corruption probes ordered through FIA. Before we insist that the Americans leave us alone, let us mobilise some domestic revenue resource that is currently yielding revenue intake at levels that are too embarrassing to quote. Is there room for improvement in revenue generation? There is not just room for improvement; there certainly is room enough for adding a multiple storey complex in the revenue collection chart. The problem is caused by political expediencies and business pressure groups, particularly the juvenile social attitude of the largely illiterate wholesale and retail traders in main urban shopping markets, who line up to support Nawaz Sharif in wholesale numbers as their tax evading role model. They wish to have a system in which people can be selectively investigated and squeezed for non-tax reasons. For top politicians a system at best that has the inherent flexibility to "exclude" special ones and concentrate on all others. Well that accommodating tax system has been in place for decades now despite several tax reforms soap theatricals. The end product has not changed, not because remedies are not known but simply because the honest determination needed for that is unaffordable for the owners of the country.

Having served on more than one tax reforms committee in the past, from my experience the common denominator approach in all the committees was to appear to be sincere in the pursuit of additional revenues but ensure that they did not offend or step on the toes of those who have had the power or influence to stay above the application of fiscal laws. The truth of the matter is that no new or additional powers are needed to enforce tax laws. The existing tax law provides for penalties and prosecution for tax avoidance and evasion, for violation of other fiscal provisions; the power to raid business premises, inspect books and records; appoint receivers aided by the local police to enforce collection of outstanding tax dues, freeze bank accounts, attach immovable as well as immovable assets of tax defaulters and to put them to public auction, even issue warrants of arrest through tax recovery officers. That only leaves room for public floggings and beheadings!

The problem is not with tax laws, just as it is not with the national constitution. The theory part is pretty much okay. It is the application and enforcement of fiscal laws that is full of dangers and booby traps. The constitution provides for capital punishment for any military overthrow of an elected government. In practice, their lordships in their collective wisdom have repeatedly passed judgement saying "*well done*" for coming through with a successful takeover despite the inherent dangers in attempting to overthrow lawfully elected governments. A sickening argument which states "*a successful revolution has its own justification*" has being regularly employed to justify military takeovers repeatedly. In tax matters too, in spite of the fact that provisions for criminal prosecutions have always been on the statue books, in real life not a single taxpayer has ever been successfully prosecuted in any court of law in the land. Neither the problem nor its solution requires knowledge of rocket science. The missing ingredient is the political will and intellectual honesty of those in positions of power, and a higher sense of social responsibility on the part of society as a whole. The former factor will not change for obvious reasons; the latter is an option that society collectively needs to take charge of without waiting for any approvals. Until these two remedies remain out of reach, the fiscal soap opera will continue to run meaninglessly as it has done for decades. Information about taxes paid by taxpayers should be the right of every citizen under a now common "*Right of Information Act*". Short of that, our revenue generation and tax evasion problems will never be resolved effectively.

Striking "Delete" for past; Pressing "Enter" for future

In today's dynamic world and exhausting pace of daily lives, any individual or nation standing still at any stage is effectively going backwards because others continue to move on. At the same time, moving on but getting distracted from time to time means progress will suffer setbacks with each distraction.

Air travel these days is less tiresome than a decade ago because of better flying machines and the availability of in-flight entertainment for the duration of flights. Some airlines leave passengers spoilt for choices. During a chance viewing of a Bollywood production based on a story built around India's national hockey team for women, there was an inspiring song that went very well with the situation. However, one part of it had a general message of inspiration expressing a burning desire to do something about problems instead of being used and exploited all through life. That somehow got stuck in my memory like an old broken record that refuses to go away or move forward. That bit was:

کـکچھ کریئ نس نس میری بولے
کوئ تے چل ضد پھڑئے
ڈوبے ترئے یا مرئے
پسنا یونھی پسنا یونھی بس کرئے

Kuchh kariye, nas nas meri boley
Koi tey chal zidd phariye
Dubey taryey ya mariyey
Pisna yuunhi, pisna yuunhi bus karye

Apologies to the lyricist if a word or two from his original piece have been incorrectly reproduced but the message is unmistakably clear. The spirit and essence of determination in the message is unambiguous. The musical composition and vocal rendering were equally brilliant and did justice to the intended mood. It rang in my ears as an obsession until I got down to this project and therefore it gets a mention before the endeavour ends with a note of gratitude to the writer. A bit of "*zid*" [*passion*] is fundamental to the pursuit of a committed cause provided the "*zid*" is constructive and a driving motivation; not a hate filled vendetta.

A lot of young people as well as those not so young need to take a firm decision to start something positive. An old Chinese proverb states, "**Better to light one small candle than to curse the darkness**".

A lot of people seem to be waiting for another Jinnah to come back or for some miraculous rise of an indigenous Kamal Ataturk or Martin Luther King. While letting that dream live in us, those living today cannot allow themselves the luxury of living in that dream. That will not happen. They came in their times and enacted their roles brilliantly and their contributions still impact and influence many lives even today. Today belongs to those who live in present times. We cannot change our existence but we can certainly try to change our essence. It is time for **Kuchh kariye!**

Gripe water prescription

There is too much grumbling or moaning in the air to allow positive influences to flourish. When a person is tense and exhausted, it is generally helpful to sit back for a while to take a few deep breaths and exhale slowly and gently each time. In doing so the body relaxes and sends a message to the brain to take a short break. People cannot understand the instant impact of this short drill until it is actually done. This can be done in a matter of minutes, in a train or bus seat, in an office chair or while watching a television programme. In very much the same way, some exercise or drill needs to be undertaken to release years of stress generated free flowing anxiety from the system. Let us decide to observe a week in which complaining and moaning of all sorts is officially banned without exception. If it cannot be done, nationally, let us try it at lower levels; in a particular office, even in a single family. That will spare the mind and body time for recovery from accumulated psychological bruising and battering. It may not sound like a big deal but if done once, the mind and body will demand a replay soon. That sabbatical from moaning generated stress allows space in the mind for some positive thoughts. In our vision of grand designs and projects, small opportunities for rest and relaxation are sacrificed. In the end, while the pursuit of a national lottery winning number may not come to fruition, smaller joys of watching our young ones playing in front of our eyes are lost too.

If we were all a nation of minors, perhaps I might have been tempted to prescribe the famous "*gripe water*" drink for babies mixed with a bit of laughing gas as a national drink for that week. May not be desirable to prescribe the miracle drug for a longer period in any case because the next batch of delivery will almost certainly contain a substantial percentage of contaminated fake versions from the generic masters of that particular art! It is most important to somehow get the disproportionate anger and aggression out of our system before we can be ready for any creative pursuit.

Multi-faith activities and pursuits

Very few persons amongst us will disagree that one of the biggest causes of present national upheaval is the result of divisions and sub-divisions of the population into religious sub groups that cannot co-exist, nor do they wish to co-exist because each is an independent and self-centred vested interest that runs the risk of extinction in the event of a grand merger. The perpetuation of these divisions was ensured through the instrument of indoctrination of each sub-group to levels of never ending confrontational intolerance and inflexibility in posturing that will keep them apart as long as they live. That kind of mind set can only be sustained through hatred of others. That hatred has now engulfed minorities too which are hardly capable of the kind of retaliation that other Muslim sub-groups can inflict on each other, as is regularly seen in Shia & Sunni vendettas. While it is the responsibility of the state to take care of law and order matters, civil society needs to play its part in addressing the ethnic and religious divides by encouraging multi-faith [including intra-faith] and multi-cultural activities. We need to find minimum common denominators to bring people together in common causes and celebrations. Instead of banning Christmas, New Year, Basant and Diwali celebrations, the state must play a proactive role in promoting such activities and deal firmly with those who are accustomed to disrupting all celebratory occasions. If our levels of governance have dropped to where the writ of the state cannot be applied to protect social events in a fight against fundamentalism, then thinking about the future, peace and prosperity is a meaningless exercise. The problem is home grown, solutions will have to be home made too. The essential ingredient is taking bold decisions at the top, honesty of purpose and a vision for the future that transcends petty party politics. When a disease is serious and potentially terminal, the treatment too is difficult and long term.

Problems can only be solved by bringing parties and leaders together, tackling issues jointly, issues that are too complex and greed driven for local solutions. If this possibility seems too unmanageable at the national level, the approach can be tested through limited pilot projects in a selected area or areas. If successful, it will give hope and encourage others to replicate the effort; a few pilot projects that set the trend in religious and social harmony. These types of reconciliatory pursuits are inconsistent with larger agendas of current political leaders and military strategists. Any leader who can take the first step might suddenly find himself in popular demand because by now the vast majority of the population is exhausted and disgusted with current events of violent infighting.

Edhi's law of political irrelevance

Many of us should take a leaf of out *Abdul Sattar Edhi's* workbook of social and humanitarian service. He has never waited for a *Musharaf* to relinquish office, a *Zardari* to fall from power or the Americans to leave Afghanistan. So many have lived in fantasy land for years believing that Musharaf leaving the seat of power will signal the end of religious extremism and now hoping for a similar miracle if the Americans leave Afghanistan or if Zardari is removed from power in the traditional mid-term mould. Musharaf left a number of years ago but the rot continues. What will change if through an unlikely change of heart Zardari says goodbye today and the United States pack up their bags at the same time and leave the region after wishing good luck to our country? The present problems are far deeper rooted than some experts and politicians seem to understand. All that is, however, irrelevant to Edhi and he carries on, as he has been doing for ages now on his larger than life anonymous projects of selfless and dedicated social service. He is almost a freak existence in his surroundings, a refreshing oasis in the middle of a punishing desert.

According to the Guinness Book of World Records, as of 1997, Edhi Foundation's ambulance service is the largest volunteer ambulance service in the world, in addition to literacy-training courses for all ages, free medical clinics and a soup kitchen that serves 1,000 free meals a day. Those who have the resources and the inclination to do something constructive for the welfare of the common man and indeed for their own long term survival need to follow in the footsteps of Edhi; not rest on sitting room sofas waiting for a leader of their wishful dream to come to the throne before the evil curse holding back the nation can be lifted. Edhi is a tailor made illustration of **Kuchh kariye!**

"Khutbas" of national consensus

If religious leaders have a shred of sincerity in their souls about the welfare of the nation and the suffering millions, they now have to demonstrate some evidence of their claims. The country cannot sustain their divisive and mutual hate generating agendas for too long now. The only way this might work in a peaceful manner is to have the same unanimously agreed "*Khutbas*" sermons delivered before Friday prayers at every mosque in the country. After all, there is a national committee which gets together to decide whether the festivals of Eid are to be celebrated or not on a particular day. So why cannot there be a national committee to agree on a minimum common *Khutba* which is so vital to long term national interests?

There is no way all religious sects will ever collectively agree as the much trumpeted national "*ummah*" on every aspect of religious belief and interpretation. Ideally, the way this card is flagged regularly at opportune times, the entire *Ummah* should be speaking with one voice and from a single platform. If we cannot do that, let us stop talking about the *Ummah* completely because in the face of so many splits and divisions, the concept has ceased to be relevant in the current global context for quite some time now. Setting aside complete agreement, there have to be minimum areas of agreement and common ground. For the sake of argument, let us say that most religious sects have disagreements over 75 per cent of religious beliefs and interpretations. Let us forget about the 75 or 80 per disagreements and agree to talk about only those remaining 20 per cent issues on which these people have no disagreements till the national situation on the ground improves. If these people cannot even agree on 20 per cent of the Islamic religion for the sake of collective good in despairingly desperate times, which Islamic religion is then left to talk about from a single platform? This minimum consensus supported by strict implementation by the government and more importantly society should be taken as the first building block to reinvent religious tolerance and peaceful co-existence. The imams of all mosques will then not need to nor have the option to propagate negative sentiment against each other.

That kind of surge of national interest might appeal to a handful of preachers given the terrible dangers that loom, but voluntary universal acceptance of the proposal from the present unruly confrontational crowd will remain a mirage. For once in recent decades, let us involve every citizen of the country in decision making. We can have a national referendum on the issue to determine whether the development of common text for sermons delivered in mosques should be enforced by national consensus. If there is overwhelming support, religious parties will be put on the spot to either demonstrate some degree of national spirit or be further exposed for what they are really worth in that case. As for areas of discord or disagreement between various sects, those can be temporarily suspended or set aside during the period of these types of nation bonding campaigns.

These are desperate times and call for an unusual show of vision, tolerance and a spirit of sacrifice of self and party interest. If we cannot agree on basic minimums for the sake of survival, then history will take its own course, teach its causal lessons and even the suggested type of attempts might be too late to consider once the nails start to go into the national coffin. There is a lot of talk about impending revolutions, even talk by industrial tycoons like

Nawaz Sharif and his business associates but revolutions too need the right kind of leadership to control and navigate their course. In our politically bankrupt milieu, the foolishly talked about revolution will be nothing more than an uncontrolled state of anarchy and it will certainly not accept Nawaz or a feudal lord as its head. That deluded arrogance of revolutionary role playing reflects nothing more than empty heads incapable of anticipating the causal course of events that usually follow collective despair and revengeful anger. If and when anarchy sets in, these revolutionary leaders will be amongst the first to flee the country to settle in the comfort of their luxury flats in various parts of the developed world.

So let us cut this silly crap and try a few quick, sane and rational measures with national consensus to show the world and more importantly ourselves that there is still some light at the end of a long and dark tunnel. If any success is achieved, no one will need to go west or east to inform the world about it. The world will itself take notice of positive signals because right now the eyes of the whole world are focused on us in any case, more in anxiety than hope. If we cannot be dragged out of our current opium trance now to act instantly with responsibility, then the following sign post at an entry point to a wild life park in Africa may aptly symbolise the thinking process at the moment:

"TAKE NOTICE: WHEN THIS SIGN IS UNDER WATER, THIS ROAD IS IMPASSABLE"!

The importance of discarding the appearance syndrome

When every smuggler is a Haji, when most businessmen who deal in smuggled and counterfeit goods also simultaneously say their prayers five times a day, when the most corrupt civil and military state officials present themselves in public appearance as devoted Muslims, when the symbols of political decay only dress up in "jacket potato" attire as conscience clearing certification of patriotism, and despite pathetic levels of accountability in society a minister in charge of Haj affairs manages to get behind bars for misappropriation of public funds and extortion of money from genuine Haajis, it is NOT evidence of failure of religion, it is manifestation of the overbearing mania for social role playing wherein religion is not practiced as a faith but is worn as a social mask and dress [persona] because of society's obsession with visible form and physical appearance over substance and spirit of actions and behaviour. If it were not so, those practicing religion with such display of religious symbols should be exemplary role models for society and the young generation in terms of integrity, best values, practices, etc. but in reality they are the exact opposite because the display of religious symbols is their minds' rationalisation of their otherwise perverse mental pursuits. It is high time for the citizens of the state to understand that this "*structural*" obsession is largely responsible for them being fooled continually for over six decades. It needs to be discarded and the only criteria for judgement of individuals must be actual performance in life. Both *Abdul Sattar Edhi* and **the fictional** *Maulana Ramzan Khan Chaudhry* charged with corruption in Haj affairs wear equally long beards. Whereas *Edhi* is known and revered for his moral values and unqualified devotion to service of mankind, the latter has made himself a champion for everything wrong with society at the moment; similar physical personas with completely opposite end products! When society starts to understand that the physical appearance of men and outward expression of all sorts of socio-religious practices should always be considered secondary to the real spirit and rationale of why something is meant to be done, better times will come automatically. As long as any society is content or stupid enough to be so easily misled by mental billboards and not actual products, the downhill slide will continue.

Taking on mini pilot projects

When uncertainty and despair are the lead emotions, it is not a wise approach to experiment on mega national projects. It is safer and prudent to start mini-projects and if successful, the lessons can be applied subsequently on larger scales. A street or group of streets can be taken up as pilot projects by political parties as show cases of excellence, peaceful co-existence, mutual respect, good governance, clean and hygienic environment, rule of law, etc. as practical illustrations of vision for the future of each political party; a practical demonstration of manifestos rather than vague theoretical slogans.

If for instance there is a mosque in the jurisdiction of such a pilot project, let it welcome every Muslim of any sect in joint prayers. We need to work on solutions that address real life issues with realistic solutions, those that bring people closer, trying to work together, using common strengths and energies. A successful project might attract neighbouring streets to replicate that. All of this assumes that most men, if not all, are well meaning and carriers of goodwill but in need of sober guidance. Rogue elements in selected localities who do not join welfare initiatives could well be exposed for their true worth as an externality. This is not a detailed master plan; merely a barebones structure on which flesh and muscle can be added with careful consideration of details, but it is a possible and hopeful start and certainly better than not doing anything as the clock in the time bomb clicks on.

Back to basics

Like the suggested strategy for religious harmony, there is an equally important need for some kind of unifying political anchorage. The only approach that could possibly make sense and draw national acceptance in setting revised directions has to be under the clear vision of the nation's future as spelled out by the father of the nation. Support for that cause will only be meaningful if it has a national outreach that engages the thus far ignored and marginalised commoner in society. That support can also come through the national referendum proposed in the context of religious harmony. The nation must overwhelmingly support the strategy of following **ONLY** Jinnah's clear guidelines on political philosophy **as stated directly in his own words and speeches** and scoff at all those who try to twist Jinnah's words to confuse the population so that their fraudulent political ambitions can be put in place instead. Those who fail to respond to the popular view in this critical hour must be excluded from all popular political support and be left alone to rot away in their solo flights against a popular national sentiment.

Burning siege mentality effigies

A popular past time in public demonstrations on various issues, even some non-issues is burning effigies. The only effigies that currently need to be burnt as regular rituals are those of general hatred, siege mentality and conspiracy theories, tax evaders, bribery fed social parasites, religious imposters, smugglers, etc. The national calendar should have specially earmarked occasions when such effigies are set alight publicly without a muscle moved in silly violence but as symbolic social condemnation of various criminal actors in society. At the moment, there is no collective social pressure or reprimand on all wicked characters and role players whom we condemn in lip service only. These types of symbolic gestures may seem innocuous or meaningless but they do put psychological pressure on guilty parties and redirect mind sets in the requisite directions. For a tax evader or black marketer in real life watching the burning of a symbolic effigy of his unlawful existence in the company of friends and family will make uncomfortable viewing. Not too long ago there used to be bill boards on busy commercial roads in major cities with very derogatory slogans directed at people involved in bribery, dishonesty, smuggling, etc. They were gradually made to disappear. Someone must have felt uncomfortable getting reminded of his misdeeds at every street corner!

When for instance, an anonymous effigy representing a "*rishwat khoor*" [*bribe taker*] whether involved in political bribery, as a functionary of the state or even as a private sector parasite is publicly burnt, it will privately embarrass if not rattle the mind of guilty parties. Those guilty themselves know it, their friends and families know it, even the spouses, sons and daughters of such persons often know the factual details. That kind of socio-cultural pressure or reprimand is non-existent today. Unless a combination of effective governance and social censor is in place, social criminals will continue to operate guilt free and bleed the nation into an economic coma.

In each of these symbolic demonstrations, it is paramount that no act of violence in the slightest is committed. The moment it is done, the guilty parties will be in celebration and will bring media focus only on any violent act. Therefore it is up to organisers to maintain a vigil and apprehend every trouble maker for action in accordance with the law. It will be equally important for the same organisers to ensure that the consequential actions of police functionaries in such cases are kept under observation and reported to the public at large through the media.

Compulsive transparencies

Ensuring accountability in public offices becomes more difficult when the standard of transparency and access to information is difficult, if not completely denied. Lack of accountability leads to underachievement and encourages corrupt practices. Lack of control and accountability in private sector performances also suffers as a consequence because those who are mandated to regulate and supervise various private sector activities get down to corrupt practices without fear of consequences. There is far too much secrecy in the way the business of the state, public service departments and most private sector service organisations operate.

The modern approach for promotion of accountability is through cost effective and user friendly web sites that offer all kinds of information that is deemed in public interest. The present judiciary repeatedly claims to be supportive of transparency in all other aspects of public life. It could set the trend by offering all types of information relating to its role, performance, criteria for appointments and promotions, etc. When candidates are considered against judicial vacancies, the public should be able to check for itself which candidates meet or fail to meet the prescribed criteria for appointment of judges. It is no secret that appointing authorities or committees for judicial posts are under tremendous socio-political pressure from lobby groups or political party affiliations. This system of public awareness of rules and criteria is a great help in resisting external pressures that cut across considerations of pure merit. Whether pure merit takes precedence over political and parochial considerations in appointment and promotions is a different matter, a classical illustration of practice undermining a sound theoretical plan.

Tax evasion is rampant and so is corruption amongst revenue staff. But it is no better or worse than in other governmental departments, public sector organisations and even in private sector bodies. Try getting a loan from most private banks and the standard of morals will be pretty much similar, or even try getting your child's "*Nikkah*" document registered with most local *Nikkah* registrars. There will be no shortage of faults and irregularities in the document until the incumbent can be persuaded in other rewarding ways. If some private sector organisations perform better, it is usually not because of higher ethical economic values in the private sector but because of better control and management in specific organisations. No one is born to order for playing specific roles in society. Every society has its share of honest and corrupt, or peaceful and troublesome characters. The ratio varies from society to society, but whatever the ratio may be, it is likely to be the same for almost all organisations and institutions across the board. An honest person will make a good policeman or a good priest. A dodgy character will manifest his attributes accordingly whether as a judge, policeman or a preacher. Two factors can change or influence that. Improving social morals of society as a whole and reducing opportunities for corrupt practices.

Modern media has the capacity to do that, but viewing numbers and moral accommodation are higher considerations than social reform and public accountability. Here is a classic illustration of that paradox. A couple of years ago, the well-known and very lucrative global brand of IPL cricket in India decided to exclude Pakistani cricketers from its financial bonanza. Many hopeful candidates were understandably upset at the loss of huge financial opportunity and some vented their frustrations in the public domain. In one such television discussion show, reputed for its police station interrogation style, a couple of aggrieved cricketers were invited and given a public roasting for allegedly putting money before national pride. They were taunted for wanting to play in an unfriendly country like India only because of huge payments involved. Then the anchor *Chaudhry Ramzan Khan* abruptly cut short the conversation saying a commercial break had to be taken; a commercial break put ahead of an issue of national importance, but the contents that followed in the break were the real hypocrisy. The commercial break showed video clips of Bollywood movies and songs; a few more video bits about juicy Bollywood gossip and scandal, not a hint of any local content. As the commercial break ended the anchor completely oblivious of what had been telecast during the break then returned to resume his tirade against his invited guests in the name of greed and nationalism. To say that social values in the current breed are muddled up and loaded with contradictions to the brim would be a massive understatement. Bring this up with the accused anchor and the accuser will be shouted down into submission.

The current level of social responsibility amongst our citizens is unacceptably low. It needs to be enhanced considerably through awareness and media education for the good of the citizen himself, repairing image abroad but above all to intensify the role of civil society in ostracising the worst offenders. Those involved in well-known unlawful activities or robbing the state exchequer through tax evasion, misappropriation of bank loans, power theft, etc. must face a naming and shaming campaign to take the gloss out of ill-gotten wealth as much as possible. Recent punishments awarded to some cricketers for spot fixing should deter many others from being tempted or socialising with the kind of slimy characters who baited the cricketers into the nets of greed. The present lot of Supreme Court judges have made a bit of contribution in bringing the names of some of the top swindlers into the public domain. These people will have had a very comfortable ride till now but ever since their naming and shaming, their lives will have almost certainly changed for the worse. The role of social responsibility and civil society as a whole has never received the attention it requires and the constructive contribution it can make towards improving the collective lot of the nation.

Periodic publication of declared incomes and wealth of a selected number of top public life figures should be a mandatory annual drill through computerised random ballot, subsequently inviting the public to provide information to a dedicated cell about assets in their knowledge that are owned but not declared by the filers of declarations. It does not have to be a very large number of declarants every year. Those not selected in a computer ballot will still have to remain vigilant and discreet in the extent to which they can indulge in financial misappropriations. On its own, this may not have a massive impact but in tandem with other measures, the aggregate impact can be quite visible. It certainly will be better than doing nothing at all.

Fast forward to past culture and values

There is hardly a living soul today who has seen life in this country until the mid-1970s and still disagrees that the values, relationships and dynamics of society until that stage of our history were better than the current state of affairs by many a country mile. People were considerate, tolerant, humane, hospitable and carriers of a positive way of thinking in most matters. We need to make an honest assessment, better still a formal and objective study of all identifiable factors and variables that were present in those times but are not part of today's society or thinking patterns. Conversely, those factors or conditions that made that society a distinctly superior one to the present crowd can be identified and the nation must be re-educated about how abandonment of those values has led to these awful present times. To take just one real life example, when elections were being held for office bearers of the students union in Government College Lahore in 1966, there were two principal candidates who were widely perceived to be running neck and neck in polls assessments by students. That remained the case until almost 24 hours before actual voting. Then an unforeseen incident turned the position on its head. A supporter of one candidate allegedly slapped, yes merely slapped a supporter of the other following an argument. Very few students were present on the occasion but the news spread like wild fire and a shock wave ran through the vote bank of students. An overwhelming majority of potential supporters of the candidate whose supporter was accused of violent behaviour voted for the other side and that candidate won a landslide victory.

Compare that to today's election environment during student union elections. Candidates and supporters rampage through academic premises in possession of automatic weapons. Intimidation and violent behaviour are generally deemed the key to success. Hardly any student union election is complete these days without incidents of random firing involving bullet wounds, if not fatalities. Would anyone disagree on the desirability of reverting to practices and values of the past? Other aspects of life have similar illustrative examples to remind society about. Is reintroduction of the now abandoned value package possible at all considering how far away we have moved since then? If there is a strong will and an unwavering admission of wrong doings, everything is possible. Shaping the mental resolve is entirely up to affected persons alone. It is time for making a choice; one which could be the difference between survival and annihilation.

Self-evaluations and public feedbacks

State institutions need to develop a culture of regular feedback from the public to correct shortcomings, realigning priorities and enhancing performance. Unless that is done, the nation will continue to waste time, resource and keep going even backwards carrying on doing what we have always done. These types of systems have multiple objectives and benefits. Firstly, once such systems become up and running, they create a feeling of important relevance amongst the public and involvement in monitoring governance matters. Secondly, displaying performance results on governmental web sites at regulated periods such as every six months puts pressure on those governmental departments and state functionaries to maintain at least minimum standards of service. Successive results are an accurate reflection of whether there is actual improvement or deterioration. Thirdly, some element of a culture of accountability starts to build in society.

Assessing public perception of independent judiciary

It would be a great national service if a media channel carried out a well-structured survey to get feedback from the public to see if it feels that the present judiciary is doing what they expected from it when the nation was trying to restore judges to their previous positions. In fact, it would be even better if the judiciary itself undertakes regular feedback exercises to ascertain whether their clients are happy with the service provided to them. Particularly interesting would be feedback from those who carried the momentum of the restoration of judiciary during the punishing hot weather in Punjab. Did they envisage the kind of journey that is currently being actually undertaken by their lordships or did the nation have a different vision in mind at the time? Above all, has the condition of the miserable lot undergone an iota of improvement since restoration of the superior judiciary or are they too superior to get involved in the petty affairs of those below the national poverty line? Did the common man in his unlimited patience and ignorance hope for a change in fortunes once their lordships were liberated from their places of unlawful detentions? All this is most important because of the traditional disconnect between those who govern and those they govern.

The fact of the matter is that judges are the same flesh, blood and grey matter that the rest of higher echelons of society are. There could be and have been freak cases of real substance from time to time but expecting a different and superior breed to transform simply through change of dress is an unfounded expectation.

Taking on or making up with the world

Everyone thinks of changing the world, but no one thinks of changing himself
Leo Tolstoy

The time for a vital decision is now upon us; staring straight in our face. The choice is simple. Should we be focusing immediately on reducing or increasing our tensions and divisions, at home and abroad? Do we need to make more friends or enemies than appear in our present balance sheet? Can we afford to keep our eyes closed and let matters get even worse or to move decisively in reconstructing broken bridges? Finally, should we not make fundamental changes to our way of life and thought processes in order to give ourselves a decent chance of a better future or stay on course for relegation to the dustbins of history? We alone can answer these questions and the choices we make will shape the future.

Restoring international image

The Internet copy of the Daily Dawn newspaper reported on Tuesday, 17 Nov, 2009 that the international watchdog Transparency International published its annual rankings naming the world's most corrupt countries. With a score of 2.7, Pakistan was ranked 139 out of the 180 countries on the list, a position it shared with fellow South Asian nation Bangladesh. The bottom five nations — Somalia, Afghanistan, Myanmar, Sudan and Iraq show that 'countries which are perceived as the most corrupt are also those plagued by long-standing conflicts that have torn apart domestic governance infrastructure. The five countries seen as least afflicted by corruption were New Zealand, Denmark, Singapore, Sweden and Switzerland. The score is based on perceptions of the degree of corruption as seen by business people and country analysts.

It would make perfect sense to study closely the common denominators in high and very low corruption countries and learn lessons for application to our own situation. Have we ever focused on matters like these that affect almost every citizen and in particular, those who are in need of immediate attention? Who is stopping us from doing so except our own misplaced or deceitful priorities? We surely cannot be so helpless being a sovereign nation that we can do nothing about it. But if we think we are totally helpless, let us stop bragging repeatedly about sovereignty or self-respect. Some time ago when there was an extreme shortage of sugar in the country, there was a positive media campaign for a complete boycott of sugar consumption in households. Has anyone, including in the media run a campaign for boycott of all types of smuggled goods for instance? As a nation, we need to get into that kind of practical grove to fight against evil practices in society.

If we cannot do it at a national level, let some individual leader, legislator or political party take a lead or initiative and start a pilot project somewhere; create an organised socio-legal "motorway" alongside the "wild life Grand Trunk Road" as a living comparable example for people to think about. Empty promises in speeches and party manifestos have run well past their expiry dates; only practical demonstrations might attract some followers.

Leaders like Imran Khan should have been focusing their attention and energies on such pursuits, but are unable to raise their head above their strong prejudices to start any productive project. Even one practical demonstration might enlist many more admirers who eventually aggregate to a broader support in the fight against corruption. The nation and especially the average disorientated citizen need a ray of hope that is visible and verifiable in real life. They need it from someone they can trust and to that extent Imran could have made a positive contribution but he needs to dust himself out very quickly from his present negatively conservative and angry mental wrangle. If he cannot, it will be a great tragedy for him and for his long term admirers because his present direction raises far too many serious concerns and promises very little encouragement.

Projects like these do not require begging for approval or support from state institutions and there is no place for violence in such schemes unless they fall into evil hands. That is where the role of citizens in identifying trouble makers amongst their respective groups from the outset is very important. At the same time these kinds of endeavours provide a great learning opportunity for young men and women to be involved in constructive pursuits thereby laying the foundation for future leadership.

RECAP

The total text covers a very wide range of topics and events. However, two elements should always be kept in spotlight. Firstly, that a few key themes run through the entire script as applicable to various situations and are therefore deliberately repeated to drum in the point. Secondly, it may appear that many sub-themes have been unnecessarily listed for decorative criticism. The principle consideration in bringing up dozens of such issues is to highlight that a lot of seemingly insignificant aspects of life, behaviour or society require serious review and reconsideration by individuals and civil society without waiting for bigger developments or for a change in government to happen first; a kind of "*burning a candle instead of cursing the darkness*" approach.

Key themes to remember and focus on are:

1. Concentrating on the spirit and reasons for actions and beliefs should always take precedence over the current obsession with physical manifestations in order to get better outcomes in future.
2. Repeating the same mistakes and policies that have brought us to our present state of affairs will only bring more of the same outcomes and consequently more misery.
3. Never confuse criticism of socio-political religious actors with religion itself, nor let anyone fool you into falling for that cunning trap.
4. Very often, problems are caused or persist because of faulty implementation either due to poor comprehension or dishonest intentions. Those who benefit from such misuse will always drag others into believing that a new system is required to draw attention away from real solutions that depend on honest implementation. That deceptive web is brilliantly described in the following quotation **"Everything must change so that everything can stay the same and we can remain masters."**

5. Minds preoccupied with negative thoughts, hatred, anger and the like are destined to generate only unhealthy influences and undermine the ability to think and analyse matters rationally.

6. Having seen the results of divisive forces at work for decades now, there is no option than to pursue life based on finding common ground home and abroad that encourages everyone to join in pursuits of joint interests.

7. Controlling minds and freedoms eventually end in no good for all parties involved. The on-going violent events against excessive controls in many Middle East countries are good examples to learn from.

8. To be respected in this world, the only way forward is to show respect to others.

9. A lot of issues raised and points made are meant to create awareness or realisation that to put it mildly things are not right at present, offer an invitation to think and to think again about current processes that are not working; to ask questions about choices made and the consequences of those choices. Reactivating deactivated minds towards analytical thinking is a crucial endeavour of this project and therefore is one of the repetitive key themes.

10. "**Extremism**" in any form or faith is not good for any individual or nation. If there was any doubt in any mind about that, the very recent inexplicable mass killings in Norway should leave no doubt whatsoever. **Extremism** is not any one religion plague. It is a common to all humanity, state of individual or collective mind and a very acutely disturbed one at that. Moderation, tolerance and above all the ability and willingness to adapt to diversity and the changing world are the golden key to peace and prosperity.

References

Adler Alfred, 1968; 2nd edition, ***The Practice and Theory of Individual Psychology,*** Littlefield Adams, USA

Adler Alfred, 2009 - Reprint edition, ***Understanding Human Nature - The Psychology of Personality,*** Oneworld Publications, London

Aristotle, 1955, ***On Sophistical Refutations [Translated by E. S. Forster & D. J. Furley],*** Cambridge, Massachusetts

Atkinson A B, 1989 - 2nd Edition, ***The Economics of Inequality,*** Oxford University Press, Oxford – UK

Berne Eric, 1973, ***Games People Play: The Psychology of Human Relationships,*** Penguin Classics, London

Bhutto Zulifiqar Ali, 1969, ***Myth of Independence,*** Oxford University Press, New York

Dostoevsky Fyodor, 2011, ***The Idiot,*** Simon & Brown, UK

Dostoevsky Fyodor, 1997, ***Crime and Punishment [Translation by Richard Pevear],*** Penguin Classics, London

Dostoevsky Fyodor, 2002, ***The Brothers Karamazov [Translation R. Pevear& L. Volokhonsky],*** Farrar, Straus and Giroux, New York

Dostoevsky Fyodor, 1994, ***Notes from Underground [Translation R. Pevear& L. Volokhonsky,*** Vintage Books, New York

Dr AjmalMakhdoom Mohd., ***Comparison of Jungian and Freudian Analysis,*** Ph.D.Thesis: U.C.L., London

Faiz Ahmad Faiz, 1997, ***"Nuskhahe-wafa",*** Karawan Press, Lahore, Pakistan

Festinger Leon, 1957, ***Cognitive Dissonance***, Stanford University Press, Palo Alto – CA

Freud Sigmund, 1980 [Original 1899], ***The Interpretation of Dreams***, Avon, New York

Freud Sigmund, 2003 [Original 1905], ***Jokes and their Relation to the Unconscious (Penguin Classics)***, Penguin, London

Freud Sigmund, 1973 – New edition, ***Introductory Lectures on Psychoanalysis***, Penguin Books Ltd, London

Jung Carl Gustav, 1976 – Rev. edition, ***Psychological Types; The Collected Works of C.G. Jung, Vol. 6***, Harcourt, Brace & World, New Jersey, USA

Jung Carl Gustav, 1960, ***Psychology and Religion***, Yale University Press, New Haven

Jung Carl Gustav, 1981, ***The Archetypes and the Collective Unconscious; Collected Works of C.G. Jung Vol.9 Part 1***, Princeton University Press, New Jersey, USA

Jung Carl Gustav, 2006, ***The Undiscovered Self***, Signet, Colchester – UK

Jung Carl Gustav, 2009, ***The Red Book: Liber Novus***, W.W. Norton & Co, London

Jung Carl Gustav, 1955, ***Modern Man in Search of a Soul***, Harcourt Harvest, Boston, USA

Jung Carl Gustav, 2010 (reproduction), ***Synchronicity: An Acausal Connecting Principle. (From Vol. 8. of the Collected Works)***, Princeton University Press, New Jersey, USA

Kaufmann Walter, 1975- Revised Edition, ***Existentialism from Dostoevsky to Sartre***, New American Library, New York City

Koffka Kurt, 1963, ***Principles of Gestalt Psychology***, Harcourt, Brace & World, New York Moore Michael, 2002, ***Downsize This***, Pan Books, London

Krishna Murthy T. S., 2008, ***TheMiracle of Democracy***, Harper Collins Publishers, New Delhi

Musgrave Richard A, 2000, ***Public Finance in a Democratic Society***, Edward Elgar Publishing Ltd., Cheltenham – UK

Nietzsche Friedrich, 1997, ***Beyond Good and Evil,*** Dover Publications, New York

Nietzsche Friedrich, 2006 [2nd edition], ***On the Genealogy of Morals,*** Cambridge University Press, Cambridge – UK

Pirie Madsen, 1985, ***The Book of the Fallacy: A Training Manual for Intellectual Subversives,*** RoutledgeKegan& Paul, London

Russell Bertrand, 2004 [New edition], ***Power: A New Social Analysis,*** Routledge, New York

Sartre Jean-Paul, 1993, ***Being and Nothingness: An Essay on Phenomenological Ontology,*** Washington Square Press, Linden, USA

Services Club Book, 1977, ***Quaid's Correspondence,*** Pap-Board Printers (Pvt) Ltd, Rawalpindi, Pakistan

Shahid-ur-Rahman, 1999, ***Who owns Pakistan,*** Printers & Distributors, Pakistan

Shaw Bernard, 1944, ***Everybody's Political What's What,*** Constable and Company, London